UNJUST ENRICHMENT AND CONTRACT

This book examines the role of unjust enrichment in the contractual context, defined as contracts which are (a) terminated for breach, or (b) subsisting, or (c) unenforceable. The book makes three claims in relation to the orthodox common law account of restitution (founded on unjust enrichment) in the contractual context. First, the orthodox account correctly proceeds on the basis that the restitutionary claim in the contractual context is founded on an independent cause of action in unjust enrichment, rather than some equitable notion of unconscientiousness or the law of contract. Secondly, the book departs from the orthodox account by rejecting the unjust factors approach and endorsing the absence of basis approach for the law of unjust enrichment. Finally, the book argues that the right to restitution in the contractual context should be determined by the conditionality of the transfer of the benefit rather than a requirement such as the termination of the contract, as the orthodox account dictates. To that end the book proposes the following model, under which the right to restitution in the contractual context is determined by the resolution of the following two questions: (1) Was the transfer of the benefit (eg of money or services) conditional? (2) Was there a qualifying failure of condition? A condition can be, and often is, the other contracting party's counter-performance, but it may also be an event not promised by either party. What qualifies as a failure of condition depends on the type of contract in question. This book identifies two types of contracts, namely those which are apportioned (eg instalment contracts) and those which are unapportioned. It is only in relation to the latter that termination is required. It is a particular strength of the book that it is underpinned by detailed and original historical analysis which makes a novel and distinct contribution to the history of the laws of unjust enrichment and contract.

Unjust Enrichment and Contract

Tariq A Baloch

·HART·
PUBLISHING

OXFORD AND PORTLAND, OREGON
2009

Published in North America (US and Canada) by
Hart Publishing
c/o International Specialized Book Services
920 NE 58th Avenue, Suite 300
Portland, OR 97213-3786
USA
Tel: +1 503 287 3093 or toll-free: (1) 800 944 6190
Fax: +1 503 280 8832
E-mail: orders@isbs.com
Website: http://www.isbs.com

Hart Publishing Ltd, 16C Worcester Place, Oxford, OX1 2JW
Telephone: +44 (0)1865 517530 Fax: +44 (0)1865 510710
E-mail: mail@hartpub.co.uk
Website: http://www.hartpub.co.uk

British Library Cataloguing in Publication Data
Data Available

ISBN: 978-1-84113-908-1

Typeset by Hope Services, Abingdon
Printed and bound in Great Britain by
TJ International Ltd, Padstow, Cornwall

Foreword

This book, based on an Oxford doctoral thesis, is about the borderland between the law of contract and the law of restitution. That borderland raises important and difficult questions about the relationship between a predominantly consensual obligation and an obligation imposed by law. In particular, does recourse to the law of restitution and the principle of unjust enrichment subvert the contractual allocation of risks and allow an escape from a bad bargain and, if so, when? In the case of a valid contract, what role, if any, does the contractual allocation of risks have after the contract has been discharged?

Dr Baloch's work addresses these and other questions about the role of unjust enrichment in a contractual context. He considers valid and unenforceable contracts. His starting point is a detailed historical analysis of the position from the late seventeenth century to the nineteenth century, when the view that restitutionary obligations are based on an implied contract became influential. He argues the 'implied contract' view was not as deeply embedded as some thought. He also argues that the lesson from history is that modern attempts to re-integrate the innocent party's right to restitution after a breach of contract into the law of contract or to explain them as based on equitable notions of unconscionability are flawed on both historical and analytical grounds. But, while he argues that the basis of such obligations is the principle of unjust enrichment, it is not the traditional common law approach based on grounds for restitution, but the approach in the civilian jurisdictions of Continental Europe adopted by Peter Birks shortly before he died, which Dr Baloch refers to as the 'new Birksian approach'.

This is a valuable book, thoughtful and well researched. It is concerned to build a model that fits comfortably with the cases, and its focus is on the work of modern commentators. Those concerned with the relationship of contract and the law of restitution whether at a theoretical level or in practice will benefit by careful study of what Dr Baloch has to say, whether or not they agree with it.

Royal Courts of Justice, 14 February 2009   JACK BEATSON

Preface

It would be difficult to write this preface without mentioning the late Peter Birks, who was to be my supervisor for the doctorate upon which this book is substantially based. Suffice it to say that although I did not know him as well as many others who have written about, or in memory of, him, my interactions with Peter leading up to the commencement of my doctoral studies perfectly illustrated his passion, generosity, clarity of vision and loyalty. Whatever view one may take of his work (and I leave it to the reader to decide where I stand), Peter's standing as a great teacher cannot be denied. I can only wonder how he would have reacted to the thesis and book in its final form.

Some of the qualities I mentioned were evident in the way Peter, even in his last months, ensured that I would not be without a suitable supervisor when I entered the University of Oxford in 2004. It was my good fortune to have Andrew Burrows and, later, Mike Macnair, as joint supervisors for the doctorate. Their generous, careful and learned supervision has hugely benefitted the thesis. I am indebted to them and hope that I can follow their example as a teacher. I am also grateful to my thesis examiners, David Ibbetson and Jamie Edelman (and at the interim stage, Ewan McKendrick), for engaging with the thesis in a way that a doctoral student hopes for when toiling over their project for 3 years or so. Outside these formal relationships, I have also learnt a lot from Robert Stevens.

For their personal and financial support I must also thank the two colleges that I have called home during my stay in Oxford: Lady Margaret Hall and, for the majority of my stay, Corpus Christi College. At Corpus, I really enjoyed the support and friendship of the law fellows, Lucia Zedner and Elizabeth Fisher. More generally, I am grateful to the fellows and staff of Corpus for welcoming me as a student and member of the Senior Common Room.

The journey towards a doctorate was made possible by many people but I would like to record my appreciation for four teachers in particular. As an undergraduate within the Law School of Queen Mary, University of London, Shelley Lane and Ian Yeats gave me the chance and space to believe that a career in law might actually be a possibility. Shelley's career switch deprived the Law School of one of its best teachers. And Ian Yeats' contribution to the Law School, from its inception no less, is truly difficult to measure. As a postgraduate it was Charles Mitchell who set in motion events which culminated in my commencing doctoral studies at Oxford. He has been a source of support throughout. It was during the brilliant restitution course, co-led by Charles and Sarah Worthington, on the inter-collegiate University of London LLM, that I was first exposed to, and became interested in, the subject. Finally, the most crucial influence and contribution has come from Alison Firth. Without her, it would have been difficult to contemplate and then negotiate the transition from undergraduate to postgraduate law student. Under her guidance and support, I was able to secure funding for the LLM, see my name in print (probably too soon), enrol on the restitution course and teach my first university class.

A number of institutions have made important contributions to the thesis and this book. My former colleagues and students at the London School of Economics and Political Science provided the kind of stimulating environment in which it was easy to put the finishing touches on the thesis and then convert it into a book. The argument in the book is underpinned by detailed historical research. The interest in legal history was first stirred in the library of Lincoln's Inn, which houses some of the most important manuscripts on the common law. These sources provided invaluable information on the period this book covers. In using the library during the course of my legal education, I have learnt, and benefitted, a great deal from the librarian, Guy Holborn and his assistant, Catherine McArdle. The trustees of the Kennedy Memorial Trust provided the first opportunity to investigate the history of restitution in the place where the subject took on its modern form—Harvard Law School. I am grateful to Harvard for their financial assistance by way of the Mark DeWolfe Howe Fellowship, which provided the funds to complete my research in Boston. At Harvard I also encountered another set of first class librarians led by David Warrington, who looked after the Law School's special collection. Although the research I carried out at Harvard is not very visible in the book, it did provide a framework for the historical work that I pursued subsequently. The research also provided the first inkling that more work would have to be done on the eighteenth century. The germ of this idea came from some questions during a lecture based on my research, and delivered under the auspices of the Harvard European Law Centre, titled, *Of Dogs and Dingoes: The Intellectual History of Restitution*. I am grateful to the lecture participants and the centre for their invitation.

Chapter 3 is an expanded version of an article which was first published in the *Law Quarterly Review* ('Unjust Enrichment Pyramid' (2007) vol 123, p 636), and is reproduced here by kind permission of the editor, Francis Reynolds. I would also like to thank the Harrowby Manuscript Trust for allowing the reproduction of parts of Chief Justice Ryder's notebook. These notebooks provide a vital and unique insight into the workings of the common law in the mid-eighteenth century. It has also been a pleasure to work with Richard Hart and his team at Hart Publishing.

On a personal note, the writing of the thesis and book has been a lonely and consuming process, and I have therefore been very grateful for the moments of welcome distraction and support provided by friends and family. I am afraid that they may have come out badly from the bargain since for large periods I have been an absent son, brother, friend and, most recently, uncle. I hope to make it up to them, especially my siblings, Mahreen, Shahzeen and Bilal, and nephew, Aaryan.

Finally, I dedicate this book to my parents, Mohammed Bux and Hassina, whose sacrifices, love and support made all this possible.

Paris, 5 November 2008   TARIQ A BALOCH

Contents

Foreword   v
Preface   vii
Table of Cases   xv
Table of Statutes and Foreign Legislation   xxiii

Introduction   1

1. An Historical Analysis of the Independence of Unjust Enrichment   5

   I.   Introduction   5
   II. Myth, Mystery and Illusion   10

     A. The Two Senses of 'Contract': a Source of Rights and as a
        Method of Classification   10
     B. Procedure and the Development of Indebitatus Claims   13

   III. Development of the Law before *Moses v Macferlan*   19

     A. Holt CJ and Indebitatus Claims   20
     B. Role of Equity in the Development of the Law   29
     C. Encouraging Indebitatus Claims   31

   IV. Lord Mansfield's Decision in *Moses v Macferlan*   33
   V. The Period After *Moses v Macferlan*   37

     A. Case Law   38
     B. Legal Discourse   41

   VI. Learning from the Past: Concluding Comments   44

2. Rejecting the Role of Unjust Enrichment in the Contractual Context   47

   I.   Introduction   47
   II. A Critical Appraisal of the Three Models   48

     A. Kull and the *Third Restatement of Restitution*   48
     B. Hedley   59
     C. Jaffey   64

   III. Conclusion   67

3. What is the Best Organisation for the Law of Unjust Enrichment:
Unjust Factors or Absence of Basis?   69

I.	Introduction	69
II.	New Birksian Approach	72
	A. Objective and Subjective Tests of 'Basis'	72
	B. Notion of Basis	74
	C. Greater Unity	76
III.	The Pyramid	77
	A. Wrong reasons: the Swaps Cases	78
	B. Wrong Basis: *CTN Cash and Carry v Gallaher*	79
	C. Clashing Obligations: *Roxborough v Rothmans of Pall Mall Australia Ltd*	82
	D. Enhancing Choice: *Deutsche Morgan Grenfell v Inland Revenue Commissioners*	83
IV.	Three Criticisms of the New Birksian Approach	85
	A. By-Benefits	85
	B. Negative Formulation	86
	C. Retrospectivity of Termination	87
V.	Conclusion	87

4. The Role of Unjust Enrichment in the Contractual Context: an Introduction to Chapters 5 and 6   89

I.	Background	89
II.	The Model Proposed in this Book	93
III.	Overview of Chapters 5 and 6	95

5. Historical Foundations of the Modern Law of Unjust Enrichment in the Contractual Context   97

I.	Introduction	97
II.	Evolution of the Dominant Model	97
	A. Background: Independency	98
	B. Antecedents of *Kingston* and *Boone*	100
	C. The *Boone* Principle in Detail	106
	D. Reception of *Boone* and Establishment of the Dominant Model	111
III.	Rescission and Total Failure of Consideration	122
	A. Total Failure of Consideration	123
	B. Rescission	124
IV.	Apportioned Contracts and Quantum Meruit	128
	A. Apportioned Contracts	128
	B. Quantum Meruit	129
V.	Conclusion	139

6. The True Role of Unjust Enrichment in the Contractual Context   141

   I.   Introduction   141
   II. Core Principles   142

       A. Meaning of 'Condition'   142
       B. A Qualifying Failure of Condition   146
       C. Accrued Rights   156
       D. Prevention   164

   III. Distinctiveness of Quantum Meruit   167

       A. Infringing the Freedom of Choice   169
       B. Entire Contracts   170
       C. Valuation   172

   IV. Unenforceable Contracts and Claims by the Party in Breach   174
   V. Failure of Condition and Absence of Basis   175
   VI. Restitution upon Failure of Condition: Contract or
       Unjust Enrichment?   178
   VII. Conclusion   180

Conclusion   183

Bibliography   191
Index   203

Table of Cases

Adams v Fairbain (1817) 2 Stark 277, 171 ER 845 121
AG v Blake [2001] 1 AC 268 1
AG v Stevens (1737) West t Hard 50, 25 ER 814; 1 Atk 358, 26 ER 228 28
Alexander Popham v Bampfeild & Al (1682) 1 Vern 80, 23 ER 325 105
Ambrose v Rowe (1684) 2 Show KB 421, 89 ER 1018 138
Amory v Broderick (1822) 5 B & Ald 712, 106 ER 1351 56
Anon (1704) 6 Mod 131, 87 ER 887 23
Arris & Arris v Stukeley (1677/8) 2 Mod 260,
    86 ER 1060 ....12, 21, 22, 23, 30, 41
Astley v Reynolds (1731) 2 Barn K B 40, 94 ER 343 26
Attorney-General v Perry (1735) 2 Comyns 481, 92 ER 1169 26
Atwood v Maude (1868) LR 3 Ch App 369 154
Baber v Harris (1839) 9 Ad & E 532, 112 ER 1313 116
Baltic Shipping v Dillon (1993) 176 CLR 344 152
Bank of Boston Connecticut v European Grain Shipping [1989] AC 1056,
    1099 158
Banque Financiere de la Cite v Parc (Battersea) Ltd [1999] 1 AC 221 ....45, 69
Barr v Gibson (1838) 3 M & N 390, 150 ER 1196 119
Basten v Butter (1806) 7 East 479, 103 ER 185 136
Batard v Hawes (1853) 2 El & Bl 287, 118 ER 775 41
Beale v Thompson (1803) 3 Bos & Pul 405, 127 ER 221; 4 East 546, 102
    ER 940 133
Beany v Turner (1670) 1 Lev 293, 83 ER 413 100
Beed v Blandford (1828) 2 Y & J 278, 148 ER 924 124
Behn v Burness (1863) 3 B & S 751,122 ER 281 ....120, 121
Behrend & Company v Produce Brokers Company [1920] 3 QB 530 ....129, 148
Belfield v Bourne [1894] 1 Ch 521 155
Benjamin Ward & James Ward v Sir Stephen Evans (1702) 2 Ld Raym 928,
    92 ER 120; 6 Mod 36, 87 ER 799; 1 Com 138, 92 ER 1002 and BL Add
    MS 35980, f 79 25
Bentsen v Taylor [1893] 2 QB 274 121
Blackwell v Nash (1722)1 Str 535, 93 ER 684 ....102, 104
Bolton v Wills (1650) Style 214, 82 ER 655 23
Boomer v Muir (1933) 24 (2d) P 570 173
Boone v Eyre (1778) cited in argument in *Duke of St Albans v Shore* 1 H
    Bl 270, 273; 126 ER 160; LI Dampier MS APB 41; LI Hill MS 11,
    ff 380-381 ....98, 100–102, 104–112, 119, 121, 122, 124, 185

Bornmann v Tooke (1808) 1 Camp 376, 170 ER 991...144

Bosanquet v Earl of Westmoreland (1738) West T Hard 598,
    25 ER 1104...26

Bovey v Castleman (1794) 1 Ld Raym 69, 91 ER 942 ....21, 30

Bowdell v Parsons (1808) 10 East 359, 103 ER 811 56

Bright v Boyd (Circuit Court, D, Maine 1841) 4 F Cas 127 43

Brocas' case (1588) 3 Leonard 219, 74 ER 644 104

Brown v Bullen (1780) 1 Doug 407, 99 ER 261..38

Brown v St Paul, Minneapolis & Manitoba 36 Minn 236, 31 NW 941 (1886) 59

Buckley v Collier (1692), 1 Salk 113, 91 ER 406 130

Bull v Sibbs (1799) 8 TR 327, 101 E.R. 1415 138

Buller v Crips (1703) 6 Mod 29, 87 ER 793..24

Burkmire v Darnell (1704) 6 Mod 248, 87 ER 996; 2 Ld Raym 1085, 92
    ER 219 (*Buckmyr v Darnell*); 1 Salk 27, 91 ER 27 (*Birkmyr v Darnell*);
    3 Salk 15, 91 ER 663 (*Bourkmire v Darnell*)...23

C&P Haulage v Middleton [1983] 1 WLR 1461...67

Camilla Cotton v Granadex [1976] 2 Lloyd's Rep 10 127

Campbell v Jones (1796) 6 TR 570, 110 ER 708 108

Caswell v Coare (1809) 1 Taunt 567, 127 ER 954..117

Chandler v Webster [1904] 1 KB 493..176

Chanter v Hopkins (1838) 4 M & W 399, 150 ER 1484..118

Chater v Beckett (1797) 7 TR 201, 101 ER 931 ....114, 115

City of New Orleans v Fireman's Charitable Association 9 So 486 (1891)............149

City of York v Toun (1699) 5 Mod 444, 87 ER 754...23

Clerk v Mundall (1698) 12 Mod 203, 88 ER 1263 23

Clerk v Shee & Johnson (1774) 1 Cowp 197, 98 ER 1041 30

Clerke v Martin (1702) 2 Ld Raym 757, 92 ER 6 24

Coggs v Barnard (1703) 3 Ld Raym 163, 92 ER 622; 1 Com 133, 92 ER
    999; BL Add MS 34125 18

Cole v Shallet (1682) 3 Lev 41, 83 ER 567 ....102, 104, 106

CTN Cash & Carry v Gallaher [1994] 4 ALL ER 714...79-81

Cunnigham v Buchanan Jardine [1988] 1 WLR 678..127

Curling v Long (1797) 1 Bos & Pul 634, 126 ER 1104 133

Curtis v Hannay (1799, 1801, 1819) 3 Esp 82, 170 ER 546.....................................117

Cutter v Powell (1795) 6 TR 320, 101 ER 573...133

Dale v Sollet (1767) 4 Burr 2133, 98 ER 112 34

Dawson et UX v Myer Mil' (1726) 2 Str 712, 93 ER 801..102

De Bernales v Fuller (1810) 2 Camp 426, 170 ER 1206 127

De Havilland v Bowerbank (1807) 1 Camp 50, 170 ER 872 127

De Oleaga v West Cumberland Iron & Steel (1879) 4 QBD 472.............................148

Decker v Pope (1757) LI MS 129 (unfol) and Inner Temple Misc MS 96,
    f 37 ....20, 21, 26, 29, 34

Deglman v Guaranty Trust Co of Canada and Constantineau [1954]
    3 DLR 786..174

Denison v Ralphson (1682) 1 Ventris 365, 86 ER 235; 2 Shower KB 250,
  89 ER 921 (*Beningsage v Ralphson*); Skinner 66, 90 ER 32 (*Bevingsay v
  Ralston*)..12
Devaux v Conolly (1849) 8 CB 640, 137 ER 658 ....129, 148
Dies v British and International Mining and Finance Corporation [1939]
  1 KB 724 170
Dimond v Lovell [2000] 2 WLR 1121 175
Duncomb v Tickridge (1648) Aleyn 94, 82 ER 933..116
Ellen v Topp (1851) 6 Exch 424,155 ER 609 ....108, 119, 120
Ellis v Hamlen (1810) Taunt 52,128 ER 21 136
ERDC Group v Brunel University [2006] EWHC 687 168
Farnsworth v Garrard (1807) 1 Camp 38, 170 ER 867 ....135, 136
Fenner v Meares (1746-1779) 2 Black W 1269, 96 ER 746............................116
Ferguson (D O) & Associates v Sohl (1992) 62 BLR 95 156
Fibrosa Spolka v Fairbairn Lawson [1943] AC 32 ....124, 176
Fielder v Starkin (1788) 1 H Bl 17, 126 ER 11...136
Fielding v Serrat (1696) Comb 375, 90 ER 537...23
Fits v Freestone (1676) 1 Mod 210, 86 ER 834 23
Floyer v Edwards (1774) 1 Cowp 112, 98 ER 995; Lofft 595, 98 ER 817...............38
Ford v Tiley (1827) 6 B & C 325, 108 ER 472 56
Foreman State Trust & Savings Bank v Tauber (1932) 180 NE 827 166
Franklin v Miller (1836) 4 Ad & E 599, 111 ER 912 134
Fruhling v Schroeder (1835) 2 Bing NC 77, 132 ER 31.................................127
Gamerco SA v ICM/fair Warning (Agency) Ltd [1995] 1 WLR 126.....................154
GEC Marconi v BHP Information Technology (2003) 128 FCR 1 169
Gillett v Mawman (1808) 1 Taunt 137, 127 ER 784 138
Glazebrook v Woodrow (1799) 8 TR 366, 101 ER 1436 ....103, 111
Goodisson v Nunn (1792) 4 TR 761, 100 ER 1288........................100, 103, 104, 111
Goodman v Pocock (1850) 15 QB 576,117 ER 577; 14 Jurist O.S 1042........131, 137
Gosbell v Archer (1835) 2 Ad & El 500, 111 ER 193................................121, 174
Goss v Chilcott [1996] AC 788 90
Grant v Vaughan (1764) 3 Burr 1516, 97 ER 957...25
Graves v Legg (1854) 9 Exch 709,156 ER 304..108, 119
Green v Crane (1704) cited in *Williams v Gun* (1710) Fort 177, 180;
  92 ER 808...23
Ha v New South Wales (2001) 189 CLR 465...147
Hagedorn v Laing (1815) 6 Taunt 163, 128 ER 996.......................................126
Harbour Assurance v Kansa General Insurance [1993] 1 QB 701.....................127
Hayes v Bickerstaff (1675) Freem KB 194, 89 ER 138...................................104
Hazell v Hammersmith & Fulham [1992] 2 AC 1..69
Henty v Schroeder (1879) 12 Ch D 666 128
Hervey and others v Aston and others (1737-38) West T Hard 350,
  25 ER 975...105
Heyman v Darwin [1942] AC 536 127

Hoare v Rennie (1859) 5 H & N 19, 157 ER 1083...108

Hochster v De La Tour (1853) 2 El & Bl 678, 118 ER 922. ....55, 56, 57, 58, 137

Holme v Guppy (1838) 3 M&W 387, 150 ER 1195...166

Honck v Muller (1881) 7 QBD 92...108

Howis v Wiggins (1792) 4 TR 714, 100 ER 1261..115

Hulle v Heightman (1802) 4 Esp 75, 170 ER 647; (1802) 2 East 145,
    102 ER 324 ....131, 133–138

Hunlocke v Blacklowe (1670) 2 Wms Saund 156, 85 ER 893 ....100, 104

Hunt v Silk (1804) 5 East 449, 102 ER 1142..123, 124

Hussey v Fiddall (1698) 12 Mod 324, 88 ER 1353 23

Hussey v Jacob (1696) 1 Ld Raym 87, 91 ER 954 23

Hyundai Heavy Industries v Papadopoulos [1980] 1 WLR 1129 ....162, 163

Icely v Grew (1836) 6 Nev & Man 467...126

Isaak Mattos v Parker (1756) LI Harrowby MS doc 17, p 35.....................................27

Jacob v Allen 1 Salk 27, 91 ER 26...116

Jestons v Brooke (1778) 2 Cowp 793, 98 ER 1365 ....30, 38

Johnson v Collings (1800) 1 East 98, 102 ER 40 116

Jones v Barkley (1781) 2 Doug 684, 99 ER 434 ....98, 116, 185

Kelly v Solari (1841) 9 M & W 54, 152 ER 24..2, 81

Kingdom v Cox (1848) 5 CB 222, 136 ER 982..151

Kingston v Preston (1772) cited in argument in *Jones v Barkley* (1781)
    2 Doug 684; 99 ER 434; LI Dampier MS APB 17; LI Hill MS 10,
    ff 180-186..26, 98, 100–103, 105, 106, 109, 185

Lamond v Davall (1847) 9 QB 1030, 115 ER 1569 126

Leers, Ex Parte (1802) 6 Ves Jun 644, 31 ER 1237 39

Leigh v Dickeson (1884) 15 QBD 60. ....169, 170

Leigh v Paterson (1818) 8 Taunt 540, 129 ER 493 57

Lickbarrow v Mason (1787) 2 TR 63, 100 ER 35...18

Lindon v Hooper 1 Cowp 414, 98 ER 1160..22

Little v Courage (1995) 70 P & C 469 166

Lodder v Slowey [1904] AC 442 173

*Lord Gilbert Kennedy v The Panama, New Zealand, and Autralian Royal
    Mail Company* (1867) LR 2 QB 580..120

Lovelock v Franklyn (1846) 8 QB 358, 115 ER 916 56

Lovett v Hobbs (1679) 2 Show KB 127, 89 ER 836...133

Mackay v Dick (1881) 6 App Case 251 166

Maclean v Dunn (1828) 4 Bing 722, 130 ER 947 126

*Maredelanto Compania Naviera SA v Bergbau-Handel Gmbh (The Mihailos
    Angelos)* [1971] 1 QB 164..121

Martin v Court (1788) 2 TR 640, 100 ER 344...115

Martin v Sitwell (1691) 1 Shower KB 156, 89 ER 509 26

Martin v Weedon (1754) LI Harrowby MS doc 12, p 6..27

Mavor v Pyne (1825) 3 Bing 285, 130 ER 522...121

Menetone v Athawes (1764) 3 Burr 1594, 97 ER 998...138

Miles v Wakefield [1987] AC 539..151
Monnickendam v Lease (1923) 39 TLR 445 174
Morgan Grenfell v Inland Revenue Commissioners [2003] EWHC 1779,
    [2003] 4 ALL ER 645; [2005] EWCA Civ 78; [2006] 2 WLR 103; [2007]
    1 AC 558..83–84
Moses v Macferlan (1760) 2 Burr 1005, 97 ER 676 ....7, 8, 12, 26, 27,
                                         29, 30, 33–37, 113, 183
Keck's case (1744) 132
Newall v Tomlinson (1871) L R 6 C P 405 81
Nichols v Raynbred (1615) Hob 88, 80 ER 238 99
Oxendale v Wetherell (1829) 9 B & C 386, 109 ER 143 ....129, 150
Oxendale v Wetherell (1829) 9 B & C 386, 109 ER 143
Palmer v Stavely (1701) 12 Mod 510, 88 ER 1483 23
Palmer v Temple (1839) 9 Ad & E 508, 112 ER 1304 ....125, 126
Parker v Palmer (1821) 4 B & A 387, 106 ER 978...117
Pavey & Matthews Pty Ltd v Paul (1986) 162 CLR 221...174
Payne v Whale (1806) 7 East 274, 103 ER 105...112
Peake v Oldham (1775) 1 Cowp 275, 98 ER 1083 15
Peck v Wood (1793) 5 TR 130, 101 ER 75 115
Peeters v Opie (1671) 2 Wms Saund 350, 85 ER 1144...98
Pierson v Atkinson (1672) Freem KB 70, 89 ER 52...133
Pilkington v Peach (1680) 2 Show KB 135, 89 ER 841...................................23, 130
Planche v Colburn (1831) 5 Car & P 57, 172 ER 876; (1831) 8 Bing 14,
    131 ER 305...55, 122, 130, 132, 134,
                                      137–139, 165, 167, 169
Pordage v Cole (1669) 1 Wms Saund 219, 85 ER 449.....................98, 104, 108–110
Power v Wells (1778) 2 Cowp 818, 98 ER 1379 ....112, 113
Pulbrook v Lawes (1876) 1 QBD 284...121, 174
R v Mayor and Burgesses of Lyme Regis (1779) 1 Doug 135, 99 ER 89 15
Rambux Chittangeo v Modhoosoodin Paul Chawdhry (1867) 7 WR
    (India) 377...41
Renard Constructions (ME) Pty Ltd v Minister for Public Works (1992)
    26 NSWLR 234. 173
Rex v Nunez (1736) Cases T Hard 265, 95 ER 171 30
Richardson v Dunn (1841) 2 QB 218, 114 ER 85 ....129, 150
Robert Taylor v Motability Finance Ltd [2004] EWHC 2619 172
Roberts v The Bury Improvement Commissioners [1870] L R 5 C P 310 326 164
Rover v Cannon Film Sales (No 3) [1989] 1 WLR 912.....................................160, 175
Rowland v Divall [1923] KB 500 155
Roxborough v Rothmans (2001) 208 CLR 516..............6, 46, 82, 147, 149, 160, 161
Russell v Russell (1880) 14 Ch D 471..127
Saunders v Plummer (1662) Bridg O 223, 124 ER 557 12
Sayer v Pocock (1776) 1 Cowp 407, 98 ER 1156 15
Scarisbrick v Parkinson (1869) 20 LT 175...174, 121

Schlencker v Moxsy (1825) 3 B&C 789, 107 ER 926..116

Shipton v Casson (1826) 5 B & C 378, 108 ER 141 ....129, 150

Short v Stone (1846) 8 QB 358, 115 ER 911 56

Shuttleworth v Garnet (1689) 3 Mod 239, 87 ER 156; 3 Lev 261, 83
    ER 680; Comb 151, 90 ER 398; Carth 90, 90 ER 657; 1 Show KB 35,
    89 ER 431..21, 22, 30

Sinclair v Brougham [1914] AC 398, 415 40

Sir Lindsay Parkinson v Commissioners of Works [1949] 2 KB 632....................169

Sir Richard Hotham v The East India Company (1787) 1 TR 638, 99
    ER 295 166

Smith v Airey (1704) 2 Ld Raym, 92 ER 187, 6 Mod 128, 87 ER 885;
    3 Salk 175, 91 ER 760..21, 30

Smith v Hayward (1837) 7 Ad & E 544, 112 ER 575 131

Snelling v Lord Huntingfield (1834) 1 CM&R 20, 149 ER 976 121

Somes v British Empire Shipping Co (1860) 8 HL Cas 338 80

St Albans v Shore (1789) 1 H.Bl 270, 126 ER 158 ....98, 108, 120, 185

Staples v Alden (1678), 2 Mod 309, 86 ER 1091 102

Starke v Cheeseman (1699) 1 Ld Raym 538, 91 ER 1259; 1 Salk 128,
    91 ER 121; Carth 509, 90 ER 891 23

Stevenson v Snow (1761) 3 Burr 1237, 97 ER 808...........................128, 148

Stocznia Gdanska SA v Latvian Shipping [1998] 1 WLR 574 ....90, 163, 179

Stratton v Rastall (1788) 2 TR 366,100 ER 197................................30

Street v Blay (1831) (1831) 2 B & Ad 456, 109 ER 1212......................117

Stuart v Wilkins (1778) 1 Doug 18, 99 ER 15 113

Sumpter v Hedges [1898] 1 QB 673 ....165, 168, 170–74

*The London, Chatham and Dover Railway Company v The South
    Eastern Railway Company* [1893] AC 429 127

Thomas v Brown (1876) 1 QBD 714..174

Thomas v Cadawallader (1744) Willes 496, 125 ER 1286 ....100, 103

Thompson v ASDA-MFI plc [1988] Ch 241 166

Thornton v Place (1832) 1 M & Rob 218, 174 ER 74............................172

Thorp v Thorp (1701) 12 Mod 455, 88 ER 1448; 1 Salk 171, 91 ER 157;
    Holt KB 28, 90 ER 913; Holt KB 96, 90 ER 951;1 Ld Raym 662,
    91 ER 1341..98, 99, 100, 104, 106

Tindal v Brown (1786) 1 TR 167, 99 ER 1033 17

Tomkyns v Barnet (1694) Skinner 411, 90 ER 182 26

Tootal Clothing Ltd v Guinea Properties Ltd (1991) 64 P & C R 455 75

Toussaint v Martinnant (1787) 2 TR 100, 105; 110 ER 55. ....114, 115, 116

Towers v Barett (1786) 1 TR 133,99 ER 1014 31

Townsend v Crowdy (1860) 8 C.B (ns) 477, 141 ER 1251 81

Trench Executor of Squire v Trewin (1696) 1 Ld Raym 124, 91 ER 980..........102

Ughtred's Case (1591) 7 Co Rep 96, 77 ER 425 ....99, 101

Waddington v Oliver (1805) 2 Bos & Pul NR 61, 127 ER 544....................151

Walker v Dixon (1816-1819) 2 Stark 281, 171 ER 647 151

Walker v Walker (1694) 5 Mod 14, 87 ER 490...12, 21

Wallis v Hirsch (1856) 1 CB NS 316,140 ER 131 127

Ward v Bignall [1967] 1 QB 534...127

Weaver v Boroughs (1725) 1 Str 648, 93 ER 757 ....116, 132

Weston v Downes (1778) 1 Doug 21, 99 ER 19 ....31, 39, 112, 113, 135

Whincup v Hughes (1871) 24 LT 76 ....129, 148, 149, 153, 154

White Arrow v Lamey's Distribution Limited, The Times, 21 July, 1995 149

Wilson v Johnson (1873) LR 16 Eq 606 154

Withers v Reynolds (1831) 2 B & Ad 882, 109 ER 1370..134

Wright v Newton (1835) 2 CrM & R 124, 150 ER53...124

Yates v Carlisle (1761) 1 Black W 270, 96 ER 150 15

Young v Taylor (1818) 8 Taunt 315, 129 ER 404. 116

Table of Statutes and Foreign Legislation

United Kingdom

3 & 4 Anne C9 25
9 & 10 Will 3 c 17 25
Bankrupts England Act 1825
  s 110 39
Law of Property (Miscellaneous Provisions) Act 1989
  s 2 75
Law Reform (Frustrated Contracts) Act 1943 ....1, 153
Partnership Act 1890 ....
  s 40 155
Sales of Goods Act 1893 ....
  s 11 (1)(c) 118, 120
  s 18, r 1 118
Sale of Goods Act 1979
  s 11(4) 118
  s 15A 121
  s 17(1) 118
  s 30 (1) 150

Germany

German Civil Code
  § 812 BGB 72

Introduction

THIS BOOK EXAMINES how the law of unjust enrichment can be employed to claim restitution of the value of benefits transferred under a contract that is *not* void, voidable or frustrated. It is therefore concerned with the role of unjust enrichment in the context of contracts which are (a) terminated for breach, (b) subsisting, or (c) unenforceable. Taken together these different situations make up what is referred to in this book as 'the contractual context'. The primary focus is on restitution (founded on unjust enrichment) for an innocent party where he or she has terminated a contract for breach. The book is also underpinned by detailed and original historical research which sheds new light on aspects of the history of the laws of unjust enrichment and contract.

The justification for limiting the scope of this book in the way described above is that the reason for restitution in these situations is, so it will be argued, failure of condition (what has traditionally been called 'failure of consideration' in the leading works on restitution). This contrasts with the reason for restitution being a vitiating factor (eg duress or undue influence) or that the contract is void so that restitution, in line with Birks' new approach, follows 'directly from the invalidity of the supposed basis of the payments'.[1] A contract discharged for frustration is very similar to the contracts considered and, arguably, fits within the failure of condition model advocated (indeed traditionally frustration cases have been covered within chapters dealing with failure of consideration). However, in the context of frustrated contracts the common law approach has been significantly altered by statutory intervention (the Law Reform (Frustrated Contracts) Act 1943). For this reason, frustrated contracts are not dealt with in this book.

The traditional account in Anglo-American jurisprudence, which in this book will be referred to as 'the dominant model', is that, provided the innocent party has terminated the contract for breach, he or she can elect to claim restitution of the value of the benefits transferred under the contract, instead of expectation damages. This is said to be a claim outside the contract, based on unjust enrichment for (total or partial) failure of consideration.[2] This model has been challenged and the task of this book is to assess this challenge and, more widely, to analyse what is the best framework for deciding whether restitution is available in the contractual context (as defined above).

The analysis which follows is heavily reliant on history. By adopting this methodology, no excuses are made, for it is not one which in any way conflicts

---

[1] P Birks, *Unjust Enrichment* (2nd edn, Oxford, OUP, 2005) 110. Birks' new approach is discussed and defended in Chapter 3.

[2] Exceptionally, it is also possible to claim the profits made from the breach of contract: *AG v Blake* [2001] 1 AC 268 (HL). This type of claim (for restitution for a wrong rather than restitution of an unjust enrichment) will not be discussed in this book.

with that applied by the leading works on the law of restitution. Taking the first edition of Professor Burrows' popular book on restitution[3] as an example, out of the 773 cases collected in the table of cases, just over one-third, about 260, are from the nineteenth century or before. If we then factor in that many of these cases are not only the foundation of the later cases in the twentieth century, but also underpin the analytical structure of the whole subject,[4] we begin to see that the older cases are of even greater influence than the bare numbers above suggest. It is in this sense that restitution scholars can be described as 'historians'. Accordingly, this book goes into considerable historical detail to find the context, and lines of reasoning around, the foundational cases of the earlier period, which are mainly from the eighteenth and nineteenth centuries. Extensive reference will be made not just to secondary sources but primary sources too (such as manuscript law reports, judges' notes and unpublished treatises). The historical analysis will enable us to test and understand the dominant model as well as the aspects of the competing models put forward by those challenging it.

Chapter 1 establishes that, historically, the standard claims for restitution (that is, the indebitatus claims, in particular, the action for money had and received) were viewed and understood as having been founded on a cause of action that was independent of contract (and wrongs). Moreover, it will show why attempts to shape that independence around equitable notions of unconscientiousness rather than unjust enrichment would be misconceived. The chapter will also show how the influence of Lord Mansfield, Blackstone, Roman law or equity on the development of indebitatus claims has been exaggerated.

Chapter 2 focuses specifically on restitution after termination for breach. It looks at the argument, made particularly by Professor Kull (who is the Reporter for the proposed United States' *Third Restatement of Restitution and Unjust Enrichment*) that restitution after termination for breach is contractual, rather than a claim founded on unjust enrichment. It will be shown that the historical and non-historical arguments made in support of such a position are unpersuasive.

The view that the law can *never* escape from its historical 'shape' must, however, be resisted. The present arguments about the best approach to determining whether an enrichment at the claimant's expense is unjust, is a controversial and fascinating example. This is the subject matter of Chapter 3. It shows that, even though one of the messages from Chapter 1 was that the unjust factors approach may be a defensible rationalisation of the cases, the best way forward for the law of unjust enrichment is to adopt a civilian 'absence of basis' approach, as advocated by Birks in his final work. However, it is important to appreciate, and indeed an imperative feature of any convincing model of the law, that Birks' model broadly fits with the decided cases.

With the independence and preferred general model for the law of unjust enrichment clarified, Chapters 4 to 6 work towards elaborating the details of the

[3] AS Burrows, *The Law of Restitution* (1st edn, London, Butterworths, 1993).
[4] Professor Birks' recent work puts the case of *Kelly v Solari* (1841) 9 M & W 54, 152 ER 24 at the centre of the subject: Birks (n 1 above), ch 1 generally.

role of unjust enrichment in the contractual context. A new model will be proposed, under which it will be argued that the key to determining the availability of a restitutionary claim in the contractual context requires the resolution of the following two questions: (a) was the transfer of the benefit conditional?; and (b) was there a qualifying failure of condition?

Chapter 4 introduces the main arguments that will be developed in Chapters 5 and 6. The historical analysis in Chapter 5 provides valuable insights on the evolution and establishment of the dominant model, specifically how the rules on the termination of contracts developed, the quantum meruit claim, the total failure of consideration requirement, the meaning of rescission in the older cases and the operation of the money had and received count in the contractual context. This chapter lays down the foundation for the new model by showing that in order to bring claims for a quantum meruit or money had and received (which today form the basis of a claim founded on unjust enrichment) the presence of a conditional transfer was always necessary, but rescission (which today is described as termination) of the contract was not. More generally, one of the lessons of Chapter 5 will be that greater attention needs to be paid to the law relating to conditions and performance. How the law would then look is mapped out in Chapter 6.

Chapter 6 defines the meaning of 'condition' and shows that what qualifies as a failure of a condition depends on whether the contract is apportioned or unapportioned. It is only when the contract is considered unapportioned that termination of the contract is needed to meet the qualifying failure of condition requirement. This chapter includes discussion of accrued rights to receive performance, the prevention principle and quantum meruit claims. Overall, it is submitted that the proposed failure of condition model is not only to be preferred to the dominant model applicable to an innocent party's claim for restitution after breach but, more widely, provides a convincing account of the role of unjust enrichment in the contractual context.

1

An Historical Analysis of the
Independence of Unjust Enrichment

I. Introduction

F ROM THE MOMENT that Ames announced in his historical survey of assumpsit, that a large class of indebitatus assumpsit claims ('indebitatus claims') were based on unjust enrichment and not implied contract,[1] scholarship on restitution has been marked by a distinctly historical turn. Jackson, in one of the early studies on the subject, accurately observed: 'But there can be no clear dividing line between legal history and exposition of current law, and the attempted distinction is often merely an expression of the fact that a writer has to stop somewhere'.[2]

This is particularly true of the subject of the present chapter about the existence, foundation and exposition of unjust enrichment, as an independent cause of action

---

[1] JB Ames, 'The History of Assumpsit' (1888) 2 *Harv L Rev* 1, 53, 64. The second part, from 53, deals with what Ames calls 'implied assumpsit' and which mostly comprised what in the eighteenth century were referred to as the indebitatus assumpsit claims. The indebitatus formula would be used mainly to make the following types of claim: (1) for goods sold; (2) for work done; (3) for money lent; (4) for money paid (that is, laid out to the claimant's use at his request); (5) for money had and received to the claimant's use; (6) for money due upon an account stated; and (7) for the use and occupation of land: JH Baker, 'The Use of Assumpsit for Restitutionary Money Claims 1600–1800' in E Schrage (ed), *Unjust Enrichment: the Comparative Legal History of the Law of Restitution* (Berlin, Duncker & Humbolt, 1995) 34–5.

[2] RM Jackson, *The History of Quasi Contract in English Law* (Cambridge, CUP, 1936) preface, xxiii. Despite its title, Jackson does discuss the current law and its interpretation in light of the historical material, a feature which is evident in the earliest works to the most recent. In the United States, Ames' work was followed by two treatises and a casebook of text and materials: WA Keener, *A Treatise on the Law of Quasi-Contracts* (New York, Baker, Voorhis & Co, 1893); FC Woodward, *The Law of Quasi Contracts* (Boston, Little, Brown, & Co, 1913); and JB Scott, *Cases on Quasi-Contracts* (New York, Baker, Voorhis & Co, 1905). In England, as well as Jackson's book, there were PH Winfield, *The Province of the Law of Tort*, Tagore law lectures,1930 (Cambridge, CUP, 1931) and PH Winfield, *The Law of Quasi-Contracts* (London, Sweet & Maxwell 1952) as well as JH Munkman, *The Law of Quasi-Contracts* (London, Sir Isaac Pitman & Sons, 1950). The modern standard works also rely heavily on historical materials: AS Burrows, *The Law of Restitution* (2nd edn, London, Butterworths, 2002); G Virgo, *The Principles of the Law of Restitution* (2nd edn, Oxford, OUP, 2006); P Birks, *Unjust Enrichment* (2nd edn, Oxford, OUP, 2005) and the main practitioner's work R Goff of Chieveley and GH Jones, *The Law of Restitution* (7th edn, London, Sweet & Maxwell, 2007). The historical tendency of restitution scholarship is more generally discussed in D Ibbetson, 'Unjust Enrichment in English Law' in E Schrage (ed), *Unjust Enrichment and the Law of Contract* (The Hague/London, Kluwer Law International, 2001) 50.

within the law of obligations. The debate around this subject has given rise to diverse streams of argument. Some argue that many of the claims covered by unjust enrichment are better described as contractual.[3] Even where there is agreement on the existence of an independent category, there is division over its formulation. One group seek inspiration from equity and particularly unconscientiousness.[4] Another, adopting an unjust enrichment model, differ over its best rationalisation: should it be on the basis of unjust factors[5] or, following Birks' recent work, absence of basis?[6] These questions strike at the very heart of understanding restitutionary remedies in the contractual context. These debates correctly proceed from a historical basis because it is that which, at least, sets the agenda and, in many cases, provides the best answer to the question about classifying and understanding indebitatus claims. The aim is to use history to illuminate the present.

The central battleground is the eighteenth century, and especially the chief justiceship of Lord Mansfield in the King's Bench (1756–88). As the century when indebitatus claims became very common, the focus on this time-frame is justified. It will be argued in this chapter that the best way to answer the questions posed by the debates, above, is to take a more contextual approach to the older law, especially that in the eighteenth century.

Allowing the eighteenth century to speak with its own voice enables us to resist the temptation of perceiving older law as being, by today's standards, less sophisticated. And this is all too easy when one considers certain aspects of the older civil procedure, built around the forms of action, and the lack of general legal literature compared with today, or even with the century which followed the eighteenth. This temptation, I would suggest, has played out in the present discourse about the foundation of unjust enrichment in a number of ways. One manifestation is to

---

[3] S Hedley has been the most vociferous in pushing for the contractual explanation: S Hedley, *Restitution: Its Division and Ordering* (London, Sweet & Maxwell, 2001) chs 2, 3; S Hedley, 'Implied Contract and Restitution' (2004) 63 *CLJ* 435; and S Hedley, 'Unjust Enrichment: the Same Old Mistake?' in A Robertson (ed), *Law of Obligations: Connections and Boundaries* (London, UCL, 2004). P Jaffey also adopts a contractual explanation of many of the claims, except that his theory requires the adoption of a different model of contract, one which is geared towards fulfilling the reliance interest: P Jaffey, *The Nature and Scope of Restitution: Vitiated Transfers, Imputed Contracts and Disgorgement* (Oxford, Hart, 2000) 29–33.

[4] B Kremer, 'The Action for Money Had and Received' (2001) *Journal of Contract Law* 1; B Kremer, 'Restitution and Unconscientiousness: Another View' (2003) 119 *LQR* 188; and Gummow J's strong endorsement of the equitable perspective in *Roxborough v Rothmans* (2002) ALR 335, 354–66.

[5] This is the approach taken by the standard works: Burrows (n 2 above) and Virgo (n 2 above). T Krebs argues that the unjust factor approach is better suited to English law than the civilian model (as to which see n 6 below): T Krebs, 'In Defence of Unjust Factors' in D Johnston and R Zimmermann (eds), *Unjustified Enrichment: Key Issues in Comparative Perspective* (Cambridge, CUP, 2002). This was also the essence of the argument in the discussion group reviewing this aspect of Birks' book, which attempts to reorient English law towards the civilian model (on which see note 6 below): (2004) *RLR* 260, 270–6.

[6] His new model was first put forward in P Birks, *Unjust Enrichment* (1st edn, Oxford, Clarendon, 2003) (in 2005 a new edition was published posthumously). This reorientation was in part inspired by S Meier's work: 'Restitution after Executed Void Contracts' in P Birks and F Rose (eds), *Lessons from the Swaps Litigation* (London, Mansfield LLP, 2000) 206–13; and 'Unjust Factors and Legal Grounds' in D Johnston and R Zimmermann (eds), *Unjustified Enrichment: Key Issues in Comparative Perspective* (Cambridge, CUP, 2002) 67–75.

overemphasise certain aspects of the eighteenth century either through mytholo-gising the contribution, whether good or bad, of men such as Lord Mansfield[7] or Sir William Blackstone,[8] or to exaggerate the influence of Roman law[9] or equity.[10] Another manifestation is the adoption of an attitude which dismisses the eigh-teenth century as a 'conglomerate of odds and ends of law'[11] without more.

To avert these risks, part II of this chapter will explain the features which tend to deflect the attention from the state of the law in the eighteenth century. It will be split into two parts. The first section will argue that there was a sufficiently worked out consensus theory of contract, which informed the way indebitatus claims were understood as being non-contractual. This is not appreciated in the literature, either because it is assumed that a coherent theory of contract only really emerged in the nineteenth century or because it is thought that in the eigh-teenth century the term 'contract' is used only as a tool of classification rather than something that is capable of generating a right of action. The second section will explain the relevant procedure, focussing on pleading and the jury, and its influ-ence on indebitatus claims. It will also point out that the lack of legal literature in the eighteenth century was not necessarily due to a lack of expertise or sophistica-tion but may have been due to the severe monopolies operated by the book trade during this century. This meant that legal thought, whether through law reports or law books, was not very visible on matters relevant today. However, this does not mean that no thought was given to these matters. This last point also illustrates why looking at manuscript sources becomes important, because the fact that legal material (such as cases or texts) was not printed did not mean it was unsuitable, unimportant or worse still perhaps, unreliable, as might be implied today.

The period before *Moses v Macferlan* (1760)[12] ('*Moses*') is not usually explored in any great detail and is seen as not having contributed much to the theorising of the law around the indebitatus claims and the money had and received claim ('MHR') in particular. This is partly because of the dearth of good quality law reports discussing indebitatus claims covering the end of the seventeenth and first half of the eighteenth centuries. The result is an overestimation of the contribu-tion of *Moses* and a lack of clarity about the influences on Lord Mansfield's think-ing when he handed down this decision. Part III will seek to draw a fuller picture of the law during this period through three sections and therefore place *Moses* in context. The first section will show that by Holt CJ's time, indebitatus claims were

---

[7] This would be the case predominantly with all the works in the area, many of which are men-tioned in n 2 above. The impression is reinforced by those works focusing on the history only: Baker (n 1 above) 53–7; J Oldham, *The Mansfield Manuscripts and the Growth of English Law in the Eighteenth Century* (Chapel Hill, University of North Carolina Press, 1992) esp 226–32.

[8] P Birks and G Mcleod, 'The Implied Contract Theory of Quasi Contract: Civilian Opinion Current in the Century Before Blackstone' (1986) *OJLS* 46.

[9] *Ibid* and P Birks, 'English and Roman Learning in Moses v Macferlan' (1984) 37 *CLP* 1.

[10] See references in n 4 above.

[11] J Perillo, 'Restitution in a Contractual Context' (1973) 73 *Colum L Rev* 1208, 1222. A similar assumption seems to have been made by J Gordley, 'Common Law in the Twentieth Century: Some Unfinished Business' (2000) 88 *Cal L Rev* 1816, 1817–21.

[12] (1760) 2 Burr 1005, 97 ER 676.

already perceived as non-contractual, in the sense discussed in part II. This more coherent non-contractual picture of the claim is sometimes lost because of the focus on Holt CJ's criticism of the expanding province of the actions during his time as Chief Justice of the King's Bench. The first section will also reassess Holt CJ's criticisms and will argue that his concerns were understandable and directed to specific problems that would still have been of concern when the indebitatus claims were much encouraged in Lord Mansfield's time. It will be suggested that he would not have objected to the many situations identified in *Moses*, where MHR could be employed. One of the effects of seeing the indebitatus claims as non-contractual is that the focus then shifts to the particular situations in which the different claims arise (for example, in relation to MHR, it is the mistake or the failure of consideration which generates the claim and not some contract). It was Lord Mansfield's synthesis of the relevant situations in *Moses* which is seen as one of his major contributions to the law in this area. If, as has been said so far, the non-contractual nature of the indebitatus claims was appreciated by Holt CJ's time, why did we have to wait for Lord Mansfield to provide a synthesis of the situations in which MHR could be employed? In fact we did not, and the first section will illustrate through the limited case law and manuscript sources that a synthesis of the different situations had already been reached in the cases before *Moses*.

The picture of the law before *Moses* would not be complete if we did not explain two further features of it: first, the language of equity and its potential influence on Lord Mansfield's thinking and, secondly, his desire to encourage indebitatus claims, and MHR in particular. The remaining two sections of part III deal with these two features. The second section will provide evidence, through manuscript sources, to show that Lord Mansfield was not borrowing any specific doctrines from equity in his decision in *Moses*. The law relating to restitutionary money claims at the time and before *Moses* was more fully worked out in the common law than in equity. The third section will explain why Lord Mansfield was a great 'friend' of the indebitatus claims. In a period when the majority of civil litigation continued to be taken up with debt litigation, there was a demand for quick and inexpensive resolutions to disputes, especially in the context of small debt litigation. Here, the indebitatus claims represented an attractive pleading form because of the minimum effort and expense (as compared with special assumpsit) required to employ them for a claim. Lord Mansfield understood this and wanted to encourage this more effective form of justice. There was also another motivation. One must not overlook the great gains to be made by capturing the debt litigation market, because the judges had a pecuniary interest in the litigation which passed through their court. And it is noteworthy that in Lord Mansfield's time in particular, the King's Bench enjoyed spectacular growth in its share of the debt litigation market as compared to its rival for this work, the Court of Common Pleas.

Part IV assesses Lord Mansfield's exact innovation in *Moses* in the light of the discussion in part III. We will see that couching the action in terms of equity was likely to be his main contribution, rather than a synthesis of the different situations in which MHR could be employed or holding that it was non-contractual.

Part IV will also show how, in theoretical terms, Lord Mansfield envisaged equitable principles and their relation to principles of the common law, as well as his exposure to the principle of unjust enrichment as a possible rationalisation of claims for restitution. This will be explored by examining Lord Mansfield's reaction to Lord Kames' work on equity.

Part V will track the development of the law after *Moses*, by looking at case law (first section) and legal discourse (second section). In terms of case law it will be argued that there are broadly two noteworthy periods. The first, covering the period between *Moses* and roughly the end of the eighteenth century, witnessed the highpoint in equity reasoning when the courts effectively approached the task of determining whether the MHR claim would succeed by asking whether it was unconscionable for the defendant to retain the money claimed. The uncertainty such a broad principle caused generated a backlash, such that towards the end of the eighteenth century and certainly throughout the nineteenth century there was never again a period when equitable reasoning was so dominant in MHR and indebitatus claims generally. This is the location of the second period of case law, which shows the courts focussing on the situations in which the claim arose rather than any broad principle. Contrary to modern accounts, it was during this second period where we see that sometimes the courts overlooked the fiction of the contract in the implied contract explanation, treating the indebitatus claims as genuinely contractual. It will be argued that this was something that would not have happened in the eighteenth century. In terms of legal discourse, a number of sources will be referred to, to illustrate that the non-contractual nature of the indebitatus claims was grasped and alternative explanations suggested in relation to it at various points in the late eighteenth century and the nineteenth century, before the contributions of Maine and Ames. The extremely important arguments of these two authors, especially Ames, were not as novel or as groundbreaking as is usually assumed.

Finally, part V will seek to apply the lessons of the historical account to modern debates over the exposition of the modern law of unjust enrichment. The consistent non-contractual treatment of the indebitatus claims strongly vindicates treating the law of unjust enrichment as an independent cause of action within the law of obligations, separate from the laws of torts and contract. Moreover the problems experienced by founding the indebitatus claims on broad equitable principles during Lord Mansfield's time provide ample support for those who argue against making unconscientiousness the principle which underlies the modern law of unjust enrichment. However, there are still those who argue that either all or part of the modern law of unjust enrichment should be treated as part of the law of contract. In so far as these authors raise specific arguments not covered in this chapter, they will be dealt with in Chapter 2. Moreover, defending the view of an independent law of unjust enrichment does not mean that the way it is has operated in England is correct. As Chapter 3 will argue, Birks' new approach, which is founded on a civilian 'absence of basis' conception, is to be preferred over the pure unjust factors approach currently adopted by the common law.

II. Myth, Mystery and Illusion

A. Two Senses of 'Contract': a Source of Rights and as a Method of Classification

Ames' analysis of the indebitatus claims was built on identifying that the promise or contract implied in law in many of those claims was fictional and therefore the claims were non-contractual. In the discussion which follows it will be argued that the indebitatus claims were perceived in this way throughout the late seventeenth and eighteenth centuries, which was the period when they became more commonly pleaded. In order to sustain such an argument it will have to be shown at the outset that there was a theory of contract during this period which would identify (as was the case when Ames was writing) that anything not involving a parties' actual (express or implied) agreement would be considered as non-contractual. In other words, we need to establish that there was a consensual theory of contract at the relevant time. Such a task poses three problems.

The first is that there is a considerable line of literature which effectively states that a theory or coherent law of contract—on which basis one could identify something as non-contractual—only really emerged in the nineteenth century.[13] Secondly, a cursory glance at, for example, the contemporary treatise literature in the eighteenth century shows that the indebitatus claims were discussed in terms of promises and contracts,[14] confirming the view held by some that they were perceived as variants of a contractual claim.[15] Thirdly, historians have tended to emphasise the disunity amongst the indebitatus claims, pointing to the fact that some of the counts required the express proof of request.[16] However, they also point to the potential for the request to be fictional, something which occurred more frequently from the latter part of the eighteenth century. Nevertheless, such a view tends to undermine the attempt made here to view indebitatus claims as a single category which was understood theoretically as non-contractual. The key to resolving these three problems and to supporting the broader claim made in this chapter is to appreciate the two senses in which the term 'contract' is used in the period we are focussing on. The first sense is the one which generates rights and is based on the consensual theory which we generally recognise today. The second sense in which contract is employed is as a classificatory category.

---

[13] P Hamburger, 'The Development of the Nineteenth-Century Consensus Theory of Contract' (1989) 7 *Law and History Review* 241, 245–6, identifies a number of legal historians who take this view, albeit for different reasons, including PS Atiyah, *The Rise and Fall of Freedom of Contract* (Oxford, Clarendon Press, 1979), M Horwitz, *Transformation of American Law 1780–1860* (Cambridge, Harvard University Press, 1977) and AW Simpson, 'Innovation in Nineteenth Century Contract Law' (1975) 91 *LQR* 247.

[14] See eg the references in n 101 below (where the eighteenth century literature is cited).

[15] Ibbetson (n 2 above) 38.

[16] Baker (n 1 above) 35, 41–7; DJ Ibbetson, *A Historical Introduction to the Law of Obligations* (Oxford, OUP, 1999) 270–1.

The starting point is the persuasive and powerful case made by Hamburger that in the seventeenth, and especially the eighteenth, century common lawyers used civilian sources selectively to etch out a consensual theory of contract for the common law.[17] The consensual theory attracted the attention of common lawyers because 'it provided them with what had long been absent from the common law, a description of the consensual reality of contracts'.[18] He points to a number of contemporary published and unpublished sources which evidence the recognition of this consensual reality.[19] He also explains that a number of practical constraints in the eighteenth century prevented the consensus theory from influencing and shaping contract doctrine until the nineteenth century.

For our purposes, it is sufficient to note that while the different elements were not fully elaborated, the consensual theory was employed as a way of distinguishing express promises or contracts, which were enforced through special assumpsit, and promises or contracts implied in law.[20] Gilbert's description is an excellent example:

Note the difference between an Assumpsit in Deed and an Assumpsit in Law; in the Assumpsit in Deed where the contracts are mutual, and either side declares for non performance, there he must set forth the very contract, and if he mistakes in Quantities or Sums, he fails; because his injury is in the Non performance of the very contract alledged in the declaration, and if he does not shew such a contract, he does not intitle himself to a recompence of the breach of it.

But where he brings his Action for an Assumpsit in Law, if he shews Part of the goods delivered, or Part of the money lent, 'tis good; because on every several Delivery of Goods, or receipt of money, the law implies a several Contract for Restitution, and there the gist of the inquiry is not whether such a particular contract is broken, but whether the goods were delivered, or Money paid to the defendant, and the quantities of the goods or the sum is no farther material than to increase or lessen the damages.[21]

---

[17] Hamburger (n 13 above) esp 265–9.

[18] *Ibid* 270.

[19] Including J Gilbert's unpublished treatise on contracts from around 1705 (British Library MS Hargrave 265, 266); Sir Robert Henley's (Lord Nottingham) notes in his commonplace book (unpublished, BL Additional MS 26060 f 14); H Ballow (or Bellewe), *Treatise on Equity* (London, D Browne and J Shuckburgh, 1737); W Jones, *An Essay on the Law of Bailments* (London, C Dilly, 1781); and JJ Powell, *Essay Upon the Law of Contracts and Agreements* (London, J Johnson and T Whieldon, 1790). To this list must be added W Sheppard, *Actions Upon the Case for Deeds viz Contracts, Assumpsits, Deceits, Nuisances, Trover and Conversion* (2nd edn, London, SS, 1675), a work of the second half of the seventeenth century. In ch 4 concerning 'Of an action upon the case arising upon, and conversant about a contract, or agreement; and of an assumpsit; and where an action will lie about this or not' (35), he discusses different requirements which would be recognisable to anyone familiar with the common law of contract today, starting with his definition of the subject: 'That contract (largely taken) is an agreement between two, or more, about something to be done, whereby both parties are bound to each other, or one is bound to the other' (36).

[20] It should be emphasised that contrary to Ibbetson's (n 16 above) 271–2 contention, the vocabulary of promises and contracts was used interchangeably. While most of the references in n 101 below refer to promises, for examples of the use of contract see the Gilbert extract which follows (text to n 21) and Sheppard (n 19 above) 36.

[21] J Gilbert, *The Law of Evidence* (London, W Owen, 1756) 193–4. A similar statement appears in Gilbert's unpublished treatise on contract from around 1705 (BL MS Hargrave 265 f 95) (for which see Baker (n 1 above) 55).

The distinction being made here explains why the difference between promises implied by law and those made by the parties was emphasised in the literature throughout the eighteenth century.[22] It was a difference not without significance. As will be illustrated, attempts to limit indebitatus claims through an argument that such a claim could not be used where a contract (based on consensus) between the parties was not possible, was rejected in a case as early as 1677/78.[23] The key was not whether the parties' agreement could or would arise in the circumstances, but whether there was some 'meritorious action'[24] which would generate a right to restitution.

That the essence of the indebitatus claims was that they were not founded on a consensual theory of contract also explains why, despite the difference between the counts (eg some requiring proof of request) they were treated theoretically as a unified category. The non-contractual essence was seen as the characterising feature.

The second sense of contract was that of classificatory tool. The two sources for this way of thinking were, first, the evolution of the assumpsit form of action which required a commitment to the promissory language (even though the cases we are speaking about no longer contained promises) and, secondly, the sense in which 'the whole business of human negotiations' was considered contractual by writers.[25] It was in this sense that indebitatus claims continued to be discussed in the language of promises and contracts. This is vividly illustrated in Lord Mansfield's judgment in *Moses* and the period thereafter. His judgment in *Moses*, as we will see, sought to place MHR on an equitable foundation, which he did not think contradicted his statement that the claim he was dealing with was contractual too.[26] It was, of course, contractual in the classificatory sense that all these matters of human interaction were contractual. This sense of contract did not, as the cases after *Moses* show, inform the reasoning adopted in the judgments.[27]

It is important to note that the classification of indebitatus claims as contractual had operative effects of two kinds. The first was that contractual claims (including indebitatus claims) were an exception to the rule that common law personal actions (eg tort) do not survive the death of the parties.[28] The second effect was that indebitatus claims were also considered contractual for the purposes of the rule that it was impermissible to join causes of action in contract and tort.[29]

All this is not to say that a contract was not at the root of some of the situations in which indebitatus claims were used or that some of the claims were later

---

[22] See the references in n 101 below.

[23] *Arris & Arris v Stukeley* (1677/78) 2 Mod 260, 86 ER 1060. See text around n 63 below.

[24] *Walker v Walker* (1694) 5 Mod 14, 87 ER 490. See text around n 65 below.

[25] The quote is from Powell (n 19 above) vol 1, v (message to the reader). For other similar quotes from writers see Hamburger (n 13 above) 272–3.

[26] See part IV generally. See especially the text from n 141 below onwards.

[27] See part V, section A(i).

[28] *Saunders v Plummer* (1662) Bridg O 223, 124 ER 557.

[29] *Denison v Ralphson* (1682) 1 Ventris 365, 86 ER 235; 2 Shower KB 250, 89 ER 921 (*Beningsage v Ralphson*); Skinner 66, 90 ER 32 (*Bevingsay v Ralston*).

considered to be part of the law of contract (as it expanded its horizon and became settled in the nineteenth century). For example, the action for an agreed sum is considered a contractual claim today but would be litigated in the eighteenth century through the indebitatus formula. This reality of the changing boundary of causes of action and/or the factual basis of a claim should not distract us from the fact that the existence of a contract was not a necessary precondition for the indebitatus claims. It was in this sense that the essence of the claim was non-contractual. Waiver of tort cases provide an instructive analogy. The ability of a party to waive a tort and instead rely on indebitatus claims did not change the nature of either action. In one situation, the case was presented as a tort and in another, by 'waiving the tort', as a non-contractual claim for money.

B. Procedure and the Development of Indebitatus Claims

It is hard to escape the impression from many of the accounts that the practical mind-set of the eighteenth century lawyer made him uninterested in or incapable of theorising about indebitatus claims before Lord Mansfield. The fiction of the promise within the pleadings, represented as fact on the record, civil trial by jury, and the general lack of coherent expression of any theory to rival Lord Mansfield's, reinforce this impression. As Baker has argued, the culture of fiction suppressed principle because a lawyer may be content:

> to say that in certain factual situations the law implies a promise on which assumpsit may be brought, without asking the wider question of why the law should imply promises in some situations and not in others. This short-sightedness bedevils the history of restitution in England at least down to the time of Lord Mansfield.[30]

I will deal with the lack of literature point later. Here I want to look at the relationship between procedure and the development of indebitatus claims more carefully and to suggest that it is likely that in the eighteenth century judges or lawyers did think more widely about indebitatus claims before Lord Mansfield.

Generally, the forms of action represent a repository of the older law,[31] pointing to the broad outline of facts needed to bring a claim. Within the process of pleading, near formulaic forms of action aided the tight control and management

---

[30] Baker (n 1 above) 34.
[31] Indeed, as Maitland observed, a history of the forms of action would be a 'full history of English Private Law': FW Maitland, *The Forms of Action at Common Law* (Cambridge, CUP, repr 1941) 10. Perhaps the point can be made quite clearly if we look at J Chitty's book on pleading at the turn of the century, and which Stephen lauded in his own acclaimed work on the same subject. J Chitty, *A Practical Treatise on Pleading and to the Parties to the Action with a second volume containing Precedents of Pleadings* (1st edn, London, W Clarke 1809) distilled points of principle as they arose in relation to each form of action which produced, in the section on assumpsit, what can be considered the precursor to the book on contract that Chitty's son produced in 1826. The style is one of continuous prose, rather than a series of summaries or abridgments of cases. The authorities are footnoted where relevant. This is the modern form of treatise which became increasingly popular in the nineteenth century. One cannot help but think that the preparation of this work set the foundation for the work on contracts.

over the question of law or fact that would be debated at trial. This was done primarily by the rule as to single issues: by the process of pleading the parties were required to arrive at a single issue of fact or law.[32] This was the chief object of pleading. If it was a question of fact then it would proceed to trial by jury. If it was a question of law, then the issue, a demurrer, would be placed before the bench. The process could potentially be long and arduous and since it provides the background to understanding the law, it is important to appreciate the various pleading stages.[33]

After the issue of the writ, the stages of pleading would begin. The first stage was the composition of the form of action or cause of action in the declaration. The form of action would follow the tenor of the writ. There were various counts to pick from, which could be used in the declaration. Pleadings could then proceed as follows:

(1) The defendant would consider the claim in the declaration and decide whether to raise a question of law (demur) or fact.

(2) If the defendant demurred then it would be expressed in form and tendered to the claimant, who would be obliged to join the demurrer. By this *joinder in demurrer* a question was created on the matter of the declaration's legal sufficiency and this would go to the court for decision.

(3) But if the defendant did not demur then the pleading stages continued. Leaving aside possible pleas by the defendant which, for example, could raise matters of jurisdiction, procedural objections on the writ or capacity of the parties to sue (pleas which tend to simply divert, suspend or abate the particular writ) we can move on to the next possible stage. Here the defendant could make two types of pleas. The first type was by way of *traverse*, which was effectively denying all or some essential part of the substance of the facts of the claim. The second type of plea was a *confession and avoidance* which 'admitting them [the facts] to be true, allege new facts which obviate or repel their legal effect'.[34]

(4) If the defendant traversed, this raised an issue straight away and then the question of fact would be tendered by the defendant. If it was accepted and the claimant joined in the issue, it would go to trial. Unlike a demurrer, the claimant was at liberty not to accept the traverse and could then plead in response. He would have the same options available to him: he could consider the traverse insufficient in law (either substance or form) and so he might demur at this stage as well.

---

[32] If there were multiple counts, then an issue was allowed for each count.

[33] What follows is primarily based on W Holdsworth, *History of English Law* (London, Methuen, 1922–66) ('*HEL*'), vol III (627–58) and vol IX (263–335). His account gives a historical background to the pleading rules which were applicable throughout the period we are studying and beyond. H Stephen, *A Treatise on the Principle of Pleading in Civil Actions* (2nd edn, London, J Butterworth, 1827) has also been cross-referenced, as well as JF Schiefer, *An Explanation of the Practice of Law: Containing the Elements of Special Pleading, reduced to the comprehension of every one.* (London, J Pheney, 1792).

[34] Stephen (n 33 above) 75.

(5) If the defendant confessed and avoided, again the claimant could either demur or could plead to it either by traversing or confessing and avoiding. If pleading in response to the defendant, this kind of pleading was called a *replication.*

(6) And to this replication the defendant could then either demur or plead, by traversing or confessing and avoiding. This stage of pleading was called the *rejoinder.* This kind of altercation in the pleading process continued until an issue of fact was joined upon by the parties. As an overview, the stages were as follows: declaration, plea, replication, rejoinder, surejoinder, rebutter and surrebutter (and could continue).

Once the parties had reached a triable issue, a transcript of the various pleadings that had been delivered was made up. For an issue at law the transcript was called a demurrer book, and for an issue of fact, a paper book. Reinforcing the repetitiveness (it was after all done by hand) the next stage was the entering of the issue, which was essentially copying the aforementioned transcript onto the official record (the issue roll). It was then filed at the relevant office of the court, whereupon it would proceed to trial to be heard either exclusively by judges in court (if it was a question of law) or a jury (if a question of fact).

Despite the admirable object of the process to reach a single issue on each count, what made it difficult was the law's strong commitment, particularly from the viewpoint of modern eyes, to form; indeed, a question on the propriety of the process was the equivalent to a question of law and was raised as a demurrer. This was compounded by the fact that there was a lot of scope for fatal technical errors, which were often taken and were responsible for the decline of special pleading.[35] Also, with a premium attached to the length of pleadings, there was a suspicion, often realised, that pleadings would be drawn out for gain by the lawyers.[36]

One can see that with such a system, in which the substantive issues were so tightly managed and sometimes not debated because of successful technical objections, there was a real risk for principle to be suppressed or, more aptly, straitjacketed. That is not to say that everything about the system was necessarily bad. The process of pleading certainly resembled a science and, it can be argued persuasively, provided the discipline and structure which the best lawyer/legal mind would appreciate today. Similarly, the single issue rule provides us with a reminder about the law's commitment in this period to simplicity and expediency. It is arguable that these single issues provided a sound basis on which to etch out legal principles.

---

[35] W Blackstone, *Commentaries on the Laws of England* (1st edn, Oxford, Clarendon Press, 1765–69) vol III, 305–6; W Holdsworth, 'The New Rules of Pleading of the Hilary Term, 1834' (1923) 1 *CLJ* 261, esp 267, 271–3 and Holdsworth (n 33 above) vol IX, 281–2; and JH Baker, *An Introduction to Legal History* (4th edn, London, Butterworths, 2002) 86–90. For case law commenting on how technical objections should not get in the way of justice, see *Sayer v Pocock* (1776) 1 Cowp 407, 98 ER 1156; *Peake v Oldham* (1775) 1 Cowp 275, 98 ER 1083; and *R v Mayor and Burgesses of Lyme Regis* (1779) 1 Doug 135, 99 ER 89.

[36] In *Yates v Carlisle* (1761) 1 Black W 270, 96 ER 150, the pleading devices spun out of control, making a paper book of 2,000 sheets, which was reduced to a quarter of a page when the court ordered counsel to make an issue. See also CHS Fifoot, *Lord Mansfield* (Oxford, Clarendon Press, 1936) 61–5.

Nevertheless, the system when applied to contract claims provided little space for theorising. This was in stark contrast to the pleading of indebitatus claims, as they developed in the seventeenth century. Compared to what would be a long particularised declaration, in indebitatus claims, a paragraph with few details on the nature of the claim was sufficient. The indebitatus count stated that:

the defendant, on the ... day of ... at ... in the county of ..., was indebted to the plaintiff in a named sum of money, for real property or goods sold, or for personal services or for money lent, paid, or had and received, or for interest, or for some other pre existing debt on simple contract, incurred at the defendant's request; and that being so indebted, the defendant in consideration thereof afterwards, to wit, on the day and year aforesaid, at ... aforesaid, in the county aforesaid, undertook and faithfully promised the plaintiff to pay him the said sum of money, when he, the said defendant, should be thereunto afterwards requested.[37]

In response the defendant would plead the general issue, 'non assumpsit'. This would be sufficient for the case to be tried. The noteworthy aspect is the very little amount of pleading required and the tolerance for the lack of factual information for the claim. We will come later to why such claims were popular, perhaps even encouraged. With the understanding that the promise in the count was fictional, and that the counts and the defendant did not expose the real nature of the claim or the defence, one can see that the whole burden of deciphering the case and principle to be applied was left to trial. With the pleading process bypassed, as Stephen was to rue later,[38] the rule as to single issues and the other elements pertaining to that process would not interfere with the way the case was decided. Effectively, declaring generally in this way provided greater scope for elaborating principles for recovery. There were three factors which may have limited this ability: the jury trial, the content of the count, and the judge's or lawyer's own capability. But it will be argued that these factors would not have led to there being no theorising at all. Restricting the scope for theorising does not equate to eliminating such scope.

With the indebitatus claims bypassing the pleading process, the burden on the trial would still potentially create a problem for a judge directing a jury. This could be because the jury ignored the judge's direction and so effectively expanded its role from fact-finder to one of determining the law (that is, jury nullification).[39] Or the jury could be employed as a device by a judge to avoid making decisions on the law, as was the general trend in the medieval period.[40] However, in the period with which we are concerned (late seventeenth and eighteenth centuries)[41] judge-

---

[37] Chitty (n 31 above) 334–5 is a composite count used to illustrate the common elements.

[38] Eg he described the plea of general issue as 'narrowing very considerably the application of the greater and more subtle part of the science of pleading': Stephen (n 33 above) 176. More generally see Holdsworth (n 35 above) 266–70.

[39] The negative impact this could have on the development on the law has been mapped out by Green in the criminal law context: TA Green, *Verdict According to Conscience* (Chicago, University of Chicago Press, 1985) ch 3. For civil law examples see J Oldham, *Trial by Jury* (New York, New York University Press, 2006) ch 3.

[40] Baker (n 35 above) 79–80.

[41] See text to nn 59–61 below.

jury relations were more settled, with the latter generally following the direction of the former. Furthermore, judges during this period were more confident and willing to express authoritative decisions on the law, and this was matched by the desire of the legal community and litigants to have the law clearly stated.[42] There were a number of mechanisms which enabled legal discussion and which also acted as a control over the jury's potential to act as an obstacle to theorising.[43] Indirectly, questions of fact could be withdrawn from the jury if they were seen as matters of legal definition;[44] similarly the jury's power would be limited by rules of presumption that they would be directed on, for example, rules of practice, good sense and prima facie rules of law.[45]

More direct mechanisms to raise questions of law for the court, without interference from the jury, were the devices of case reserved, special verdict, motion in arrest of judgment and motion for a new trial. Under the case reserved procedure, the jury would be directed to find a general verdict for the claimant, subject to the court's opinion on the special case or statement of facts. No verdict would be entered on the record at this stage. The statement of facts would be stated by each counsel and dictated by the court. This would be done in front of the jury so that their opinion could be taken if there was any disagreement. The case would be framed as raising a matter of law, and within four days was presented in front of the trial judge, who would decide the case. A general verdict would then be taken and entered onto the record.

Less common than the case reserved procedure was that of the special verdict.[46] Counsel would agree on notes to be given to the jury, who would then consider them and give their verdict privately to the judge. The judge would then (usually the next morning) announce the tentative verdict, and if was agreed to by counsel and then confirmed by the jury, a verdict was entered onto the record. But if it was objected to, then there would be argument.

The two most commonly employed mechanisms in the period discussed here were the motion in arrest of judgment and the motion for a new trial. Under the former, the defendant (after verdict was given for the claimant) would argue that the facts as found did not disclose a cause of action on which the claimant could succeed. Finally, there was the motion for a new trial which could be raised in a wider variety of circumstances in the eighteenth century than had been the case before, including the trial judge's determination that the final verdict was contrary to his direction on the law or evidence, or that he himself had erred in his direction to the jury or in ruling on the admissibility of material evidence.

---

[42] Baker identifies the beginning of this trend from the sixteenth century: (n 35 above) 82–3.

[43] For what follows see generally Baker (n 35 above) 71–85; and J Thayer, ' "Law and Fact" in Jury Trials' (1890–91) 4 *Harv L Rev* 147, 161–9.

[44] *Tindal v Brown* (1786) 1 TR 167, 99 ER 1033, where it was held that the question of what is reasonable notice to the indorser of a bill for non-payment was a matter of law.

[45] J Thayer, 'Presumptions and the Law of Evidence' (1889–90) 3 *Harv L Rev* 141 and Baker (n 35 above) 82–5.

[46] EG Henderson, 'The Background to the Seventh Amendment ' (1966) 80 *Harv L Rev* 289, 307–11.

It has been argued that Lord Mansfield's time was characterised by a greater willingness to employ some of the mechanisms outlined above, which played an important role in his ability to control the jury and develop commercial law.[47] His effective empanelment of special juries, usually composed of merchants, is just one example of this.[48] The relative rise in business in the King's Bench during his time provides strong support for this claim.[49] It should be emphasised, however, that since the period before Lord Mansfield in the eighteenth century has not been studied in as much detail,[50] it is difficult to assess accurately the extent to which Lord Mansfield was more willing to use these mechanisms than his predecessors.[51] Certainly, it should be noted that there are examples of judges willing to employ the mechanisms to elaborate principles of law, even though this may not have been necessary for the case before them.[52]

In sum, the accumulation of mechanisms discussed above meant that the jury was less of an obstacle to the development of the law than might be thought, and perhaps explains why, by the end of the eighteenth century, there was a move in Scotland to introduce trial by jury, something which was achieved later in the nineteenth century.[53]

The second potential limit on the ability to theorise was the count's wording. To a large extent this did place a limit on the elaboration of any principle underlying indebitatus claims, but this was by way of essentially a privity requirement which existed in these claims after Lord Mansfield as well. The general wording was not overly restrictive.

---

[47] Baker (n 1 above) 57; Baker (n 35 above) 85; and Oldham (n 39 above) esp 32–4. In *Lickbarrow v Mason* (1787) 2 TR 63, 73; 100 ER 35, after stating that during 30 years of Lord Mansfield's reign the 'commercial law of this country has taken a very different turn from what it did before', Buller J goes on to explain that before 'that period we find that in Courts of Law all the evidence in mercantile cases was thrown together; they were left generally to the jury, and they produced no established principle'. In contrast, during Lord Mansfield's time general principles were 'stated, reasoned upon, enlarged, and explained, till we have been lost in admiration at the strength and stretch of human understanding'. This statement, as is indicated by the flourish at the end, should be understood in light of a mentee's attempt to pay tribute to a mentor whose career had come to a close.

[48] Oldham's work on special juries has done much to shed light on the subject. On the historical background see J Oldham, 'The Origins of the Special Jury' (1983) 50 *U Chi L Rev* 137. On Lord Mansfield's use of special juries see Oldham (n 7 above) 96–8.

[49] See text to n 127 below.

[50] This could be partly because many of the relevant developments are not to be found in published materials: see n 88 below.

[51] See n 88 below.

[52] The MS of Holt CJ's opinion in *Coggs v Barnard* (1703) BL Add MS 34125 (the published reports are short and do not quite capture the breadth of discussion: 3 Ld Raym 163, 92 ER 622; 1 Com 133, 92 ER 999) is an excellent example. This should be kept in mind, especially when considering the potential implication in Buller's comments (n 47 above) that judges were happy to leave matters to the jury rather than laying down general principles, before Lord Mansfield's time.

[53] See JLS Swinton, *Considerations concerning a Proposal for Dividing the Court of Session into Classes or Chambers; and for Limiting Litigation in Small Causes; and for the Revival of Jury-Trial in Certain Civil Actions* (Edinburgh, 1789). For subsequent developments see 'A Short View of the Difficulties which Surrounded the Introduction of Trial by Jury in Civil Causes into Scotland; and of the Ultimate Success of the Experiment' which appears in the appendix of W Adam, *A Practical Treatise and Observations on Trial by Jury in Civil Causes* (Edinburgh, T Clark, 1836) and D Walker, *A Legal History of Scotland* (London, Butterworths, 2001) vol VI, 323–30.

Having argued that the pleading of indebitatus claims created scope for theorising, the remaining question is this: did the lawyers and/or judges take advantage of this scope and elaborate any meaningful theory or principle? The best and most direct evidence to answer this question would be the legal literature of the eighteenth century, and if one looks at the most visible evidence (published material) one is tempted to say that no thought was given towards this question (or at least any thought that was registered explicitly or implicitly) until Lord Mansfield's time. This is not just because of his decision in *Moses*, but also because his time on the bench coincided (especially in the latter part) with an explosion in the publication of better quality law reports and a more methodical treatment of law (in contrast with the abridgment form that dominated the first half of the eighteenth century) which flowered into the treatise literature that we continue to rely on today.[54] These visible signs can be seen as reflecting a more thoughtful and analytical mind. However, as I have argued elsewhere,[55] the production of legal literature was not necessarily related to the lack of legal development in this area but to monopolistic business practices of the law book trade, which created a market where the lifespan of obsolete titles was prolonged and it was extremely difficult to publish new works for a large part of the eighteenth century.

The book trade's negative impact on the printing of legal literature has implications on the way we understand the development of the law in the eighteenth century. The lack of literature or the style adopted should not necessarily reflect on the critical ability of lawyers or judges, especially when compared to their late eighteenth century counterparts. This in turn necessitates paying closer attention, where possible, to unpublished material[56] which expressly and implicitly evidences the kind of mind we can be sure did have an idea about the way the indebitatus claims worked. As we shall see in parts III and IV, such an enquiry indicates that lawyers and judges were taking an approach that was not too different from Lord Mansfield's.

III. Development of the Law Before *Moses v Macferlan*

Moses is always seen as the starting point to unlock Lord Mansfield's understanding of, and ambition for, indebitatus claims, and MHR in particular. As a coherent and influential statement its authority is undoubted, but in order to appreciate

---

[54] M Lobban, 'The English Legal Treatise' (1997) 13 *Iuris Scripta Historica* 69, esp 73 and 82–4; and AW Simpson, 'The Rise and Fall of the Legal Treatise: Legal Principles and the Forms of Legal Literature' (1981) 48 *U Chi L Rev* 632, 652 and 658–62.

[55] TA Baloch, 'Law Booksellers and Printers as Agents of Unchange' (2007) 66 *CLJ* 389.

[56] This includes books, case reports and judges notes as well. This is important not just to discover new material but also to correct or illuminate information already possessed, especially in relation to short or unreliable published reports: J Oldham, 'Eighteenth Century Judges' Notes: How They Correct, Explain and Enhance Reports' 31 (1987) *Am J Leg Hist* 9. For examples of unpublished materials that show as great a sophistication as works which appeared later, see Baloch (n 55 above) n 7.

better the development, understanding and ambition of Lord Mansfield in relation to these claims, a preferable starting point is the case of *Decker v Pope* (1757) ('*Decker*'),[57] handed down by Lord Mansfield very soon after his elevation onto the bench in 1756:

> Where a debtor desires [another] person to be bound with him or for him [and the] surety is [afterwards] obliged to pay [the] debt; this is a sufficient [consideration] to raise a promise in law [and] to charge the principal in an act for money paid to his use. *I have conferred with most of the judges upon this doctrine [and] they agree with the opinion—And Nothwithstanding* Holt had intimated his [opinion] that actions on the case were carried too far, *my* own sentiments were that they never could be too far extended as it was certainly [the] interest of [the] public that [the] way to justice [should] be as short and as little expensive as possible—*And as to the objection that* [the] court of chancery *is* [the] proper court for the surety to be relieved in, . . . *there are many cases in which a* Court of Equity *may be necessary* to come at facts, *yet if a* Court of Law *is* once *possessed of the* facts *I* [know] of no case where it could not give relief in an [action] on [the] case. *The jury must find for the plaintiff.*[58]

Three striking features emerge from this quotation, which will now be discussed in greater detail: the first is the reference to Holt CJ; the second is the reference to equity in the case; the third is Lord Mansfield's contrasting opinion on the benefits of the action.

A. Holt CJ and Indebitatus Claims

Within the period of innovation for indebitatus claims (especially MHR) in the second half of the seventeenth century,[59] it is likely that such claims were being pleaded more frequently during Holt CJ's time on the bench.[60] This may support the view that the increased activity during this time coincided with a period of greater development of the law in relation to these claims.[61] Within the history of indebitatus claims, Holt CJ's time on the bench is sometimes considered to have been noteworthy (amongst other reasons) for his general resistance to the plead-

---

[57] The case is referred to in a footnote by W Selwyn, *An Abridgment of the Law of Nisi Prius* (2nd edn, London, W Clarke & Sons, 1810) 86, n 27. Two manuscript reports survive: Lincoln's Inn MS 129 (unfol) and Inner Temple Misc MS 96, f 37. Both date the case from 1757, and provide a very similar report of the passage that is quoted.

[58] As it clarifies the decision, I have combined the reports in the extract which follows. I have taken as my base the report from the Inner Temple (IT Misc MS 96, f 37). The main differences between this report and that from LI MS 129 (unfol), which clarifies the quote, are shown in italics.

[59] Baker (n 1 above) 49–53.

[60] This argument is supported by a keyword search (keying in 'indebitatus' and different counts) on the English Reports (CD version; the online version is less helpful and more unreliable), which show that during Holt's Chief Justiceship there was a rise in the number of reported decisions considering indebitatus claims. Although the measure is crude and focuses on published reports, it tends to confirm the observations of a number of authors: Jackson (n 2 above) 39, Holdsworth (n 33 above) vol viii, 88; AW Simpson, *A History of the Common Law of Contract* (Oxford, OUP, 1975) 489; and Winfield (1952) (n 2 above) 6. I am indebted to M Macnair for his help in generating these statistics.

[61] See the authors noted in n 60 above.

ing and development of such claims, as Lord Mansfield's observation in *Decker*, above, shows. Without more, the dearth and low quality of reporting could lead to the impression that Holt CJ's resistance was unthinking or uncritical[62] and/or deflect attention from the way the claims were perceived at the time. Such an assumption would perhaps do a disservice to one of the great commercial judges of that era. A closer look at the evidence illustrates a more nuanced picture.

By Holt CJ's time it was firmly established that indebitatus claims were not contractual in any real sense; the promise was provided by law. So in *Arris and Arris v Stukeley* (1677/78),[63] one of the arguments considered and rejected by the court was that the claimant's indebitatus claims for profits wrongly obtained by the defendant could not be brought because this would mean implying a contract 'against the will' of the parties, who clearly did not agree to receiving or giving over these profits. This argument, as we will see, is more likely to have been persuasive in the course of the nineteenth and into the twentieth century[64] than at this time where the court was strongly committed to, and understood, the principle that the promise was a fiction, and that the better analogy was to be drawn with debt and account. These latter two provided a better reflection of the direction of the indebitatus claims. Holt CJ's general understanding of the action is best gleaned from a series of cases discussing whether indebitatus can be employed to recover on a wager:

> it is merely a wager and no indebitatus lies for it; for to make that lie, there must be work done, or some meritorious action for which debt would lie; but it does not for this wager, because this is due in a collateral respect: it is true, the cast of a die alters the property if the money be staked down, because it is then a gift on condition precedent, and indebitatus precedent lies against him that holds a wager, because it is promise in law to deliver it if won ... Though on the loss of a wager, the defendant had promised the next day to pay it, yet an assumpsit would not lie on it, because it wants consideration, it being but executory.[65]

The distinction being drawn in this extract shows that a clear idea of indebitatus claims even at this stage was being applied, namely that it could not be used to enforce purely executory promises, as some form of *executed* consideration or 'meritorious action', for which debt would lie, was needed. Indeed, it was this realisation of the claim and its potential to enable circumvention which was behind Holt CJ's resistance, but only in specific circumstances, as we shall see.

The first example of Holt CJ's resistance comes in the case of *Shuttleworth v Garnet* (1689) ('*Shuttleworth*'),[66] where the claimant employed an indebitatus

---

[62] JS Rogers, *The Early History of the Law of Bills and Notes* (Cambridge, CUP, 1995) 177–8.

[63] 2 Mod 260, 86 ER 1060.

[64] See part V, section A(ii).

[65] *Walker v Walker* (1694) 5 Mod 14, 87 ER 490. This report gives the fullest recorded judgment of Holt CJ; however, the other reports are not inconsistent with it: 12 Mod 69, 88 ER 1170; 12 Mod 258, 88 ER 1306; Comb 303, 90 ER 492. See also *Bovey v Castleman* (1794) 1 Ld Raym 69, 91 ER 942; and *Smith v Airey* (1704) 2 Ld Raym, 92 ER 187; 6 Mod 128, 87 ER 885; 3 Salk 175, 91 ER 760.

[66] 3 Mod 239, 87 ER 156; 3 Lev 261, 83 ER 680; Comb 151, 90 ER 398; Carth 90, 90 ER 657; 1 Show KB 35, 89 ER 431.

claim to recover customary fines owed by the defendant. The question reserved for the court was whether an indebitatus claim could be brought in such a case. The majority agreed that it could, with Holt CJ dissenting. His main objection in the case was that indebitatus should not be employed to try what in substance is a question of title to land (real rights). The view which emerges from the reports is that he thought indebitatus claims were confined to the world of personalty, not realty[67] (in the same way that indebitatus could not be employed in the context of a specialty, but could be used for, say, debt arising out of parole contracts). It is likely that one of the reasons for this was that claims raising issues of title had specific rules and procedures which would be undermined by the very little pleading that was required in indebitatus claims, which is why in one of the reports of *Shuttleworth* he is recorded as saying 'for an indebitatus is laid generally, and the defendant can not tell how to make his defence, but debt is laid more particularly'.[68] It is unsurprising that Holt CJ was in the minority, because by the time of *Shuttleworth*, indebitatus had already been employed in cases raising issues of title.

Although Holt CJ's attempt to maintain a boundary between realty and personalty in relation to indebitatus claims was not successful, his objections were not irrelevant because, in the eighteenth century, there were pockets of cases in which indebitatus was thought to be inappropriate to try the particular title dispute. *Lindon v Hooper*[69] is a good example, because here Lord Mansfield rejected the attempt to use indebitatus instead of replevin or trespass since:

> the point to be tried and determined in this action is, whether the plaintiff's cattle trespassed upon the defendants land? That may depend upon the plaintiff's right or the defendant's right, or the fact of trespassing: or it may depend on mere form. If the distress was irregular, the amends must be recovered back again; so that, allowing of the cattle to substitute this remedy in lieu of an action of trespass, would, as between the parties, be equal and unjust; and upon principles of policy would produce inconvenience. It would break in upon that branch of the common and statute law which relates to distresses. It would create inconvenience, by having rights of common open to repeated litigation, and by depriving posterity of the benefit of precise judgments upon record.[70]

In order to avoid these 'inconveniences' it was better to plead specially, as would be required under replevin or trespass, rather than the general declaration which would only create a situation in which the defendant 'might be surprised at the trial: he would not be prepared to make his defence'.[71]

---

[67] This is why he was against the use of indebitatus assumpsit to recover profits generated by contested offices, such as *Arris v Stukeley* (n 63 above): Baker (n 35 above) 371.

[68] Comb 151, 90 ER 398.

[69] 1 Cowp 414, 98 ER 1160.

[70] *Ibid* 418.

[71] *Ibid* 418. It is arguable that the attempt to distinguish this case and reasoning from other cases in which indebitatus was allowed in the context of realty is not very strong. It may be that in the background, the surprise objection here is an admission that indebitatus was being expanded too far: on which see text to nn 167–8 below.

Similar to *Shuttleworth* are those cases in which Holt CJ's objection was that allowing indebitatus claims for fines by custom was a step too far and was surely too hard 'for it was to leave matter of law to a jury'.[72] As to what he meant here, the answer comes in *City of York v Toun* (1699),[73] in which we are told that indebitatus claims to recover fines are resisted on the basis that there was no privity or implied assent 'when a fine is imposed on man against his will'.[74] Neither was there any right shown to this fine or some precedent consideration. And Holt CJ concurred: 'We will consider very well of this matter; it is time to have these actions redressed. It is hard that customs, bye-laws, rights to impose fines, and everything should be left to the jury'.[75] The problem in these cases is that the legal right to the customary payment or fine was going to turn on issues of public law and the interpretation of statutes and of medieval charters, which would be very difficult for a lay jury to understand and apply. Had such charters, for example, been specifically pleaded there would be no necessity for jury trial (the judge would simply be called upon to apply the relevant instrument), and the potential such a trial brings of bias based on local politics (since the jury was drawn from the locality).[76]

There are a line of cases in which Holt CJ is reported to have said 'there is no such thing as a contract or promise in law, though there be such an expression in the books' or a variation of it.[77] It seems that only Holt CJ held this view (and perhaps Powell in one case),[78] which is against the general trend in the case law and text at the time, in which promises/contracts in law were recognised as a category in which indebitatus claims fell.[79] Indeed, Holt CJ recognised promises in law in other cases.[80] What seems likely in these cases is that the tag was being used instrumentally with reference to what were genuine implied-in-fact contracts rather than something about the nature and foundation of indebitatus claims. The one exception may be the anonymous case from 1704 which on one

---

[72] *Hussey v Fiddall* (1698) 12 Mod 324, 88 ER 1353.

[73] 5 Mod 444, 87 ER 754.

[74] *Ibid.*

[75] *Ibid.*

[76] Holdsworth (n 35 above) vol ix, 170–7; and also M Macnair, 'Vicinage and the Antecedents of the Jury' (1999) 17 *Law and History Review* 537, esp 549–51.

[77] The quote is from *Burkmire v Darnell* (1704) 6 Mod 248, 250, 87 ER 996. Note that the other reports of the case do not mention such a wide-ranging remark, although there is nothing in them to suggest that such a remark could not have been made: 2 Ld Raym 1085, 92 ER 219 (*Buckmyr v Darnell*); 1 Salk 27, 91 ER 27 (*Birkmyr v Darnell*); 3 Salk 15, 91 ER 663 (*Bourkmire v Darnell*). Other cases in which Holt CJ is reported to have commented on the non-existence of promises/contracts in law are *Fielding v Serrat* (1696) Comb 375, 90 ER 537; *Starke v Cheeseman* (1699) 1 Ld Raym 538, 91 ER 1259; 1 Salk 128, 91 ER 121; Carth 509, 90 ER 891; *Green v Crane* (1704) cited in *Williams v Gun* (1710) Fort 177, 180; 92 ER 808; and Anon (1704) 6 Mod 131, 87 ER 887.

[78] See the quote from Burkmire (n 77 above) which is reported to have been made by Powell too: 6 Mod 248, 250; 87 ER 996.

[79] See n 101 below; and in terms of cases see the argument of the Solicitor General (Winnington) accepted by the court in *Arris and Arris v Stukley* (n 63 above) 262. See also *Bolton v Wills* (1650) Style 214, 82 ER 655; *Fits v Freestone* (1676) 1 Mod 210, 86 ER 834; and *Pilkington v Peach* (1680) 2 Shower KB 135, 89 ER 841.

[80] *Hussey v Jacob* (1696) 1 Lord Raym 87, 91 ER 954; *Clerk v Mundall* (1698) 12 Mod 203, 88 ER 1263; and *Palmer v Stavely* (1701) 12 Mod 510, 88 ER 1483.

interpretation could be seen as Holt CJ expressing the view that MHR was based on a genuine implied promise. However, given the poor quality of the report and, as was said above, his comments elsewhere on the existence of promises in law and the general consensus at the time that indebitatus claims were based on promises in law, such an interpretation is unlikely.

The large category in which negative remarks were expressed was in cases concerning bills and notes. The first point to note about these cases is that they were not strictly about indebitatus claims, but the onerabilis assumpsit count.[81] As the duty to pay under bills of exchange was founded on the customs of merchants, it could not strictly be described as a debt for the purposes of indebitatus claims. And so the indebitatus formula was adopted to say that the defendant was chargeable (onerabilis) under the custom rather than indebted. From the perspective of the commercial community, actions on bills of exchange provided shorter and quicker routes to recovery. All that the claimant needed to prove was that the instrument was signed by the defendant and then recovery could be had. Unlike a usual indebitatus claim, the underlying facts (albeit brief) did not have to be proved.

This form of pleading was thought to be restricted to merchants. However, in 1689 the King's Bench effectively extended the category to non-merchants too. An extension of a different kind was sought in 1702, when it was argued that the class of instruments to which onerabilis assumpsit applied should be extended to cover promissory notes as well as bills of exchange. Holt CJ was extremely critical of this extension:

> That the maintaining of these actions upon such notes, were innovations upon the rules of the common law; and that it amounted to the setting up of a new sort of specialty, unknown to the common law, and invented in Lombard street, which attempted in these matters of bills of exchange to give laws to Westminster Hall. That the continuing to declare upon these notes upon the custom of merchants proceeded from obstinacy and opinionativeness, since he had always expressed his opinion against them, and since there was so easy a method, as to declare upon a general indebitatus assumpsit for money lent, &c.[82]

Holt CJ's concerns in these cases were practical and defensible rather than a theoretical attack on the nature of indebitatus or onerabilis claims. The proposed extension threatened the boundary between commercial rules in relation to bills and those governing general monetary obligations. This was worrying because in relation to the latter, the law could at least ensure that bare promises were not upheld, but this question of the consideration was taken away by treating any written evidence (following the custom of merchants) like a specialty.[83] The instinct was that with the prospect that promissory notes within the alleged custom (and

---

[81] Baker (n 35 above) 369–70
[82] *Clerke v Martin* (1702) 2 Ld Raym 757, 758; 92 ER 6. See also *Buller v Crips* (1703) 6 Mod 29, 87 ER 793.
[83] Rogers (n 62 above) 180–4.

even within 3 & 4 Anne c9) were almost devoid of cautelary formality (as was the case with instruments like bonds, which required seal, witness and delivery, or bills of exchange, that required a particular form of words), it was quite possible for parties to find themselves bound to a negotiable instrument without quite realising its effects.

Holt CJ's concerns were not shared by the legislature who passed Acts expanding the class of negotiable instruments.[84] But, as Rogers has shown, Holt CJ's fears were vindicated because, throughout the eighteenth century, the courts were often confronted with the difficulty of distinguishing commercial from non-commercial instruments. And the 'complicated, and not wholly satisfactory' rules which fell from these cases persist in the law today.[85] Another vindication of Holt CJ's position comes from Macnair's analysis, which suggests that the real problems with bills and notes were visible in equity. This is because the negotiability of an instrument allowed the claimant to bar standard defences like set-offs and cross-claims. However, relief could be had in equity and the relative increase in these types of applications (with allegations involving fraud) at the end of the eighteenth century suggests that Holt CJ's fears of extending the class of negotiable instruments were justified.[86]

In sum, we can see that Holt CJ's concern in these cases was related to a wider issue about the class of instrument to be considered as like bills of exchange. Indeed, one effect of his argument was that the facts on which the onerabilis claim was based should be pleaded. This is why he wanted these instruments to be used as *evidence* of the debt rather than, as the merchants desired, the beginning and end of the claim.[87]

From this account we can see that Holt CJ's resistance was a manifestation of the kind of teething problems expected with an increasingly frequent use of indebitatus claims (or onerabilis assumpsit) in different situations. His general view is likely to have been that the claim was non-contractual and available in certain circumstances where debt usually is allowed. He had a vision of it that, it is submitted, was not in many respects radically different from that applied throughout the eighteenth century. He would not have disagreed with many of the circumstances collected by Lord Mansfield in *Moses* in which the action may apply. His concerns were directed more at insuring that indebitatus claims were not employed in a way which threw difficult legal or policy questions onto the jury, or prevented courts

---

[84] 9 & 10 Will 3c 17 (relating to inland bills of exchange) and 3 & 4 Anne c9 (promissory notes).

[85] Rogers (n 62 above) 184.

[86] M Macnair, 'The Court of Exchequer and Equity' (2001) 22 *J Leg Hist* 75, 80.

[87] This is also how Lord Mansfield understood Holt CJ's decisions: *Grant v Vaughan* (1764) 3 Burr 1516, 1525; 97 ER 957. Within the context of bills of exchange or notes treated in the same way, Holt CJ had shown himself to be quite willing to entertain indebitatus claims, provided there was a debt to be recovered. This was so even in complex three party situations: *Benjamin Ward and James Ward v Sir Stephen Evans* (1702) 2 Ld Raym 928, 92 ER 120; 6 Mod 36, 87 ER 799; 1 Com 138, 92 ER 1002 and BL Add MS 35980, f 79. The manuscript report shows Holt CJ laying down a more general principle, in three party cases such as these: 'if [A] be indebted to B, A gives the money to C to pay B, B may have an indebitatus assumpsit [against] C yet [A] is not discharged until C hath paid to B but B may have his action [against] A notwithstanding'.

from considering important issues such as the status of promissory notes. In so far as he had a specific limitation on it, it was, as intimated in *Shuttleworth*, that indebitatus claims were confined to the world of personalty, and not realty.

Whether within Holt CJ's time or after there was an idea in which kind of circumstances recovery would be allowed, like Lord Mansfield's account in *Moses*, is not easy to track from the reports.[88] But it is highly unlikely that thought was not given to this question until Lord Mansfield's decision. The first piece of evidence comes from the reports that do exist, and which show, in isolated instances, the application of MHR in circumstances that were collected in *Moses*.[89] Out of these cases, *AG v Perry* (1735) contains a synthesis of the circumstances in which MHR could be used and it is not dissimilar from the list in *Moses*:

> whenever a man receives money belonging to another without any reason, authority or consideration, an action lies against the receiver as for money received to the other's use; and this, as well where the money is received through mistake under colour, and upon an apprehension, though a mistaken apprehension of having a good authority to receive it, as where it is received by imposition, fraud or deceit in the receiver.[90]

The second piece of evidence comes from the notebooks of Sir Dudley Ryder, covering the period when he was Chief Justice of the King's Bench (1754–56),[91]

---

[88] This is probably because much of the law on indebitatus claims, especially in the crucial and unchartered period between Holt CJ and Lord Mansfield, is not to be found in published reports but was subject to oral transmission, common (uncited) wisdom amongst the bench and bar, and manuscript reports. A note should be made about manuscript reports, which were often published much later, usually in the second half of the eighteenth century. Although such reports were often available in manuscript form before publication and closer to the period when the case was decided, this cannot be readily assumed: see, eg Grose J's comment in 1799 that he did not know about the case of *Thomas v Cadwallader* (1744), at the time he argued (as counsel) *Kingston v Preston* (1772), since a report of the decision had not been printed at the time: ch 5, n 34. The manuscript may have been simply unavailable, too expensive (see J Oldham, 'Underreported and Underrated: the Court of Common Pleas in the Eighteenth Century' in H Hartog and W Nelson (eds), *Law as Culture and Culture as Law: Essays in Honour of John Phillip Reid* (Madison, Madison House Publishers, 2000) 121–3) or in limited circulation. All these forms of unpublished transmission make it difficult to track contemporary legal thought, especially in relation to indebitatus claims, before Lord Mansfield. One way to illustrate this point about sources of law when *Decker* and *Moses* were decided is to take what was, in the first half of the eighteenth century, a state of the art work in terms of the reports which it covered, namely Viner's 23 volume *Abridgment* (see n 101 below). At around the same time that the final volume of Viner's work was published, there appeared *Indexes to Mr Viner's General Abridgment of Law and Equity* (Oxford, 1757), which included, at i–vi, a list of 'reporters abridged by Mr Viner' together with the editions used. Out of around 118 or so reports listed, only 16 cover the period after Holt CJ's time as Chief Justice (after 1710). Within this, only eight relate to cases from courts of law. Tellingly, these eight reports contain few if any cases on indebitatus, and the ones that do appear are not noteworthy. This may explain why the majority of the cases referred to in *Moses* are from or before Holt CJ's time. Oldham's work shows that the situation in relation to the Court of Common Pleas was worse, particularly in the first half of the eighteenth century: Oldham, *ibid*.

[89] *Tomkyns v Barnet* (1694) Skinner 411, 90 ER 182 (mistake, fraud and perhaps failure of consideration); *Martin v Sitwell* (1691) 1 Shower KB 156, 89 ER 509 (failure of consideration); *Astley v Reynolds* (1731) 2 Barn KB 40, 94 ER 343 (mistake); and *Bosanquet v Earl of Westmoreland* (1738) West T Hard 598, 25 ER 1104 (mistake and deceit).

[90] *Attorney-General v Perry* (1735) 2 Comyns 481, 491; 92 ER 1169.

[91] The trial notes of this period (LI Harrowby MS docs 12–18), which are on permanent loan to Lincolns Inn, were noted in a shorthand which has been deciphered and transcribed by KL Perrin. The following discussion is based on the Perrin transcript. The established form of shorthand means that

just before Lord Mansfield was elevated to that position. A large number of the cases in the notes from his time on the King's Bench are indebitatus claims (quantum meruit, goods sold and delivered, MHR, money lent, etc). There is also a relatively high turnover of cases, reflecting the fact that trials were by modern standards extremely rapid.[92] Moreover, when submissions of counsel are noted, they show, whatever the quality of the argument, some structure in terms of the relevant issues in the case and their argument towards it.[93] Similarly, the judge when directing the jury or discussing the relevant issues took the kind of structured approach evident in other manuscript sources.[94] As observed earlier, despite the notion of implied promise in the counts, the promise was understood as being fictional. This is confirmed when we see that the promise did not in any way influence the trial in these notes, either in the way the witnesses were examined, the submissions made and the direction to the jury. Instead, we can be confident that it was understood that indebitatus claims followed on certain kinds of defined situations. For example, in *Isaak Mattos v Parker* (20 March 1756), the claimant's counsel is noted as making the following submission in law: 'Wherever money paid by mistake, fraud, deceit or extortion without consideration, the law makes it money to the use of the payer'.[95]

This list closely follows the one enumerated by Lord Mansfield some years later in *Moses*.[96] This suggests that Lord Mansfield's list was not a groundbreaking event necessarily, and was more common knowledge than is usually assumed. This is not to underplay the coherence of Lord Mansfield's statement, and its broader potential, to which we come later,[97] but simply to put his decision in context of common law thought current at the time. If this is right then we need to revisit those accounts which assumed that Lord Mansfield's statement was more exceptional and therefore must have been inspired less by the development in the common law and more by external sources. The primary examples here are the early writings of Birks, in which the Roman law is placed at the forefront of Lord Mansfield's mind when he was deciding *Moses*. In his first article,[98] he argued that Lord Mansfield consciously borrowed the categories in which MHR could be employed from the

---

these notes perhaps are the closest we are likely to get to a fully contemporary note of the trial in this period, or the essence of what was said. For general background on the civil caseload in the Ryder Notebook see J Langbein, 'Historical Foundations of the Modern Law of Evidence: a View from the Ryder Sources' (1996) 96 *Colum L Rev* 1167, 1176–81.

[92] The turnover of cases was not as high as that during Lord Mansfield's time, when there was an increase in King's Bench business: see text to n 127 below and Oldham (n 7 above) vol I, 124.

[93] Eg *Martin v Weedon* (25 May 1754) LI Harrowby MS doc 12, at 6. In what appears to be an indebitatus assumpsit claim for money for timber delivered to the defendant by the claimant, Ryder CJ's notes show that the submissions made for the claimant were structured around key questions in the way a lawyer would recognise today. This is also true of the occasional more fully reported arguments from the Restoration onwards.

[94] As well as *Martin v Weedon* (n 93 above), see also MS opinions of Holt CJ's opinions in BL Add MS 34125 and 35979; and LI Misc MS 809.

[95] LI Harrowby MS doc 17, at 35.

[96] See text to n 132 below.

[97] For which see in part IV and part V, section A(i).

[98] Birks (n 9 above).

Roman law. This statement was based on what was considered the exceptionality of Lord Mansfield's exposition, the assumption that such categories were not thought about before. As has been shown, since they were thought about, we can accept the more realistic picture that Lord Mansfield, rather than importing wholly new categories into the law, was undertaking a synthesis, not unfamiliar to lawyers at the time. This is not to dismiss the influence of Roman law, but to place it in the background, a place it is likely to have occupied in an educated lawyer's outlook in the eighteenth century.[99]

In a second article, Birks, with McLeod,[100] argues that Blackstone imported into the common law from the civilian tradition the implied contract rationalisation of indebitatus claims. His fame secured the survival of the implied contract theory well into the twentieth century, before Goff and Jones sought to explode it.

There are two problems with placing responsibility on Blackstone. The first is discounting the similar implied contract type analyses before the publication of Blackstone's works and *Moses*. The printed literature, reflecting the case law, illustrates that Blackstone was following an established tradition of explaining indebitatus claims as being based on a contract implied in law.[101] The second problem is the assumption that Blackstone's explanation was necessarily so influential. As one of the most successful writers of his age it may be easy to assume this to be the case. However, his work was not perceived as the best reference for the law as applied in

---

[99] Indeed many student guides recommended the study of the civil law as an essential element in the student's legal education: R Campbell, *The London Tradesman, being a compendious view of all the trades, professions, arts, both liberal and mechanic, now practised in the cities of London and Westminster calculated for the information of parents, and instruction of youth in their choice of business* (1st edn, London, T Gardner, 1747) 75; and *Considerations on Various Grievances in the Practick Part of our Laws; with some observations on the Code Frederick, the Roman Law, and our own Courts of Equity, etc* (Dublin, 1756) 32–3. There was also the potential Roman law influence through Scottish law, for an example of which see Hardwicke LC in *AG v Stevens* (1737) West t Hard 50, 53; 25 ER 814; 1 Atk 358, 26 ER 228: 'as where A pays money upon such a consideration, and it is not performed, an action at law lies for A for money had and received to his use, which is expressed thus by Scotch law, *causa data non secuta*'.

[100] Birks and Mcleod (n 8 above).

[101] A good way to illustrate this is to take the works contained in the catalogue in J Worrall, *Bibliotheca Legum: or, a new and compleat list of all the common and statute law books of this realm, and some others relating thereunto* (London, J Worrall, 1753) as being representative of the state of the knowledge before Lord Mansfield's elevation to the King's Bench. This was the only exclusive law catalogue during this period and was updated regularly (it had been first published in 1732). The following sample of works from the 1753 edition of the catalogue speak of a theory not dissimilar to Blackstone's (they rationalise the claim as implied promise in law): M Bacon, *A New Abridgment of the Law* (London, H Lintot, 1736–66) vol I, 163; J Lilly, *The Practical Register: or, a general abridgement of the law, as it is now practised in the several courts of Chancery, King's Bench, Common Pleas and Exchequer* (2nd edn, London, J Walthoe *et al*, 1735) vol I, 132; W Nelson, *An Abridgment of the Common Law: being a collection of the principal cases argued and adjudged in the several courts of Westminster-Hall* (London, R Gosling *et al*, 1725–26) vol I, 82-, esp 85; C Viner, *A General Abridgment of Law and Equity, alphabetically digested under proper titles with notes and references to the whole* (Aldershot, C Viner, 1742–57) vol I (published 1746) 263; W Bohun, *Declarations and Pleadings, in the most usual actions brought in the several courts of King's Bench and Common Pleas at Westminster* (2nd edn, London, Samuel Birt *et al*, 1743) (the book is careful to distinguish between express promises, parol promises and implied promises in relation to the different declarations and pleadings, so that when discussing indebitatus it has 'implied' (see eg 141) in the margins).

the courts.[102] We have a wonderful snapshot from the correspondence of law students from the end of the eighteenth century,[103] which show that the wise student of the law would supplement his reading with other works.[104] All this should force us not to focus exclusively on him, a point reinforced by the other sources that expressed the same idea.

Finally, there is a silent assumption in the article by Birks and McLeod that the implied contract explanation was understood in the same way in or about Blackstone's time and much later, when it was dismantled by scholars. Although it is impossible to track every step of how a term or terms is or are understood or used, it will be argued that eighteenth century lawyers were clearer about the fiction of the implied in law contract than lawyers much later, when Ames sought to reveal the fiction and place the claims on the unjust enrichment basis. This is the story of the subsequent development to which we return in part V.

B. Role of Equity in the Development of the Law

The reference to equity in the quote from *Decker* above provides a good departure point to discuss the influence of equity on Lord Mansfield's thinking at the time he laid down *Moses*. We revisit the influence of equity when discussing the developments of the law during and after the handing down of *Moses*.[105]

The first point to note is that the reference to equity in *Decker* was specific to its facts and not a general statement about the foundation or origin of indebitatus claims. At the time that *Decker* was decided it was unclear whether the common law had abandoned its uncompromising position of not allowing claims of contribution between sureties under the indebitatus formula. But courts of equity were providing such a remedy and Lord Mansfield's decision in *Decker* confirmed that the common law would too.[106] In the terms in which he expressed himself, one should note that his decision would increase business in the King's Bench, a point which will be taken up in the next section.

---

[102] M Lobban, *The Common law and English Jurisprudence 1760–1850* (Oxford, Clarendon Press, 1991) 41–6.

[103] The letters were written by three young men embarking on a law career as clerks in the 1790s. Some of these are in the Crabb Robinson Correspondence 1725–99 held at Dr Williams' Library, Gordon Square, London. I will refer to these as 'DWlib CRcor'. The letters were between Thomas Amyot, Henry Crabb Robinson and William Pattisson. Some of their letters are published (with discussions on the law edited out) in PJ Corfield and C Evans (eds), *Youth and Revolution in the 1790s: Letters of William Pattisson, Thomas Amyot, and Henry Crabb Robinson* (Stroud, A Sutton, 1996).

[104] In DWlib CRcor letter 57 (19 August 1795), Amyot paints a vivid picture of his early days as a legal clerk and how in an attempt to master his profession, he began 'to read Blackstone's Commentaries', but that 'I cannot say I edified greatly from it'. He confesses that it was only when a senior clerk devised a plan for him which entailed reading the 'practical parts of Blackstone' followed by 'separate and by way of commentary some good professional treatise on that or chapter' did things become clearer.

[105] Part IV and part V, section A(i).

[106] GH Jones, 'The Role of Equity in the Law of Restitution' in E Schrage (ed), *Unjust Enrichment: the Comparative History of the Law of Restitution* (Berlin, Dunker & Humblot, 1999) 162.

Generally, it has been difficult to assess the relationship between equity and indebitatus claims. This is particularly so when one reads the consistent mention in *Moses* and in numerous cases thereafter to the action being like a bill in equity.[107] Buller J in *Stratton v Rastall* sought to resolve the issue as to the availability of MHR in the case by laying down that 'in order to recover money in this form of action, the party must shew that he has equity and conscience on his side and that he could recover in a court of equity'.[108]

In so far as this suggests that specific doctrines were borrowed from the courts of equity, this has been dismissed.[109] But no clear reason has been given for why this is the case, and therefore the suspicion persists, not least because there are obiter dicta which can be interpreted as suggesting that some borrowing may have occurred.[110] The reality is that it is highly unlikely that Lord Mansfield was borrowing any doctrine from the courts of equity when he made his statement in *Moses*: the law in this area was, as has been shown, generated and worked out in the common law courts.[111] In fact, during the development of indebitatus claims in the late seventeenth and early eighteenth centuries, cases often made analogies with the medieval actions of debt and account, rather than any equitable doctrine.[112]

While there were restitutionary type claims entertained by the courts of equity,[113] they were disparate and not developed in the coherent way that they were in the common law courts. It is difficult to assess the truth of this from the printed sources.[114] However, strong evidence of equity theory on the subject survives in Sir Thomas Sewell's manuscript[115] of materials on equity 'which he

---

[107] *Jestons v Brooke* (1778) 2 Cowp 793, 795; 98 ER 1365; and *Clerk v Shee & Johnson* (1774) 1 Cowp 197, 199; 98 ER 1041.

[108] (1788) 2 TR 366, 370; 100 ER 197.

[109] Kremer (2001) (n 4 above) 29–30.

[110] The interpretation being that the recovery of money paid under an illegal contract can be explained as copying equity's 'clean hands' principle: Hardwicke CJ in *Rex v Nunez* (1736) Cases Temp Hard 265, 266; 95 ER 171: 'As to the cases of usury, the rule has been upon indictments for usurious contracts, not to admit the party in the contract unless the money claimed thereon has been paid; and the reason is, because then he is unconcerned in interest, there being no remedy either in law or equity to recover that money back again; for my Lord Chief Justice Treby was of opinion, that where there had been an unlawful contract of a bad nature, the party should not be admitted to bring an action as for money had and received to his use, because he is *particeps criminis,* and a Court of Equity would not encourage a remedy, not even for the surplus interest, because that would give encouragement for such contracts'.

[111] See text to nn 88–97 above.

[112] This comes through vividly in Jackson's account (n 2 above). See, eg *Shuttleworth v Garnet* (n 66 above); *Arris and Arris v Stukely* (n 23 above); *Bovey v Castleman* (n 65 above); and *Smith v Airey* (n 65 above).

[113] Jones (n 106 above); and Ibbetson (n 16 above) 273–6.

[114] Nothing which echoes the statement in *Moses* appears in the following works: Lex Praetoria in G Gilbert, *The History and Practice of the High Court of Chancery* (London, J Worrall and W Owen, 1758); *A General Abridgment of Cases in Equity* (London, H Lintot and H Shuckburgh, 1734) (known as *Equity Cases Abridged*); Prolegomena of chancery and equity in D Yale (ed), *Lord Nottingham's Two Treatises* (Cambridge, CUP, 1965).

[115] Held in the Inner Temple, known as the 'Mitford Collection', and referred to hereinafter as 'IT Mitford MS'.

worked upon, and arranged in subjects and sections, doubtless with a view to the production of a major work on equity'.[116] The first 13 volumes resemble a self contained abridgment which Francis Hargrave described thus:

> The scale of the collection of references is much larger than that of the references to be met with in either of the printed abridgments of equity cases or under Chancery in Lord Chief Baron Comyns' justly admired digest, containing not only more heads and titles but also a far greater variety of divisions and references. This may be strongly exemplified as to the titles under letter A in first *Equity Cases Abridged* with Sir Thomas's under the same letter 'A', the former contains nine titles but the latter *twenty seven*.[117]

Fulfilling its promise of greater scope, it contains a head 'where the party who has received money shall or shall not be obliged to refund'[118] in volume 12, chapter 17. And in the reported and unreported cases abridged and collected there, no clear-cut principle or elaboration of discrete categories in which a refund is ordered emerges. There are in the cases references to natural justice, but since the reporting is poor, it is difficult to discern whether this was a conclusory gloss or something which was more fully worked out. The lack of any succinct categories or theory in this chapter makes the latter unlikely. As a compendium to 'chancery principles and practice in the second half of the eighteenth century',[119] this lack of coherent principle compares unfavourably to the way indebitatus claims were being handled by the common law courts.

As to what was then meant by the reference to equity in the cases, this will be discussed in parts IV and V, which assess the decision in Moses and the development of the law thereafter. This is because these references were the direct product of Lord Mansfield's decision in *Moses* and give us some indication of the true nature of his innovation.

C. Encouraging Indebitatus Claims

Very little, if any, attention is paid to Lord Mansfield's 'friendship'[120] with indebitatus claims (MHR in particular) and his proclamation that it was somehow a greater route to justice than, one assumes, other actions that were available. The answer lies in a greater appreciation of the complex procedural and institutional background of Lord Mansfield's time in the eighteenth century. Some of these we have touched upon already, namely the considerable simplicity of indebitatus claims compared with, for example, special assumpsit, which was often a needlessly

---

[116] JC Davies (ed), *Catalogue of Manuscripts in the Library of the Honourable Society of the Inner Temple* (Oxford, OUP, 1972) vol I, 72.

[117] Quoted Davies (n 116 above) vol III, 1144.

[118] IT Mitford MS vol 12, ch 17.

[119] Davies (n 116 above) vol III, 1084.

[120] *Towers v Barett* (1786) 1 TR 133, 134; 99 ER 1014; *Weston v Downes* (1778) 1 Doug 23, 24; 99 ER 19.

long, arduous and very expensive process.[121] A good starting point is that during the eighteenth century, available figures show that between 1740–1840, the vast majority of the civil caseload continued to involve debt litigation.[122] As well as simplified pleading, greater control over juries, the all or nothing costs rules, and the shortness of trial all encouraged and facilitated this kind of litigation. And there was a strong motivation. The first was the long tradition of reform movements that consistently sought to improve the recovery of small debts.[123] For example, between 1729–41 three bills were printed and presented to the House of Commons, all proposing schemes to make the recovery of small debts 'more easy and speedy'.[124] And the story is not quite captured by the recorded and printed bills but also those that failed.[125]

The clamour for more effective procedure was a response to the delay and expense of enforcing these claims in the court; it may even have been seen as a threat to the court's role and revenue.[126] The word 'threat' is apt here, albeit odd to modern eyes, because courts' and judges' revenue was generated by the amount of litigation which passed through the courts. The ensuing competition between the courts for attracting work was a very real factor and influence on common law development. In the case of debt litigation, the competition was being won by the King's Bench and in particular when that court was presided over by Lord Mansfield. It has been estimated that whereas in 1740, the Court of Common Pleas commanded a larger market share of debt litigation than the King's Bench, by 1765, the caseload of the Common Pleas had declined to roughly half that of the King's Bench.[127] If this was dramatic, then the growth thereafter was considerably greater.[128]

---

[121] Some aspects of the costs relating to special pleading are discussed by C Francis, 'Practice, Strategy, and Institution: Debt Collection in English Common Law Courts' 80 *Northwestern U Law Rev* (1986) 807, 860–1.

[122] *Ibid* 814 which breaks down into the following types of cases: (1) money bonds; (2) bills of exchange and promissory notes; (3) common counts for money lent and rent for use and occupation; (4) common counts for goods and work and counts for special assumpsit; and (5) warranty actions, common counts for food and lodging and actions of indebitatus assumpsit for MHR

[123] B Shapiro, 'Law Reform in Seventeenth Century England' (1975) 19 *Am J Leg Hist* 280, 285, 290, 294, 296, 305; and H Horwitz, 'Changes in the Law and Reform of the Legal Order: England (and Wales) 1689–1760' (2002) 21 *Parliamentary History* 301, 318.

[124] S Lambert (ed), *House of Commons Sessional Papers of the Eighteenth Century* (Wilmington, Scholarly Resources, 1975) vol VII, 13–21, 159–70 and 459–82. These bills generally envisaged a scheme in which actions would be easier to initiate by something akin to a bill of equity, and trials without a jury and lawyers.

[125] Lambert's collection (*ibid*) is not representative of the legislative activity because she only includes those bills that were ordered to be printed, which she says represent 'a tiny part of the legislative production' (vol I, ii). Another major source, which takes in a wider range of legislative material, is J Hoppit, *Failed Legislation, 1660–1800, extracted from the Commons and Lords Journals* (London, Hambledon, 1997). The following references from this work relate to proposals presented in Parliament that dealt with improving the collection of small debts: 24.026, 25.001, 27.001, 34.019, 38.007, 74.015, 91.004, 119.032, 119.034, 119.035 and 137.058.

[126] The legal community was capable and confident to express the threat such schemes would present to revenue: J Mallory, *Objections Humbly Offer'd Against Passing the Bill, intitled, A bill for the more easy and speedy recovery of small debts, into a law* (London, J Roberts, 1730) esp 46–7.

[127] Francis (n 121 above) 847–8 n 167.

[128] *Ibid* 909.

Many factors must account for this reversal of market share. The main reason given by the profession when the issue was examined by a parliamentary commission in early nineteenth century was the exclusive rights of audience enjoyed by serjeants over motions in banc in the Common Pleas.[129] Such exclusivity brought an extra layer of cost since lawyers would have to hire serjeants to argue cases in the Common Pleas. In contrast, the King's Bench had no such restrictions and was open to the bar generally. Another reason given to the commission was the higher fees charged by protonotharies of the Common Pleas.[130] The monopolies enjoyed by serjeants in the Common Pleas does not provide a full explanation of the relative success of the King's Bench over the Common Pleas by 1765. This is because this factor was also present during the period when the Common Pleas had a greater share of the market. Therefore, an additional reason must be sought for the rise in the King's Bench's share of the market, and the figures provide strong support for the view that Lord Mansfield's willingness to employ mechanisms to make more effective the application and development of commercial law, as well as his more general management of the court, made his court the most attractive.[131] For our purposes, it is impossible to ignore in *Decker* and then again in *Moses*, that synthesising the applicable principle and (as we will see in the next part) couching it in such broad terms must have helped to make his court even more popular.

IV. Lord Mansfield's Decision in *Moses v Macferlan*

The clarity and detail of Burrow's report enabled Mansfield's decision to be accorded fame. It was an important decision, and the background discussed above enables us to assess more accurately the innovation and ambition of Lord Mansfield in this decision. To remind ourselves of the key passages:

> If the defendant be under an obligation, from the ties of natural justice, to refund; the law implies a debt, and gives this action, founded in the equity of the plaintiff's case, as it were upon a contract ('quasi ex contractu' as the Roman law expresses it) ...[132]
>
> This kind of equitable action, to recover back money, which ought not in justice to be kept, is very beneficial, and therefore much encouraged. It lies only for money which ex æquo et bono, the defendant ought to refund: it does not lie for money paid by the plaintiff, which is claimed of him as payable in point of honour and honesty, although it could not have been recovered from him by any course of law; as in payment of a debt barred by statute of limitations, or contracted during his infancy, or to the extent of principal and legal interest upon a usurious contract or for money fairly lost at play: because in all these cases, the defendant may retain it with safe conscience, though by positive law he

---

[129] *Ibid* 849, citing *First Report of Commissioners on Courts of Common Law* (1829) 9 Parl Papers 149.
[130] *Ibid* 849–50.
[131] See Fifoot (n 36 above) ch 3 generally; and Oldham (n 7 above) esp 140–60. And see also text to n 47 above.
[132] See n 12 above at 1008.

was barred from recovering. But it lies for money paid by mistake; or upon a consideration which happens to fail; or for money got by imposition, (express or implied) or extortion or oppression; or an undue advantage taken of the plaintiff's situation, contrary to the laws made for the protection of persons under these circumstances.[133]

We can now see that this decision's emphasis on the non-contractual nature of the claim and its availability in discrete situations, was something that was very likely well established before this decision.[134] Recognising the real benefit of encouraging and sending out a very positive signal that the court would embrace such actions[135] (in contrast to the way the profession may have viewed Holt CJ's opinion of these actions),[136] he sought to make a very clear statement of the law. The circumstances of the case suggest that he was waiting for an opportunity to make this statement, because he engineered its appearance before the judges for further argument.[137] The tool he used, and where he probably did break new ground, was his commitment to the explanation that at the heart of these cases lay the key question whether *aequum et bonum* the defendant ought to refund the money.[138] As an illustration of his commitment, consider the case of *Dale v Sollet* (1767),[139] in which he held that the defendant was free to rely on defences at trial which would reduce the claimant's claim, without a formal plea or notice of set-off (as may have been the case under a system less driven by notions of equity and conscience). This was because 'the plaintiff can recover no more than he is in conscience and equity entitled to do'.[140] More generally, by couching the claim in terms of equity and natural justice in this way, one was left with the impression that the categories in which the claim could be employed were generally open.

But it is important to stress, as Jackson has pointed out that '[t]he *aequum et bonum* theory was not the basis of the action but the basis for deciding when the law will imply a contract'.[141] Those that argued otherwise[142] assumed that, as was the case much later,[143] implied contract here meant a genuine implied contract, in which case the *aequum et bonum* idea would be contradictory because it would be a competing basis for the contractual claim. However, as has been argued here, implied contract in the context of these claims was understood firmly in the eighteenth century to mean that the promise was imposed and did not form part of the claim that the claimant needed to establish. It was a formal requirement that needed to be satisfied for pleading purposes. It was understood as a symbol for the

---

[133] See n 12 above at 1012.

[134] See part III, section A, esp text to nn 88–97 above.

[135] See part III, section C.

[136] An indication of this is Lord Mansfield's own comment in *Decker* (n 57 above).

[137] Baker (n 1 above) 56–7.

[138] In later cases, his reference to the equitable nature of the action or whether in conscience the defendant ought to retain or return the money speaks of the same principle he discussed in *Moses*.

[139] 4 Burr 2133, 98 ER 112.

[140] *Ibid* 2134.

[141] Jackson (n 2 above) 119.

[142] Jackson cites Winfield and Hanbury as holding this view: *ibid* 118. Ibbetson (n 16 above) seems to make this assumption about Lord Mansfield's innovation: 272–3.

[143] See part V, section A(ii).

fact that these claims were *non-contractual.* And Lord Mansfield's principle simply explained the basal principle for when these non-contractual claims (read contract implied in law) would arise.

It is worth for a moment appreciating why the language of equity and natural justice may have been resorted to by Lord Mansfield as a rationalisation of MHR claims. One possible explanation arises from the instances Lord Mansfield identified in which MHR succeeded. Leaving aside the list which went on to become the centrepiece of the modern law of restitution (what I shall call 'list 2' and begins: 'But it lies for money paid by mistake; or upon a consideration which happens to fail . . .'), it repays attention to focus instead on the instances which appear first ('list 1'), reflecting perhaps their importance in his scheme:

> it does not lie for money paid by the plaintiff, which is claimed of him as payable in point of honour and honesty, although it could not have been recovered from him by any course of law; as in payment of a debt barred by statute of limitations, or contracted during his infancy, or to the extent of principal and legal interest upon a usurious contract or for money fairly lost at play: because in all these cases, the defendant may retain it with safe conscience, though by positive law he was barred from recovering.[144]

This list speaks of cases in which the defendant's retention of the money cannot be justified *at law,* because the transfer suffered from some form of invalidity: it fell foul of the statute of limitation or the laws against contracting by infants or because the transfer was under a usurious or gaming contract. Yet in all these cases, at the time *Moses* was decided, the courts had recognised the defendant's right to retain the money. The question was on what basis if not strictly in law? From this perspective one can then see why Lord Mansfield may have looked to ideas of equity in contrast to the position of law (which caused the invalidities) to explain the defendant's retention of the money in these cases.

Insufficient attention is usually paid to Lord Kames' *Treatise on Equity* ('*Treatise*')[145] and the correspondence it generated between its author and Lord Mansfield at around the time *Moses* was handed down. This is unfortunate because the correspondence shows that Lord Mansfield did think about equity in more theoretical terms and that he had been exposed to the principle of unjust enrichment in relation to gain-based claims.

Some background on Kames' work will better illuminate the letters. Kames' *Treatise* was a groundbreaking work,[146] which sought to go beyond other books in Scotland and England through its desire to present equity in a principled philosophical way, while at same time remaining true to its historical origins. The province of his work is the province of equity, which he sets up as contrasting or in opposition to the common law since it 'commences at the limits of the common law'. It is aimed at both a Scottish and English law audience, for its ambition was to present principles common to both.

---

[144] See n 133 above.

[145] H Home, *Principles of Equity* (1st edn, London/Edinburgh, A Millar and A Kincaid, 1760).

[146] M Lobban, 'The Ambition of Lord Kames' in A Lewis and M Lobban (eds), *Law and History*, Current Legal Issues vol 6 (Oxford, OUP, 2004) 102.

Two particular features are worth emphasising. The first is that since it takes the common law as its departure point, it is particularly interesting how he perceives the common law. One of the revealing groups of cases is 'founded on the will', and contains contract-generated rights.[147] This supports the view that this way of thinking about contract law was already present in the eighteenth century.[148]

The second and most directly relevant to the present discussion is his use of Pomponius's maxim, *quod nemo debet locupletari aliena jactura,* to rationalise the restitutionary claims not covered by the common law.[149] Although the discussion is not to be found in one place in the book, it is clear that all gain-based remedies are viewed as based on the maxim.[150] And this is the first known use of this maxim in English law. As we will see, it is likely to have played a large part in the nineteenth century, when unjust enrichment was used to rationalise the indebitatus claims.[151] Finally, on this point, it is worth emphasising that the maxim is not used superficially because Kames shows it informs his analysis on the types of benefits recoverable,[152] the privity between the parties (whether loss and gain needs to be the same)[153] and problems of valuation.[154] The presence of the maxim in the *Treatise* thus takes us immediately into issues which are still present in debates in modern restitution scholarship.

Extracts from the two letters[155] which follow see Lord Mansfield responding to Kames' book and ideas:

> I read ev'ry thing yr L[ordshi]p writes with great satisfaction. The best of our Judges are delighted with some of yr Law Pieces. You have taught Men to trace Law to its true noble sources: Philosophy & History. Your Principles of Equity are very ingenious; but the Opposition of Equity to Law as now administered in England by different Courts, is not to be learnt from anything yet in Print & is not deducible from Reason. It can only be explained positively and by Historical Deductions. I wish we had a Pen & Genius & Diligence like yr L[ordship]s to do it.[156]

---

[147] Home (n 145 above) 39–58 and 70–124.

[148] See especially part II, section A and part III, section A.

[149] Home (n 145 above) pt 1, ch 2, s 2, 92, 101 and 117.

[150] Eg recovering mistakenly paid debts (*ibid* 92), recovering benefits passed under a contract set aside for fraud (*ibid* 101), and other circumstances which result in the transaction being set aside (*ibid* 117).

[151] See part V, section B.

[152] Home (n 145 above) 31.

[153] *Ibid* 21–2.

[154] *Ibid* 32.

[155] Both are extracted in I Ross, *Lord Kames and the Scotland of his Day* (Oxford, Clarendon Press, 1972).

[156] *Ibid* 238 quoting Lord Mansfield from a letter dated 27 February 1762. Ross speculates about whether Lord Mansfield had seen manuscripts of the first edition before publication, as had Lord Hardwicke. Perhaps the strongest evidence for this is that in the second edition, Kames reveals that he had Lord Mansfield in mind when he wrote the work. And this is the basis for the argument that it was Lord Kames' work that influenced the decision in *Moses*: H Macqueen and W Sellar, 'Unjust Enrichment in Scots Law' in E Schrage (ed), *Unjust Enrichment: the Comparative Legal History of the Law of Restitution* (2nd edn, Berlin, Dunker & Humblot, 1999) 316. But the problem with this thesis is that it assumes the exceptionality of the statement in *Moses*, which in turn forces it to look for obvious external sources, in this case Kames' work, as Birks' work did with Roman law influences (see text to

To reduce principles of Equity into a System of Science, & to illustrate them by Examples, from all times and Countrys, is a Lesson of Jurisprudence to the whole World; and worthy of your L[ordshi]p. It equally suits parliament of Paris, the Court of Session, & the Courts in England whether called of law or Equity, but the plan of a distinct Court of Equity, upon natural or political Principles may embarrass the Subject; & any allusion to the Case in England, upon a supposed natural division of law and Equity into two Sciences can only lead to mistakes.[157]

These letters show Lord Mansfield's wholehearted endorsement of Kames' project, especially on representing equity in a principled rule-based way. He potentially goes further, emphasising that equity should not be in opposition to law and both should be based on the same principles, rather than distinct rules. All this suggests that Lord Mansfield's reference to equity was not an invitation to employ MHR in a broad discretionary way, because it would be anathema to proceeding on a principled basis. However, as the next part will show, this is exactly how MHR claims were employed—often by Lord Mansfield—in the period after *Moses* and the end of the eighteenth century. So, was Lord Mansfield's endorsement of Kames' project merely an exercise in politeness? It is submitted that this would be an unfair conclusion, and perhaps pragmatic considerations prevented him from realising the kind of model Kames had envisaged. It may be that his views in these letters expressed what would be the ideal destination of the law. Moreover, one must not forget that, as will be argued in the next part, there is evidence to show that Lord Mansfield did resile from the position of employing MHR claims in a broad discretionary way.[158] Finally, the lists of situations in which the action would apply and which he made visible through *Moses* did form an important infrastructure for the theoretical work that was to come at the end of the nineteenth century, and especially the last two decades of the twentieth century.

V. The Period After *Moses v Macferlan*

The development of the law in the period after *Moses* has rightly been described as schizophrenic.[159] The reader who tries to discern clear lines of development is bound to be frustrated. The approach taken here is to identify key patterns in the case law and legal discourse.

---

n 98 onwards). Apart from the dating problem (which relies on them showing that he had seen the work before publication), the correspondence extracted and the Preface to the second edition suggest that Lord Mansfield was not just internalising everything Kames had to say, but had something to contribute. This suggests strongly that he was also thinking about these topics independently from Kames' work. Ibbetson (n 16 above) 272 n 50, comes to the same conclusion but for different reasons, namely that the Roman law and Scots influence in *Moses* is likely to have predated Kames' work.

[157] Ross (n 155 above) 242 quoting from letter, 26 May 1766.
[158] See text to nn 167–8 below.
[159] Ibbetson (n 16 above) 277.

A. Case Law

There are broadly two noteworthy phases in the case law, which will be dealt with in the two sections which follow.

(i) High Point in Equity Reasoning

The first phase, which can be described as the high point in equity reasoning, is most clearly visible in the period following *Moses* and leading up to the end of the eighteenth century. During this period we see a high frequency of MHR cases whose reasoning was mediated through what was effectively an inquiry into whether it was unconscionable or not for the defendant to retain the money claimed.[160] Such a broad-based principle expanded the province of the MHR claim beyond anything that was suggested by the two lists Lord Mansfield had been working from. The potential for uncertainty such an open-ended principle provided was great. Three types of problems can be identified in the case law during this period. The first is that, driven by a notion of fairness, the court could become too ready to interfere in otherwise valid contracts, thereby upsetting commercial bargains. This is likely to have been the case in *Floyer v Edwards* (1774).[161] Here the claimant employed the count of MHR to claim the price and interest owed to him for goods sold to the defendant.[162] The defendant argued that the contract under which the sale took place was usurious because the interest it claimed was beyond the statutory 5 per cent. Lord Mansfield held the contract was not usurious because the statute only applied to loan agreements and not those for the sale of goods. In a subsequent case involving the same customary term, Lord Mansfield forced the seller to accept the debtor's payment into court of the principal and 5 per cent interest, not because of the usury laws but because he thought the term was more generally unconscionable.[163]

Secondly, a broad-based jurisdiction threatened to overrun other areas of law and the appropriate limitations they may have in place to deal with particular cases. In *Brown v Bullen* (1780),[164] the claimant was allowed to use MHR to claim the debt he had proved under the commission of bankruptcy against Fox (the defendant was his assignee). The defendant tried to resist this claim on the grounds that if the action was allowed it would 'tend to disturb the execution of bankruptcy laws'.[165] It was also argued that if the action was allowed then it should follow usual bankruptcy proceedings and allow the defendant to claim a set-off. It

---

[160] See the many cases collected by Kremer (2001) (n 4 above) in his article.

[161] 1 Cowp 112, 98 ER 995; Lofft 595, 98 ER 817. See also *Jestons v Brooke* (1778) 2 Cowp 793, 98 ER 1365.

[162] What today would fall within the action for the agreed sum: see paragraph following text to n 29 above.

[163] This is only recorded in 1 Cowp 112, 116; 98 ER 995.

[164] 1 Doug 407, 99 ER 261.

[165] *Ibid* 409.

was pointed out that if the argument on set-off was not allowed then the defendant would be put to the expense and risk of pursuing the claimant in a separate action, by which time the claimant may not be in a position to pay. Having shown some sympathy to the defendant's argument, Lord Mansfield nevertheless allowed the claimant's claim. It is noteworthy that this result was effectively overruled by statute early in the nineteenth century.[166]

Linked to the second problem is the third, in which the expanding province of MHR claims meant that it was being deployed in situations in which it had not been before. In a system that did not provide notice of the nature of the claimant's claim(the effect of declaring generally), this created the risk that the defendant was left in a situation where he would be ill-equipped to meet the claimant's case. In the words of the period, the defendant would be 'surprised'. This was one of the criticisms acknowledged by Lord Mansfield in a number of judgments in which he limited the MHR claim where it was deemed to cause the risk of surprise on the defendant.[167] However, it is important not to overstate the claims of the surprise objections on Lord Mansfield's thinking. This is because the procedure for claiming MHR was always susceptible to this problem throughout its existence. Indeed, one of the strengths of the MHR claim was that details could be dispensed with until the hearing. It was intentionally a system that provided no notice of the claimant's claim (the effect of declaring generally). What is likely is that the surprise objection was also an implied acknowledgment by Lord Mansfield that the equitable foundations he had laid down for the MHR claim had broadened the scope of the claim too much. And this was especially so, it seems, in those cases where there were other competing causes of actions that he felt made MHR inappropriate.[168]

In so far as Lord Mansfield did attempt to curb the breadth of the MHR, it was part of a general shift at the end of the eighteenth and early nineteenth centuries in which the courts relied less and less on equitable notions to understand and apply the MHR claim.[169] Indeed, throughout the nineteenth century, although equity is occasionally mentioned in the cases, it was more akin to lip service because there was never again a period where the courts consistently mediated their inquiry into the existence of a claim for MHR through what was or was not conscionable as they had done in the period after *Moses*. A major reason for this is likely to have been that the courts were not satisfied with the breadth and uncertainty of the equitable principle that Lord Mansfield had laid down, and which is

---

[166] Bankrupts England Act 1825, s 110. In the note to *Leers, Ex Parte* (1802) 6 Ves Jun 644, 31 ER 1237, this statute is referred to as confirming an earlier statute from 1808. However, the reference for this earlier Act is incorrect.

[167] Eg a number of what I have called the 'horse warranty' cases (see Chapter 5, text to n 77): *Weston v Downes* (1778) 1 Doug 21, 99 ER 19 and *Towers v Barrrett* (1786) 1 TR 133, 99 ER 1014.

[168] Eg the horse warranty cases.

[169] Winfield (1930) (n 2 above) 123–42; Fifoot (n 36 above) 154; Jackson (n 2 above) 121; Ibbetson (n 16 above) 272–3; and W Swain, 'Moses v Macferlan' in C Mitchell and P Mitchell (eds), *Landmark Cases in the Law of Restitution* (Oxford, Hart, 2006) 29–31.

illustrated by the three examples above.[170] The result was that the inquiry became more conservative and was built around the discrete circumstances which Lord Mansfield had identified in *Moses*. Indeed, it would not be inaccurate to conclude that Lord Mansfield's true innovation of equity-driven MHR was not as successful as he would have hoped. So while the experiment with equity did not succeed, the clear and compelling language in which he drew the map of the MHR claim in *Moses* provided an important foundation for the future development of the law in this area. Evans perfectly captures this impression of Lord Mansfield and his contribution in *Moses* at the beginning of the nineteenth century, in modest tones that are nonetheless revealing: 'In some instances the particular decisions may be *reasonably questioned,* but the utility resulting from his general discussions must be universally allowed' (emphasis added).[171]

(ii) Fiction of the Promise Flickers into Life

In the account above, it has been shown how, in the development of the law during the seventeenth and eighteenth centuries, the idea of implied contract was understood as a fiction within the pleading: the promise was imposed in law and importantly did not inform how the indebitatus claims were understood. As the outline of the first phase shows, in so far as a genuine theory emerged it was in the period after *Moses* when equitable notions were employed to shape the MHR count. In contrast, during the second phase in the nineteenth and part of the twentieth centuries there was a greater incidence of cases when courts would inform their understanding of the indebitatus claims by reference to a *genuine* implied contract.[172] This manifested itself in a number of ways, including, in one often quoted example, the acceptance by the House of Lords that even if the promise was imposed in law, and to that extent a fiction, one still needed to ask if the contract *could* exist in the circumstances:

> When it speaks of actions arising quasi ex contractu it refers merely to a class of action in theory based on a contract which is imputed to the defendant by a fiction of law. The fiction can only be set up with effect if such a contract would be valid if it really existed.[173]

---

[170] See the references in n 169 above. See also Junius' letter to Lord Mansfield (17 November 1770), where he complains, among other things, 'Instead of those certain, positive rules, by which the judgment of a court of law should invariably be determined, you have fondly introduced your own unfettered notions of equity and substantial justice ... In the mean time the practice gains ground; the court of King's Bench becomes a court of equity, and the judge instead of consulting strictly the law of the land, refers only to the wisdom of the court, and to the purity of his own conscience': Anon, *The Genuine Letters of Junius* (London, 1771) 245.

[171] WD Evans, *Essays: On the Action for Money Had and Received, on the Law of Insurances, and on the Law of Bills of Exchange and Promissory Notes* (Liverpool, Merrit & Wright, 1802) 7. This essay is reprinted with helpful annotations in (1998) RLR 1.

[172] See the examples from the nineteenth century collected by Ibbetson (n 16 above) 278–81.

[173] *Sinclair v Brougham* [1914] AC 398, 415.

This type of reasoning created awkward burdens (evidential and procedural)[174] and had substantive negative effects, not least because it denied an otherwise valid claim if a genuine contract could not be found to exist.

We can be sure that the idea of whether a contract could or would exist in a situation would not have been entertained in the eighteenth century.[175] As to why, then, these kinds of questions were asked more frequently during the second phase is not a question that is easy to answer. One likely reason could be that this was the inevitable consequence of the long-term usage of the implied contract terminology. And at some point, especially in a period where there was no alternative foundation put forward for these claims, as equity had been for MHR in the first phase, the fiction of the promise was bound to flicker into life in some cases. But it is also important not to represent the second phase as a period when there was a widespread impression that the indebitatus claims were founded on a genuine implied contract. This would be overly simplistic and would tend to overlook, as the next section will show, the evidence from this period that lawyers understood the fiction of the promise and even went as far as suggesting an alternative foundation for the indebitatus claims.

B. Legal Discourse

More modern accounts have rightly identified Ames, rather than the first *Restatement of Restitution* (1937),[176] as the catalyst for the idea that a large majority of the indebitatus claims could be explained through the principle against unjust enrichment.[177] His main insight made the work of the first drafters of the *Restatement* easier by giving them a ready-made organising principle. However, the period leading up to Ames's work is often not accurately captured.

In broad outline the standard account[178] is that in contrast to the law of contract and tort, unjust enrichment was a very late developer in the nineteenth and twentieth centuries. Before Ames, English lawyers had 'never got close to articulating an abstract idea of unjust enrichment or anything like it'.[179] This was for a combination of reasons, the main one being the persistent belief, encouraged by English writers from the eighteenth century, that the indebitatus claims were

---

[174] Eg the rationalisation that co-sureties were contractually liable for their share meant that in a multiparty case, a court would have to navigate through a very large number of implied contracts: see the examples and discussion by Ibbetson (n 16 above) 278 of *Batard v Hawes* (1853) 2 El & Bl 287, 118 ER 775; cf *Rambux Chittangeo v Modhoosoodin Paul Chawdhry* (1867) 7 WR (India) 377.

[175] See, eg *Arris and Arris v Stukeley* (n 23 above), where the argument that the contract could not exist on the facts of the case was rejected: see text to nn 63–4 above. Also see *Moses* (n 12 above) 1008, where a similar objection was made and rejected.

[176] American Law Institute, *Restatement of the Law of Restitution: Quasi Contracts and Constructive Trusts* (Reporters: WA Seavey and AW Scott) (Philadelphia, American Law Institute, 1937).

[177] Ibbetson: (n 16 above) 286–7and (n 2 above) 45–8. The story is told in A Kull, 'James Barr Ames and the Early Modern History of Unjust Enrichment' (2004) 25 *OJLS* 297.

[178] A detailed representative example is Ibbetson (n 2 above).

[179] *Ibid* 37.

founded on genuine implied contracts (hereinafter referred to as the 'implied contract theory'), something which it was easy to think because many of the counts
that made up the indebitatus category had a contractual core. But in the course of
the nineteenth century the fallacy of the implied contract theory was revealing
itself interstitially through legal texts and was most clearly and famously exposed
by Maine who observed 'But a Quasi Contract is not a contract at all'.[180] It was
against this background that Ames stepped in and provided an alternative explanation, one which was further elaborated upon in the twentieth century.

This account overestimates the hold of the implied contract theory in the nineteenth century and before. I have already argued that such an observation would
not be accurate in relation to the eighteenth century. In relation to the nineteenth
century, it was shown that there were cases which support the implied contract
theory idea. However, as was argued, the implied contract theory was not so widespread and did not have such a hold on the mind-set of lawyers that they failed to
appreciate and think more broadly (in terms of alternative models) about the fiction that lay at the heart of such a theory. The observations of Maine were not so
novel. Similarly with Ames, although his work was groundbreaking, it would be
unfair to suggest that he was the first to think about an alternative theory along the
lines of unjust enrichment or something similar.

An excellent insight into the view of the legal community of the indebitatus
claims in the first half of the nineteenth century is available from the parliamentary reports inquiring into the procedure of the courts of common law in the 1830s
and again in the 1850s. In a series of reports, where the point was raised directly or
indirectly, we see those consulted evidencing a clear understanding that there was
a fiction involved in the pleadings in these cases, something which was noted by
the commissioners.[181] One consultee, serjeant Edward Lawes, went as far as rec-
ommending that indebitatus assumpsit be abolished and replaced by debt to avoid
reliance on a fiction.[182]

As well as Lawes' suggestion, there is evidence that others thought about alternative explanations for the indebitatus claims too. For example, Evans in his
essay[183] at the beginning of the nineteenth century employed Pomponius' maxim

---

[180] H Maine, *Ancient Law* (London, John Murray, 1861) 344.

[181] *Second Report made to His Majesty by the Commissioners Appointed to Inquire into the Practice
and Proceedings of the Superior Courts of Common Law* (1830) vol XI, 547, 680 (JL Dampier); *Third
Report made to His Majesty by the Commissioners Appointed to Inquire into the Practice and Proceedings
of the Superior Courts of Common Law* (1831) vol X, 375, 542 (J Manning) and 703 (E Lawes); and *First
Report of Her Majesty's Commissioners for Inquiring into Process, Practice, and System of Pleading in the
Supreme Courts of Common Law* (1851) vol XXII, 567, 587.

[182] He had submitted a report in which one of the sections is dedicated to arguing 'Abolishing
Assumpsit in cases of Debt'. This report is extracted at Appendix E in *Third Report made to His Majesty
by the Commissioners Appointed to Inquire into the Practice and Proceedings of the Superior Courts of
Common Law* (1831) vol X, 375. The relevant discussion is at 703–4. His argument was that since the
action of debt was no longer afflicted by wager of law, it could, with some amendments, behave with
the same advantages and effect as indebitatus assumpsit, but without the fiction of the promise.

[183] See n 171 above.

(D.50.17.206)[184] as the foundation for the MHR count. This is the same maxim which is likely to have been the source of Ames' idea of unjust enrichment in his article. No attention has been paid to the great jurist Austin, who argued 'The prominent idea in Quasi-Contract seems to be an *undue* advantage which would be acquired by the obligor, if he were not compelled to relinquish it or indemnify'.[185] In an 1829 article, the author argued that Pomponius' maxim lay at the heart of the claim for the return of the money for a defective horse.[186] And as Kull has shown, Judge Joseph Story employed Pomponius' maxim to solve a difficult case he came across relating to the mistaken improver in 1841.[187] The references to the maxim in Story's judgment take us to what was arguably one of the most sophisticated uses of the unjust enrichment idea for the common law in the eighteenth, nineteenth and (before Birks' work) twentieth centuries. This is Kames' work, which made the mistaken improver one of his central examples.[188] It is highly likely that this was the source of Story's argument. Importantly, as was shown above, Kames employed unjust enrichment as a genuine cause of action (informing elements like the type of recoverable benefits and their valuation) which shaped the claim, unlike Ames' use of the idea as a conclusory gloss.

The question then is why did the momentum for change only really intensify and begin with Ames' work? This is a difficult question but the role of legal education and its influence on the development of the law must not be underestimated here. Just as the excitement, energy and popularity of restitution courses and literature were in large part responsible for the establishment of the law of unjust enrichment in a relatively short space of time in England,[189] so too in the United States a similar pattern can be traced at the end of the nineteenth and beginning of the twentieth centuries.[190] Moreover, it should be remembered that

---

[184] *Hoc natura aequum est, neminem cum alterius detrimento fieri locupletiorem* (By the law of nature it is right that no man shall enrich himself unjustly at the expense of another).

[185] J Austin, *The Province of Jurisprudence Determined* (London, J Murray, 1861–63) vol II, 944; and vol III, 134. Although they were published in the early 1860s, these lectures had taken place in the late 1820s and early 1830s: see WL Morison, *John Austin* (London, E Arnold, 1982) 21–33.

[186] 'For when a defective article is unwittingly purchased at a sound price, these principles seem to require that a bargain so unequal should be corrected by the seller's refunding a proportionate part of the purchase money. You permit him, otherwise, to obtain an undue advantage in a contract intended to be framed on the basis of equality "Nemo debet locupletari aliena jactura", is the undoubted rule of natural justice': Anon, 'On the Sale and Warranty of Horses' (1828–29) 1 *Law Mag Quart Rev Juris* 318, 325–6.

[187] *Bright v Boyd* 4 F Cas 127, 132–33(Cir Ct, D Maine, 1841). Kull argues that this case was responsible for making the language of unjust enrichment popular in mistaken improver cases, which were almost certainly read by Ames: Kull (n 177 above) esp 315–16.

[188] Home (n 145 above) 26.

[189] F Rose, 'The Evolution of the Species' in AS Burrows and L Rodger (eds), *Mapping the Law Essays in Memory of Peter Birks* (Oxford, OUP, 2006).

[190] See the extract of the letter by a student of Ames which reports 'Ames' teaching in regard to "Unjust Enrichment" was at the time a principle to be discussed with bated breath. Now it seems to have complete recognition': Kull (n 177 above) 311. It is also noteworthy that one of the prominent members of the ALI, which drafted the first restatement, was Samuel Williston, a keen proponent of unjust enrichment and a former student of Ames and Keener: *ibid* 309. Another indication of the burgeoning growth of the subject was that academics who went on to become well known in other areas initially spent time teaching or writing about quasi contract, and were directly or indirectly indebted

the cordial and more cooperative relations in Anglo-American private law in the late nineteenth and early twentieth centuries went a long way to transmitting the unjust enrichment idea initially to England.[191] Finally, it should not be forgotten that it would ultimately not be too difficult to sell an idea which sought to reveal and suppress the fictitious language of implied contract and place the claims on a non-contractual foundation, as they had been mostly understood. Whether unjust enrichment was the correct foundation for this purpose is a question which will be addressed in the final part, and will be explored in the two chapters which follow.

VI. Learning From the Past: Concluding Comments

In the modern era, it has been Birks' writings which have passionately expressed the idea that Ames was right to place many of the indebitatus claims on the unjust enrichment platform.[192] As he has shown,[193] this is right as a matter of classification because the law of obligations is not just made up of the rights generated by consent and wrongs but also unjust enrichment, as the civil law systems have long recognised. He has also argued that recognising unjust enrichment enables us to see links with other claims, usually on the equity side, which work in similar ways to many of the indebitatus claims. This makes for a more coherent picture of the law, one which breaks down (consistent with the spirit of the Judicature Acts) the equity/ law divide.

---

to Ames. Before the Law of Evidence claimed his attention, Henry Wigmore wrote an article on the subject in 1891 (H Wigmore, 'A Summary of Quasi Contracts' (1891) 25 *Am L Rev* 46); while he was waiting for a break in the field of International Law, James Brown Scott wrote one of the first casebooks (Scott (n 2 above)); and Roscoe Pound, showing his versatility in all matters of jurisprudence, seems to have taught the subject early on in his career (see the MS *Notes on Cases on Quasi Contract to be used with Scott and Keener* in the HLS special collection). Scott, in his Preface, talks about the huge debt he owes Ames for his help and notes. Similarly we know that Wigmore and Ames continued to correspond long after the former was a student at Harvard Law School. With Pound, it is a telling fact that he spent one year in the law school from 1889, just at the time when the subject was becoming public.

[191] The reporters of the *Restatement of Restitution* wrote about their project in the leading law journal in England: WA Seavey and AW Scott, 'The American Restatement of the Law of Restitution' (1938) 54 *LQR* 29. Lord Wright was an enthusiastic supporter of their insights, as he signalled in his review of the *Restatement*: L Wright (1937) 51 Harv L Rev 369. Even though many of his papers have now been lost, we know from those that survive that Ames did correspond regularly with English academics: see, eg the letter between Ames and Pollock (3 August 1905; Correspondence of Frederick Pollock, Harvard Law Library, special collections, consulted in the summer of 2004). The finding aid for this collection is available at http://oasis.lib.harvard.edu/oasis/deliver/deepLink?_collection=oasis&uniqueId=law00027. See also Ames' exchanges with Maitland, some of which are extracted in HD Hazeltine, 'Gossip about Legal History: Unpublished Letters of Maitland and Ames' (1924) 2 *CLJ* 1.

[192] His seminal book, P Birks, *An Introduction to the Law of Restitution* (revised edn, Oxford, Clarendon Press, 1989) was followed by a stream of articles; the story is told in Rose (n 189 above); although he admitted that, contrary to his earlier writings, some of the claims were not founded on unjust enrichment but wrongs: P Birks, 'Misnomer' in WR Cornish *et al* (eds), *Restitution, Past, Present and Future: Essays in Honour of Gareth Jones* (Oxford, Hart, 1998).

[193] For what follows see Birks (n 192 above) 32–4 and more recently Birks (n 2 above) chs 1 and 2.

Birks' work has also been central to building a framework for the unjust enrichment claims as they are now understood and recognised in English law. There are essentially three elements that need to be established: (1) the defendant must have been enriched; (2) the enrichment must have been at the claimant's expense; (3) the enrichment must have been *unjust* (established through unjust factors).[194] The heart of the claim is the unjust factors, which broadly echo the list ('list 2' above)[195] proposed by Lord Mansfield in *Moses*. To this extent, there is historical support for the position taken up by the modern common law, in the form of the unjust factors approach. But as was remarked in the introduction, this model of unjust enrichment still has its critics. In this debate, our historical overview is essential.

For those who argue that the spirit of the common law is better reflected if what today is described as the law of unjust enrichment is subsumed within the law of contract,[196] the message from the historical analysis is clear. In so far as anything is to be drawn from the law around the indebitatus claims (the dominant category taken over by the unjust enrichment analysis), the best representation of the jurisprudence of the past is to treat such claims as non-contractual. Moreover, history reminds us that packaging a non-contractual understanding into contractual language will in the long term have negative effects, as the second phase in the nineteenth and early twentieth centuries showed. Here, we saw that wrong results could be reached as a result of misunderstanding the fiction. The argument for abandoning the language of implied contract is therefore fully justified because it is productive of injustice. Furthermore, seeing unjust enrichment as the underpinning concept, rather than contract, allows one to appreciate the link with other gain-based remedies on the equity side. Despite these strong lessons from history, some writers continue to pursue the contractual line, at least in explaining an innocent party's right to restitution after a breach of contract.[197] In so far as these authors support their claim by specific points of history not covered in this chapter, and other non-historical points, these will be considered in Chapter 2.

Even if one accepts, as has been argued here, that there is an independent category of law not founded on contract (or wrongs), there is a debate over what framework will give content to that independence. In the common law, the dominant framework is the unjust factors approach. This has been challenged by those who seek to shape the law of unjust enrichment around equitable notions such as unconscientiousness.[198] The argument is primarily built on what is considered to be the best interpretation of Lord Mansfield's decision in *Moses* and the case law immediately thereafter. It is certainly true that the constant mention of equity and

---

[194] These elements have been recognised as the foundation of an unjust enrichment claim in numerous dicta, including the House of Lords in *Banque Financiere de la Cite v Parc (Battersea) Ltd* [1999] 1 AC 221, 227 (Lord Steyn) and 234 (Lord Hoffmann).

[195] See text to n 144 above.

[196] See n 3 above.

[197] See, especially importantly, the writings of Prof Kull referred to in Chapter 2. See also the views of Hedley and Jaffey referred to at n 3 above.

[198] See n 4 above.

the way the courts proceeded during this time-frame (what was called the first phase above) support an equitable foundation for unjust enrichment. However, any such interpretation would overlook the lessons of history because it would ignore the problems, to some extent acknowledged by Lord Mansfield himself, which occurred during this period when equitable reasoning dominated the action. Moreover, in the long term, this was just one phase in the development of the law and the broader picture does not necessarily support the idea that the indebitatus claims had an equitable foundation. One can argue that the problems that occurred in the first phase were specific to the period when the pleading of MHR was so brief that surprise was likely; and also that since there are now more settled notions of subsidiarity in the law, the risk of interfering with other causes of action, present during Lord Mansfield's time, is not such a problem today. However, in the leading modern case in which equity notions were employed to inform the unjust enrichment claim, the final result evokes exactly the kind of problem that occurred in the period after *Moses* was laid down. In the Australian case of *Roxborough v Rothmans of Pall Mall (Australia) Ltd*[199] (which will be discussed in greater detail in Chapters 3[200] and 6),[201] Gummow J's employment of the principle of unconcientiousness[202] led him to allow a party to claim back a sum paid under a contract that had not been breached nor partially or wholly set aside. That this was an unprecedented result has been recognised by many commentators, some of whom have argued that the claim should not have been allowed. Even those commentators who think the result right agree that more attention should have been paid to whether the recovery of this sum upset the contractual allocation of risk. There is another way to see Gummow J's decision in this case; namely, that the breadth of the equitable principle he applied enabled him to adopt an analysis which did not compel him to address the issue that the contract may have had something to say about whether the money could be claimed back in the circumstances.[203] This is a risk that pervades a system which has unconscientiousness at the core of its law of unjust enrichment.

However, all this does not mean that the current model of unjust enrichment, founded on unjust factors, is necessarily right. Indeed, as Chapter 3 will show, the best model is one which, applying Birks' recent work, follows the civilian absence of basis approach. This goes to show that the law can sometimes, for good reason, escape from its historical 'shape'.

---

[199] [2001] HCA 68; (2002) 76 AJLR 203, HCA.

[200] In part III, section C.

[201] In part II, section C(ii).

[202] Although he was part of the majority of the High Court of Australia (HCA) which reached the same result, he was the only one to adopt this principle to extend the existing boundaries of the law to cover this case. The other judges making up the majority (Gleeson CJ, Gaudron and Hayne JJ) did not think they were necessarily extending the law to reach their result.

[203] For a defence of Gummow J's approach, see Kremer (2003) (n 4 above).

2

Rejecting the Role of Unjust Enrichment
in the Contractual Context?

I. Introduction

THE LAST CHAPTER looked at the indebitatus claims, and the action for money and received in particular, through an historical lens. It argued that there is strong support in history for accepting that the indebitatus claims were perceived as non-contractual and many of them today are best seen as resting on the independent cause of action of unjust enrichment. Furthermore, that unjust enrichment cause of action is not best seen as dependent on equitable notions of unconscientiousness. What was there said clearly applies beyond, as well as within, the contractual context with which this book is concerned. However, in this chapter we focus more specifically on the contractual context and within that on arguments that have been made for a contractual, rather than an unjust enrichment, analysis of an innocent party's restitution after a breach of contract. In particular, we look at the important work of the influential US scholar Professor Kull, who rejects unjust enrichment as an explanation of restitution after breach. But we also examine the anti-unjust enrichment pro-contract views of Hedley and Jaffey.

What has been called the 'dominant model' is that, provided the innocent party has terminated the contract for breach, he or she can elect to claim restitution of the value of the benefits transferred under the contract instead of his or her expectation damages. This is said to be a claim outside the contract, founded on unjust enrichment for (total or partial) failure of consideration. This account has been challenged frequently and vociferously in the last three decades.[1] In the United States, the current draft of the *Third Restatement of Restitution* ('R3R'),[2] under the leadership of its Reporter Professor Kull, rejects the dominant model and builds a

---

[1] As well as those that will be referred to in the text, see R Childres and J Garamella, 'The Law of Restitution and the Reliance Interest in Contract' (1969) 64 *Northwestern U Law Rev* 433; J Perillo, 'Restitution in a Contractual Context' (1973) 73 *Colum L Rev* 1208; J Perillo, 'Restitution in the Second Restatement of Contracts' (1981) 81 *Colum L Rev* 37; E Andersen, 'The Restoration Interest and Damages for Breach of Contract' (1994) 53 *Maryland L Rev* 1; M Gergen, 'Restitution as a Bridge Over Contractual Waters' (2002) 71 *Ford L Rev* 709; and M Gergen, 'Restitution and Contract: Reflections on the Third Restatement' (2005) 13 *RLR* 224.

[2] American Law Institute, *Restatement Third, Restitution and Unjust Enrichment* (Reporter: A Kull) (Philadelphia, American Law Institute, 2000). It is still at the tentative draft stage.

picture of the law in which the restitutionary remedy after breach is seen as a contractual claim, rather than one founded on unjust enrichment. This shift from orthodoxy continues Kull's earlier work, in which he argued for a pruning back of the role of unjust enrichment in the contractual setting.[3]

More radical still are the views of Hedley[4] and Jaffey,[5] both of whom reject the role of unjust enrichment not just within the contractual setting but across the different situations in which a restitutionary remedy is awarded. But they join Kull in arguing that the dominant model can be integrated within the law of contract.[6] In order to achieve this they adopt a more expansive model of contract than is currently recognised in the common law.

Although Kull, Hedley and Jaffey are not alone in rejecting the dominant model,[7] they provide a representative spectrum of views on how an innocent party's restitution after breach of contract does, and would, work as a contractual remedy, rather than as one founded on unjust enrichment.[8] The aim of this chapter is to examine critically the models of Kull, Hedley and Jaffey. After summarising the key features of each model, it will be argued that the methodological and/or historical foundations of these models are flawed. Moreover, and partly because of the aforementioned weaknesses, the models fail the 'fit' criterion, in that they provide a less coherent picture of the law than the dominant model they try to replace. The reason why a comparison can be made against the fit criterion is because each model is ultimately aiming for the same goal. That goal is to:

> identify broader principles, often not stated in the cases, that underlie these rules and decisions and provide a basis for development of the law in such a way as to identify and eliminate anomalies and false distinctions and to make the law clearer and coherent.[9]

II. A Critical Appraisal of the Three Models

A. Kull and the *Third Restatement of Restitution*

As has already been mentioned, the R3R is the least radical of the models to be examined because it does not reject a place for a principle against unjust enrich-

---

[3] A Kull, 'Restitution as a Remedy for Breach of Contract' (1994) 67 *So Calif L Rev* 1465.

[4] Most fully worked out in S Hedley, 'Implied Contract and Restitution' (2004) 63 *CLJ* 435.

[5] P Jaffey, *The Nature and Scope of Restitution: Vitiated Transfers, Imputed Contracts and Disgorgement* (Oxford, Hart, 2000) esp ch 2.

[6] Hedley takes this further and seeks to integrate most of the law of restitution within contract: see Hedley (n 4 above) 439.

[7] See, eg Andersen (n 1 above).

[8] For Jaffey it would be through a greater protection of the reliance interest, for Hedley through implied contract and for Kull through an expansion of the contractual remedies available for breach.

[9] Jaffey (n 5 above) 24. To the same effect see Hedley (n 4 above) 439–40. Also see Gergen, speaking generally about the approach taken by him and others like Kull and the R3R: Gergen (2002) (n 1 above) 709–10.

ment within its account of the law of restitution. Moreover, it does see a role for unjust enrichment within the contractual setting. The size of the role it plays is informed by a number of general principles which are set out in the introductory chapter. It opens with the statement that 'The source of liability in restitution is the receipt of an economic benefit under circumstances such that its retention without payment would result in the unjust enrichment of the defendant at the expense of the plaintiff'.[10] The term 'unjustified enrichment' is used in preference to 'unjust enrichment' because 'unjust' implies that the application of the principle is more discretionary than is in fact the case. It is important to emphasise a number of limiting principles placed on the general right to restitution for unjust enrichment:

(1) Liability in restitution is based on and measured by the receipt of a benefit, but the receipt of a benefit does not of itself make the recipient liable in restitution.
(2) The transactions that give rise to a liability in restitution are primarily non-consensual. They take place outside the framework of an enforceable contract, or otherwise without the effective consent of both parties.
(3) The fact that a person has received or obtained a benefit without paying for it does not of itself establish that the recipient has been unjustly enriched.
(4) There is no liability in restitution in respect of a benefit intentionally conferred by the claimant on the recipient, unless the circumstances of the transaction are such as to excuse the claimant from the necessity of basing a claim to payment on a contract with the recipient.[11]

As Gergen[12] has pointed out, also detectable in the R3R is the principle against forced exchange on a defendant who is not at fault.

The R3R is split into four parts: part 1 (general principles); part 2 (grounds of liability for restitution); part 3 (remedies); and part 4 (defences). It is anticipated that part 2 will be split into five chapters (beginning with chapter 2), the projected outline of which is as follows:

Chapter 2. Transfers Subject to Avoidance

Topic 1. Benefits Conferred by Mistake
Topic 2. Defective Consent or Authority
Topic 3. Transfers under Legal Compulsion

Chapter 3: Intentional Transactions

Topic 1. Emergency Intervention
Topic 2. Self Interested Intervention

---

[10] R3R, Tentative Draft ('TD') s 1, comment a.
[11] R3R (TD) s 2 (1)–(4). See also comment to s 2.
[12] M Gergen, 'The Restatement Third, Restitution and Unjust Enrichment at Midpoint' (2003) 56 *CLP* 289, 298. For an overview of the R3R see this article and M Gergen, 'Self Interested Intervention in the Law of Unjust Enrichment' in R Zimmermann (ed), *Grundstrukturen eines Europaishen Beriecherungsrechts* (Tubingen, Mohr Siebeck, 2005).

Chapter 4: Restitution and Contract

Topic 1. Restitution to a Performing Party with No Claim on Contract

s.31. Indefiniteness or Lack of Formality
s.32. Illegality
s.33. Incapacity of Recipient
s.34. Mistake of Supervening Change of Circumstances
s.35. Performance of a Disputed Obligation
s.36. Restitution to a Party in Default

Topic 2. Restitutionary Remedies for Breach of an Enforceable Contract

s.37. Rescission as a Remedy for Breach of Contract
s.38. Restitutionary Measure of Contract Damages

Topic 3. Restitution in Cases of Profitable Breach

s.39. Profit Derived from Opportunistic Breach

Chapter 5: Restitution for Wrongs

Topic 1. Benefits Acquired by Tort or Other Breach of Duty

In the above account, only chapter 4's content has been further detailed, as it is the focus of the present chapter. It is noteworthy that unjust enrichment plays a role in topics 1 and 3. This confirms the earlier point that the R3R does not excise the principle of unjust enrichment from the contractual setting. However, it is in topic 2 that the departure from the dominant model is made, and this will be the primary focus of this chapter.

In topic 2[13] it is argued that contrary to the orthodox position, 'restitutionary remedies for breach of an enforceable contract' are (a) not founded on the principle against unjust enrichment but are alternative contractual remedies; and (b) the term 'restitution for breach' hides two different remedies. The first is the more traditional type of claim, in which the claimant may elect to rescind the contract and, as an alternative to expectation damages, seek 'restoration to the status quo ante' (s 37). The other is where damages are given as a proxy to the normal measure; analogous to the reliance measure (s 38). The noteworthy point about the relationship between the two is that where a party is trying to get the value of the non-returnable performance, the claim does not come under s 37 but under s 38k, because s 37 is limited to actually reversing the transfer.[14]

(i) Methodology

In an important early article foreshadowing his work on the R3R, Kull uses efficiency arguments based on law and economics literature to reinforce his view that the restitutionary remedies after breach are matters of contract law and not unjust

---

[13] R3R (TD no 3).
[14] R3R (TD no 3) s 37, comment a.

enrichment.[15] This is evident in relation to his discussion and objection to two features of the dominant model as laid down in the *First Restatement of Restitution* and the *Second Restatement of Contracts.* The first feature is the potential provided by the restitutionary claim to recover beyond the contract price, which has the effect of sometimes allowing a party to escape a losing bargain. And the second feature is the relaxation of the historical limitations on rescission (which he uses as a term to include termination as well as rendering a contract void ab initio).

Kull starts from the position that remedies (default rules) should as far as possible be those that parties would agree (because their agreement is voluntary and so should be the remedies).[16] It is at the stage of deciding what those remedies would be that the efficiency arguments are used. So in relation to the first feature identified above (escaping a losing bargain), Kull argues that since contracting parties expect their exchanges to be profitable, a rule which allows one party to reverse a transaction on a losing contract is one that should be rejected.[17] Moreover, any such rule would add costs to a contractual relationship as each party will have to look over its shoulder to prevent the risk of termination and restitution being realised.[18]

In relation to the second feature, Kull defends the traditional rescission requirements which acted as limitations: (1) there must be a repudiation or material breach, and (2) recovery will only be allowed if the parties can give literal restitution. He says that the unjust enrichment rationalisation has meant that, regrettably, the effect of these two important requirements has been forgotten. For example, allowing a more flexible unwinding, where the value instead of the actual thing can be returned, leaves parties very far from the status quo ante.[19] He argues that an unrestricted right to rescission and restitution (ie without the limitations placed by history) would make the life of a contract very burdensome and subject to the opportunistic threat of breach.[20] He says that, actually, the ideal rule to which parties would agree in terms of their remedies for rescission would be that it is available where it is: '(i) likely to offer advantages to the plaintiff that outweigh its cost to the defendant; (ii) likely to be less expensive to administer than enforcement; (iii) unlikely to invite costly strategic behaviour'.[21] He says that the traditional requirements on rescission meet these criteria, and are therefore the most efficient.[22]

These efficiency arguments lead him to reject both features, and are a major reason why he seeks to explain restitutionary remedies for breach as matters of contract law and not unjust enrichment. More recently, Kull's approach to restitution

---

[15] Kull (n 3 above).
[16] *Ibid* 1476.
[17] *Ibid* 1477.
[18] *Ibid* 1477–78.
[19] *Ibid* 1497.
[20] *Ibid* 1501.
[21] *Ibid* 1502.
[22] *Ibid* 1513.

for breach has been indorsed by Gergen.[23] His criticisms of the restitutionary approach, specifically the way losing contract cases are handled, are heavily based on efficiency arguments, as is evident in what he considers to be the goals an ideal solution to a legal problem should pursue. It should 'favour vindicating rights (embodied in the expectation principle) at the least cost (the mitigation principle) and the least fuss (the interest in remedial simplicity)'.[24]

Without necessarily criticising the results they reach, it is possible strongly to doubt the wisdom of pursuing the goal of efficiency in mapping out the law for the purpose of a project like the R3R. There are broadly three methodological reasons for this. The first is the general recognition that the models produced by modern law and economic theorists suffer from methodological indeterminacy because they either produce determinate predictions about the law which are wrong (they fail to explain the law) or they produce indeterminate predictions, because they require information which is not available in the form needed and/or which adjudicators do not have time to consider.[25]

The second reason arises from the evidence that the insights provided by the law and economics literature have largely been ignored by the judiciary and legislators.[26] On this basis, it would appear extremely unwise to shape a part or all of a project such as the R3R, which is aimed at clarifying and aiding the application of the law in courts,[27] by reference to efficiency concerns that have proven to be unpersuasive to the judiciary and unrepresentative of the law.

Thirdly, if efficiency is the goal, then surely the best methodology would be to ensure that the whole restatement or area of law aims towards this goal. Yet this is not the methodology pursued by the R3R or those supporting it. Take the examples of the laws dealing with supervening events, such as frustration or impossibility and general remedies for breach of contract. To meet the goal of efficiency, the law relating to supervening events and remedies for breach of contract would look very different to the way it is presented in the R3R.

---

[23] Gergen (2002) (n 1 above).

[24] *Ibid* 736.

[25] E Posner, 'Economic Analysis of Contract Law After Three Decades: Success or Failure' (2003) 112 *Yale L J* 829, 864–5. See also the responses to Posner's paper: I Ayres, 'Valuing Modern Contract Scholarship' (2003) 112 *Yale LJ* 881 and R Craswell, 'In That Case, What is the Question? Economics and the Demands of Contract Theory' (2003) 112 *Yale LJ* 903. Although they disagree with Posner's conclusion that the scholarship on economic analysis of contract law has been a failure, they do not deny the existence of methodological indeterminacy. For them, the goal of modern economic theory was never to explain the general law of contract (only early theorists like R Posner though this to be the case), but to focus on specific doctrines. As Craswell puts it, most of the modern law and economic scholarship can implicitly be read as saying 'To the extent you care about efficiency as a value, you should pay attention to the following conclusions' (906).

[26] This emerges from all three of the articles above, see, eg Posner (n 25 above) 869–70 and Ayres (n 25 above) 895.

[27] See the charter of the American Law Institute, which publishes the Restatements. It states 'The particular business and objects of the society are educational, and are to promote the clarification and simplification of the law and its better adaptation to social needs, to secure the better administration of justice, and to encourage and carry on scholarly and scientific legal work': taken from charter as published on ALI's website: www.ali.org/index.cfm?fuseaction=about.charter.

While early law and economic analysts viewed laws dealing with supervening events favourably and broadly sought to justify this approach on economic grounds,[28] subsequent work, evidencing a greater commitment to achieving efficiency, has been more critical. The analysis of M White is a very good example.[29] According to her, the most efficient remedial response to breach of contract is one which pays close attention to three different interests:

> (a) giving the promisor an incentive to perform as promised only if doing so increases economic efficiency; (b) giving the promisee an incentive to make reliance expenditures only if they are economically worthwhile given the probability that the contract may not be performed and (c) minimising the costs of risk bearing by both parties to the contract.[30]

In her model, all non-performances (this includes what we would call frustration cases; indeed many of her examples come from these situations) should be treated like a breach, with the non-performing party always liable for damages. How those damages are quantified will depend on factors including:

> the risk preferences of the contracting parties, the degree of control or influence the performing party has on whether or not the event causing non-performance occurs, the relative level of the performing party's fixed versus variable production costs, the proportion of the contract price paid in advance, and whether the event causing non-performance affects a single cost item or is due to generalised inflation.[31]

Two points are striking about her analysis. First, the 'damages remedy' that falls out from this analysis can never be equal to restitution.[32] Secondly, in the non-performance cases she does not think discharge should be allowed because this is not economically efficient.[33] This is because discharge in many instances results in (i) increasing the risk faced by both parties and (ii) incentivising a party not to perform even if it would be economically efficient.[34] Accordingly, the discharge remedy fails to satisfy criterion (a) or (c) above.[35] On her analysis therefore, an economically efficient model of the law dealing with, for example, cases of frustration or impossibility would not allow a restitutionary remedy or the parties to be discharged from their contractual obligations. This is the opposite of the Anglo-American position, which is indorsed in the R3R.[36]

Another example in the context of the law relating to supervening events will confirm the rather selective nature of R3R's methodology. In an earlier article,[37]

---

[28] From A Sykes, 'Impossibility Doctrine in Contract Law' in P Newman (ed), *The New Palgrave Dictionary of Economics and the Law* (London, Palgrave Macmillan, 1998, 2002) 265.

[29] M White, 'Contract Breach and Contract Discharge Due to Impossibility: a Unified Theory' (1988) 17 *J Leg Stud* 353.

[30] *Ibid* 353–4.

[31] *Ibid* 375.

[32] *Ibid* 367–8.

[33] *Ibid* 361.

[34] *Ibid* 362.

[35] *Ibid* 365.

[36] R3R (TD no 3), s 34.

[37] A Kull, 'Mistake, Frustration, and the Windfall Principle of Contract Remedies' (1991) 41 *Hastings LJ* 1.

Kull tries to defend the traditional common law rules on frustration and mistake.[38] He thinks that perhaps the best rule is one which leaves the losses where they lie (what he calls the windfall principle)[39] because in the end this effectively incentivises the parties to allocate the risks themselves.[40] Importantly, he is not in favour of judicial intervention either to realise the efficiency goals set down in the models put forward by law and economists[41] or the award of a monetary remedy such as restitution. For him, the great merit of the windfall principle is that it furthers the primary object[42] of contract law by respecting the parties' autonomy, since it is exclusively a matter for them how they allocate the risks of common mistake or frustration of purpose within their contract. There are a number of points to note about these arguments. First, here we see Kull rejecting efficiency arguments for reasons which could equally apply against their application to the restitution after breach context. Secondly, the rule which furthers the parties' autonomy the most is the one which leaves the losses where they fall, and does not allow a restitutionary remedy. If this is right, then why does the R3R allow a restitutionary remedy in frustration and mistake cases? If the parties' autonomy is being ignored in this context, why can it not be ignored (or is it being paid more attention) in the context of restitution after breach, where Kull (as shown above) argues that the dominant model should be rejected because it provided remedial solutions that the parties would not themselves have chosen?

Sections 37 and 38 are built upon and informed by the standard account of remedies for breach of contract in which the primary award is compensatory damages, calculated on the expectation measure. If efficiency criteria are applied by Kull in his analysis of restitutionary remedies for breach of contract, then they should also be applied to compensatory awards too. However, the problem is that efficient remedies will not comply with some uniform idea of compensation or discrete category of expectation damages.[43] Instead, modern economic theory shows that the most efficient awards are extremely variable and depend on:

> whatever measure of damages would create the best consequences—the best incentives to take precautions against accidents, for example; or the best incentives to gather information before signing a contract; or the best incentive to do any one of a hundred things.[44]

---

[38] Which he treats as addressing the same problem, namely the contractual allocation of risk: *ibid* 2.

[39] *Ibid* 6, 9–12.

[40] *Ibid*, esp 52.

[41] As the inquiry into efficiency depends on many variables, many of which are difficult to determine conclusively, the end result is that it is difficult to predict what a court may decide as an efficient allocation in any one case. And this uncertainty in turn, he argues, actually increases transaction costs either because (a) parties will try and increase certainty by trying to negotiate around the unpredictability of the court's solution or, if they fail to do this, (b) it is likely to encourage litigation (and the associated costs) because the potential for different outcomes generates conflicting expectations: *ibid* 47.

[42] In contrast to the secondary object pursued by law and economists movement in this field which is to lay down 'legal rules that will induce efficient risk spreading by contracting parties': *ibid* 42.

[43] R Craswell, 'Instrumental Theories of Compensation: a Survey' (2003) 40 *San Diego L Rev* 1135, 1179. See more generally on this R Craswell, 'Against Fuller and Perdue' (2000) 67 *U Chi L Rev* 99

[44] Craswell (2003) (n 43 above) 1137.

Consider the following example.[45] John is a manufacturer of a product which posed a 10 per cent risk of defect to its user. The risk has materialised and caused some of his customers, including Simon and Peter, losses of £200. On an economic analysis, if Simon is risk averse, it is efficient to give him a remedy of £200. But what about Peter? It does not necessarily follow that Peter should also get £200. It may be that he is risk preferring, which means that by definition he would rather go without being fully insured against the risk. So it would be more efficient to give him less than £200. Of course, this means that Peter's losses are not fully compensated but 'By definition . . . a risk preferring user will happily accept the chance of greater loss, in order to get the equal chance of greater benefit'.[46] All this is very far from how compensatory remedies for breach of contract work. But it emphasises that such compensatory awards are not efficient, and so further highlights the inconsistency that arises from applying efficiency to one group of remedies which follow breach of contract and not another. This is especially so if, as Kull argues, both sets of remedies fall within the domain of one area of law.

(ii) History

The other area of concern arises from Kull's historical claims,[47] which he uses to justify the change embodied in ss 37 and 38. For Kull, restitution after breach is an amalgam of two neglected contract remedies: quasi contract and rescission. It is in relation to the quasi contract category that he makes his main historical claims, which will be tested here.

According to Kull, the claim in quasi contract for breach (mostly in the form of a quantum meruit) of an express contract was used by nineteenth century judges to enforce promissory liability in a situation of anticipatory repudiation or one calling for reliance damages, both of which could not be accommodated in the straightforward contract scheme at the time.[48] He argues that looked at carefully, these cases were always intended to be contractual and now that the remedial scheme has caught up (because according to him the case of *Hochster v De La Tour* (1853) ('*Hochster*')[49] and Fuller and Purdue's article[50] enabled contract law to deal with, respectively, anticipatory breach and claims for reliance losses), we can drop the quasi contract, specifically unjust enrichment, explanation.[51] He argues that this is the best way to understand *Planche v Colburn* (1831).[52] In 1831, when this case was decided, there was no possible action in contract because anticipatory

---

[45] *Ibid* 1150. The example is adapted from that of Craswell.
[46] *Ibid* 1150.
[47] The most detailed account can be found in Kull (n 3 above). He also discusses it briefly in the introductory notes to R3R (TD no 3), topic 2.
[48] Kull (n 3 above) 1485–6.
[49] 2 El & Bl 678, 118 ER 922.
[50] L Fuller and W Perdue, 'Reliance Interest in Contract Damages' (1936–37) 46 *Yale LJ* 52, cont at 373.
[51] Kull (n 3 above) 1486–7, 1488–90.
[52] (1831) 8 Bing 14, 131 ER 305.

repudiation had not yet been recognised by the law. There are a number of problems with this account. Generally, it is awkward to equate quasi contract with quantum meruit, dealing with restitution after rescission as something separate. Quasi contract was known as the general legal category which covered claims beyond quantum meruit.[53] Furthermore, even if Kull is right, there is a substantial area not covered by his gap-filling thesis. This is because quantum meruit claims did not exclusively deal with anticipatory repudiation or reliance losses.[54]

More fundamentally, Kull's depiction of a conscious preference for a contractual solution rather than a non-contractual one (in the form of an indebitatus, be it a quantum meruit or otherwise), in cases of anticipatory breach or claims for reliance losses, is misconceived. This is because this underplays the general preference for indebitatus claims over contractual claims specifically in the time he is talking about (the eighteenth and early nineteenth centuries). This point is reinforced when we see that, contrary to his assertion, English law had been comfortable with, and had long recognised, the principle that a party could be in breach of their contract before performance was due (anticipatory breach). This doctrine (known as disablement at the time) had a long pedigree and was consistently recognised in the legal literature throughout the eighteenth century,[55] and in case law in the nineteenth century,[56] before *Hochster*. This shows that despite the recognition of anticipatory breach, litigants were expressly choosing an indebitatus claim on its merits rather than as a gap-filler. If this is right, then the question arises as to the attention paid to *Hochster*, and the view that it recognised the right to anticipatory breach, which would provide some support to Kull's thesis. On

---

[53] See the early work of Ames and Keener on this: JB Ames, 'The History of Assumpsit' (1888) 2 *Harv L Rev* 1, 53; WA Keener, *A Treatise on the Law of Quasi-Contracts* (New York, Baker, Voorhis & Co, 1893).

[54] The history of quantum meruit is discussed in Chapter 5, part IV, section B.

[55] G Billinghurst, *Arcana Clericalia: or, the Mysteries of Clerkship Explained; declaring, defining, and illustrating the essential and formal parts of deeds and their nature* (London, R Sare and E Place, 1705) 210; J Lilly, *The Practical Conveyancer: in two parts. Part I, Containing rules and instructions for drawing all sorts of conveyances of estates and interests* (1st edn, London, T Ward and J Hooke, 1719) vol I, 72–3; T Wood, *An Institute of the Laws of England; or, the laws of England in their natural order, according to common use* (3rd edn, London, R Sare, 1724) 230; J Lilly, *The Practical Register: or, a general abridgement of the law, as it is now practised in the several courts of Chancery, King's Bench, Common Pleas and Exchequer* (2nd edn, London, J Walthoe et al, 1735) vol I, 350; G Jacob, *Every Man His own Lawyer; or, a summary of the laws of England in a new and instructive method* (1st edn, London, J Hazard, S Birt and C Corbett, 1736) 57; G Jacob, *The General Laws of Estates; or, freeholders companion: containing the laws, statutes, and customs relating to freehold and other estates* (London, A Ward, 1740) 227; C Viner, *A General Abridgment of Law and Equity, alphabetically digested under proper titles with notes and references to the whole* (Aldershot, C Viner, 1742–57) vol V (1751), 224; and S Kyd, *Comyns' A Digest of the Laws of England* (4th edn, Dublin, Luke White, 1793) vol III, 123–4. The fifth edition published in 1822, by A Hammond, and considered a superior work in this series, follows this account: A Hammond, *Comyns' A Digest of the Law of England* (5th edn, London, J Butterworth et al, 1822) vol III, 127–8. The source of the principle in the literature was Coke's detailed report of *Sir Anthony Main's case* (1596) 5 Rep 20 b, 77 ER 80.

[56] *Bowdell v Parsons* (1808) 10 East 359, 103 ER 811; *Amory v Broderick* (1822) 5 B & Ald 712, 106 ER 1351; *Ford v Tiley* (1827) 6 B & C 325, 327; 108 ER 472; *Short v Stone* (1846) 8 QB 358, 369; 115 ER 911; and *Lovelock v Franklyn* (1846) 8 QB 358, 378; 115 ER 916. Stoljar discusses these cases in S Stoljar, 'Some Problems of Anticipatory Breach' (1973–74) 9 *Melbourne Univ L Rev* 355, 356–7.

closer inspection, we can see that, rather than recognising a new principle, this decision clarified matters.[57]

The problems began with a series of cases which generated the idea that the claimant had to *accept* the defendant's anticipatory breach before the contract could be set aside. It is likely, as Stoljar has argued,[58] that the root of this idea was the solution adopted by the courts to deal with the problem of calculating damages in cases of anticipatory repudiation. If the defendant's breach allowed the claimant to bring an action immediately, then are the damages to be calculated by reference to the market price pertaining at the time of breach or when performance would have been due? The difference in a fluctuating market could be considerable. For example in *Leigh v Paterson* (1818),[59] the defendant agreed to deliver tallow to the claimant buyer in December at a contract price of 65 shillings per cwt, but indicated in October that he would not execute the contract. The reason for this was that the price for tallow was rising: it was 75 shillings in October and 81 shillings in December. The claimant claimed damages based on the December price and the defendant on the October one. The court rightly sided with the claimant buyer, for otherwise the bargain would have been undermined: the innocent claimant would have been deprived of his expected bargain and the defendant seller would have profited from his breach, as he would then be free to take advantage of the higher prices in December. However, the reasoning employed by the court to reach this result was suspect. The court held that even though the defendant refused to deliver the tallow in October, the contract bound both parties until December, which meant that only when the time for performance passed was it truly dissolved and generated a right for the claimant to claim damages. This was because 'The contract being mutually made, could only be dissolved by the consent of both parties; it could not be dissolved by the one without the consent of the other'.[60] As a short term solution, this may have reached the right result but it had the wider problem of binding the innocent party to the contract and his performance obligation despite the clear signal that the defendant would not perform his contractual obligation. Moreover, it potentially contradicted the disablement cases[61], discussed earlier, in which a right to bring an action arose immediately upon D's breach without the need for the claimant's consent.

These two streams of cases came to a head in *Hochster*, where the defendant hired the claimant as a courier to accompany him on a tour in April 1852, to begin service on 1 June 1852. On 11 May 1852, the defendant wrote to the claimant informing him that he had changed his mind and declined his services. The claimant then, between the commencement of the action (22 May 1852) and 1 June, was able to get employment on equally good terms with Lord Ashburton,

---

[57] Although it could still be clearer, according to Treitel: G Treitel, *The Law of Contract* (11th edn, London, Sweet & Maxwell, 2003) 859.

[58] Stoljar (n 56 above) 357–9.

[59] (1818) 8 Taunt 540, 129 ER 493.

[60] *Ibid* 541.

[61] See n 56 above.

but this did not begin until 4 July. The foundation of the claimant's claim was that the defendant's 11 May letter constituted a repudiatory breach. Counsel for the defendant resisted this primarily on the basis that the defendant could not breach the contract before performance was due, unless the claimant had agreed to the repudiation. He relied on the cases that had laid down this idea of consensual repudiation. The claimant relied on the disablement cases to argue that the right arose immediately after the defendant had notified the claimant of his intention not to carry out his obligations when they arose. The court sided with the plaintiff, pointing out that if 'the plaintiff has no remedy for breach of the contract unless he treats the contract as in force, and acts upon it down to 1st June 1852, it follows that, till then, he must enter into no employment which will interfere with his promise'.[62] And this would result in the claimant 'remaining idle and laying out money in preparations which must be useless'.[63] The court expressly rejected the line of reasoning in the cases which treated the breach of the defendant as an offer that would need to be accepted by the claimant before an action could be brought. Rejecting this reasoning did not create problems for calculating damages, as the defendant had sought to argue. The court held that while the right to claim damages arose upon the defendant's repudiation, the assessment would only take into account matters after performance was due.

A number of points can then be made about this case. First, no novel principle on anticipatory repudiation was being laid down here; indeed the court followed the principle laid down by the disablement cases which had a long pedigree. Secondly, in so far as this case is a landmark, its purpose was to rid the law of the reasoning which had developed in some of the cases that sought to argue that a contract could not be set aside until the claimant had consented to the defendant's anticipatory breach.

Finally, two points can be made in relation to the argument that the quantum meruit was filling the gap left by the inability to claim reliance losses in a contractual claim. First, it is extremely difficult, if not impossible, to prove (indeed Kull does not offer any evidence) that there was a conscious idea about such a discrete type of loss at the time, such that the inability to claim such losses would be a source of frustration and the reason to employ the non-contractual quantum meruit claim, as Kull implies. As he points out, the recognition of such a discrete type of damages was hugely influenced by the Fuller and Purdue article in the twentieth century. In any event, it is highly likely, as Fuller and Purdue showed, that restitutionary awards often did capture reliance losses. In so far as this can now be done by the law of contract, it is to be welcomed and a purer definition of restitution as recovering a benefit can then be maintained. Secondly, excising reliance losses from the restitutionary regime still leaves a considerable area in which the law of restitution does not play the role of a gap-filler for the law of contract.

---

[62] *Hochster* (n 49 above) 689.
[63] *Ibid* 690.

(iii) Fit

It is Kull's interpretation of the fundamental primacy of contract over restitution[64] which drives him to say that unjust enrichment is not the cause of action in ss 37 and 38. He argues that a claim in unjust enrichment necessarily disregards the contract and subverts the contractual allocation of risk by allowing a recovery uncapped by the contract price. However, as he admits, his own model is capable of falling foul of these criteria as it allows recovery beyond the contract price under s 38, for example, in cases 'where the terms of the contract do not yield a price for interrupted performance'.[65] In one of the illustrations given of this observation, we see that it allows a party to get more than what he was paid for under the contract, for work that has been completed.[66] The example is where an agent is hired for US$2,000 per month, plus a non-exclusive agency, for the sale of completed units, but after six months the employer cancels the contract. The agent's expected income is hard to calculate but it can be shown that in alternative employment he may have been able to obtain employment in the same time for US$4,000 per month. This is US$2,000 more per month which he would have been paid over the six months, and as expectation is deemed not measurable, he is able to recover as his restitutionary damages, US$12,000.

This example emphasises that under the new model in the R3R, the contractual risk allocation is upset because the agent is getting a higher price for something he has already been paid for under the contract. Here we see a result, then, in which contract price is not a cap for the overall recovery, as Kull desires. And even if this result is defended on the basis that it only arises in exceptional circumstances, the same can be said about the incidence of recovery beyond the contract price in the dominant model of restitution after breach founded on unjust enrichment.

B. Hedley

Across more than two decades, Hedley has been a consistent critic of restitution theorists and their attempts to organise the law formerly known as quasi contract around the principle of unjust enrichment. It is fair to say that his attack has become increasingly sophisticated in the past six years with the publication of a book and an article.[67] In them, he forcefully argues the case that much of the work of unjust enrichment can be done by an expanded notion of the law of contract.[68] The fact that it has not, is down to the very conservative perspective of contract law

---

[64] R3R (TD no 3) introductory note to topic 2, note 2.

[65] R3R (TD no.3), s 38, comment c.

[66] R3R (TD no 3) s 38, illustration 3. It is based on *Brown v St Paul, Minneapolis & Manitoba*, 36 Minn 236, 31 NW 941 (1886).

[67] S Hedley, *Restitution: Its Division and Ordering* (London, Sweet & Maxwell 2001); and Hedley n 4 above).

[68] For what follows see especially his ch 3 on the '"Express Contract" Fallacy' in Hedley (2001) (n 67 above).

taken by restitution theorists, for whom the boundary of contract is defined by the parties' consent.[69] This informs the restitution scholars' approach to explaining their terrain in two ways. First, they reject the implied contract explanation because it seeks to imply consent which does not exist. Using the fiction of consent has historically proven to reach unjust results.[70] Secondly, they are then driven to seek a non- consent (read non-contractual) based explanation of claims for restitutionary awards, which in the main accounts is provided by the unjust enrichment principle.

Hedley argues that all this would perhaps be defensible if contract law was really based on consent, but this was a view that was more accurate in the nineteenth century. The growth of contract law in response to a more sophisticated market economy has meant that any notion of contract law as being founded on consent would be to commit the error of what he calls the 'express contract fallacy'. He describes this fallacy thus: 'the fallacy that contracts are intrinsically the product of the parties' wills, and so are unabridgeably divided from non-contractual liabilities'.[71] He then gives a number of examples which illustrate that the law of contract is often not concerned with reaching results consistent with what the parties may or could have agreed.[72] Examples include cases in which parties find themselves bound to contract when they may not have considered themselves to be, or the rules of damages and termination which do not flow from the parties' agreement.

The foundation of Hedley's argument is that once one recognises the express contract fallacy, it is possible to see that the boundaries of the law of contract are not defined by the parties' consent. This not only breaks down one of the central pillars on which restitution theorists build their unjust enrichment principle, but also enables us to perceive the greater potential of the law of contract to deal with 'misfiring exchanges'. One way it can realise this potential is to deal with cases which restitution theorists try and explain through their unjust enrichment principle. And the way he proposes the law of contract can do this is through reviving the doctrine of implied contract, which he argues could be used to cover four different situations that account for most of the law of restitution:[73] (1) 'almost but not quite contracts' (in this category fall cases where the contract falls foul of certain reasons such as capacity, formality or illegality); (2) 'failure of classification—contracts by other names' (covers claims for overpayment); (3) 'wrongful failure to contract—treat it as contract' (covers cases that are generally described as restitution for wrongs or disgorgement claims); and (4) 'contractual remedies—what results from contract is contractual' (this covers cases of breach, frustration and rescission).

---

[69] For what follows see especially his ch 3 on the '"Express Contract" Fallacy' in Hedley (2001) (n 67 above) 55–6.
[70] See especially Hedley (n 4 above) 436–9.
[71] Hedley (n 67 above) 55.
[72] *Ibid* 56–63.
[73] Hedley (n 4 above) 439.

This doctrine is saved from the traditional criticism of being fictional since that fiction only arises if contract law is about consent, which the express contract fallacy has shown is not the case.

(i) Methodology

By rejecting the model of contract as being based on the parties' consent, the question ultimately arises as to what then is the foundation of the law of contract or, if one is to reject a single theory, as to where the boundary of contract lies in Hedley's eyes. Hedley recognises this problem, but, it is submitted, he provides an unsatisfactory answer:

> It seems hard to lay down any general prescription for what should or should not be treated as contractual. Saying that everything which *can* be treated as contractual *should* be so treated seems foolish as saying that we should never talk of contracts unless we can be sure no fiction will result. The only safe rule seems to be to see what are the consequences of holding that a particular relationship is or is not contractual, and decide in the light of that whether that is a useful approach.[74]

This is a questionable methodology because it is very likely to be a licence for multiple interpretations on the scope of contract law. This can be seen in the rule he puts forward in the extract above as to deciding what is or is not contract: 'The only safe rule seems to be to see what are the consequences of holding that a particular relationship is or is not contractual, and decide in the light of that whether that is a useful approach'. Not only does this still beg the question as to what is contractual, but it also creates the problem as to how one decides whether something is useful or not.[75] Without any guidance, multiple interpretations are highly likely. The ensuing uncertainty at the core of an important area of law makes the application and understanding of that law difficult as well as the models that are built on it, in this case that of implied contract. Moreover, Hedley makes any possible answer difficult to discern with the different ways in which he describes the law of contract: in one account it is the law governing misfiring exchanges[76] and in another he states 'contract law *is* the law of which benefits should be paid for by the recipient (though it is other things as well)'.[77]

If, as he records earlier and the extract above implies, 'it is a matter of taste how far we can go before it can be said that we have left the law of contract entirely

---

[74] Hedley (n 67 above) 78.

[75] If by useful he means taking into account the relational, social and economic context of the parties then he is coming close to the hybrid model of contract law, which is represented most fully in H Collins' work (primarily *Regulating Contracts* (Oxford, OUP, 1999)). But if this is right then Hedley's model cannot escape the criticism faced by Collins' model: J Gava and J Greene, 'Do We Need a Hybrid Law of Contract? Why Hugh Collins is Wrong and Why it Matters?' (2004) 63 *CLJ* 605, see especially 616–20 where the authors show the difficulties judges would face, in terms of their expertise and resources, in trying to apply a hybrid law of contract.

[76] Hedley (n 67 above) 35; this is how, eg Gergen reads him: Gergen (n 1 above) (2005) 235.

[77] Hedley (n 4 above) 439.

behind',[78] why not exercise that taste in favour of the traditional understanding of the law of contract as being about the parties' consent? Taking this position is not undermined by examples of contract law ignoring the parties' consent, or as Hedley would put it, the express contract fallacy, because this does not mean that the *essence* of the law of contract is anything other than consent.[79] Thinking about the law of contract in this way provides a more secure boundary, and reflects more accurately how it is perceived in common law jurisprudence, as reflected in the majority of case law.[80]

(ii) History

There is a sense in which Hedley seeks to derive some credibility from the long-standing use of implied contract as a reason for why it is not a doctrine that should be lightly dismissed.[81] The implication from his argument is that the doctrine of implied contract symbolised the recognition by the lawyers of an earlier generation that the line between 'contract' and 'non-contract' was not so clear-cut. As he puts it, surely the lawyers from the past were not so 'stupid' as to use implied contract in a situation where there was no contract.[82]

However, the problem with Hedley's treatment and assumption is that it overlooks the different ways in which the implied contract doctrine had been used. As the historical discussion in Chapter 1 showed, in the eighteenth century the doctrine was used and understood to refer to a promise that was genuinely fictional.[83] It was firmly understood to cover non-contractual actions. However, the unfortunate label of 'implied contract' began to cause problems in the nineteenth century when the fiction gradually, and unintentionally, became forgotten. This latter usage stood in the way of justice in many cases because it implied consent when it was not relevant.[84]

Overlooking these different ways in which the doctrine was employed and the problems it caused weakens Hedley's argument to revive the doctrine. Indeed, if experience shows that it caused problems when the notion of contract was firmly

---

[78] Hedley (n 67 above) 35.

[79] Gergen (n 1 above) (2005) 239.

[80] It is instructive to note that leading theoretical or philosophical accounts of contract law see the pursuit of a general theory of contract as a virtue, even if not every detail of it can be explained. One of the criteria for a general theory is fit, and on this and a more revealing account on the mechanics of a general theory see the excellent overview provided by SA Smith, *Contract Theory* (Oxford, OUP, 2004) esp ch 2. His own analysis concludes that the promissory theory of contract provides the best explanation of the law of contract. This is because it is able to account for 'enough of the core of contract law' (105). By promissory theory he means something not too dissimilar to the consent-based explanation identified (by Hedley) with nineteenth century contract law and defended here: 'the term promissory properly emphasizes that contracts are regarded in this view not just as intentional acts (i.e., of the "will"), but as the product of acts expressing an intention to undertake an obligation' (56).

[81] Hedley (n 4 above) 435 and Hedley (n 67 above) 202.

[82] Hedley (n 67 above) 202.

[83] In part II, section A and part III, section A.

[84] See Chapter 1, part V, section A(ii).

fixed, what is to say it will not continue to be problematic when the law of contract, under Hedley's vision, is not fixed and its boundaries remain unclear?

(iii) Fit

Although Hedley claims that his implied contract model provides more reasonable results and fits better with the reasoning of the cases and the legal system generally, there are a number of problems of 'fit'.[85] These essentially stem from the insufficient attention paid to the history of the usage of implied contract reasoning and his failure to specify the boundaries of the law of contract, beyond the claim that they should be expanded and not defined by the parties' consent.

(1) By adopting a wider notion of contract, he runs into the problem that it is not only unjust enrichment theorists that accept what he calls an outmoded model of contract but a number of statutory regimes, which are frequently confronted in his 'almost but not quite contract category', as well. To get round this, he has engaged in awkward distinctions, as is illustrated by the following passage:

> So when we consider the rights and obligations arising from an underage supermarket sale, we must start by admitting that this is not 'contract' in the strict sense. Yet the law applicable to the transaction is not entirely 'non-contractual', either.[86]

This is unlikely to be helpful to the legal analysis which would need to be undertaken in court.

(2) A lack of clarity over the definition of contract is compounded by a lack of clarity over the role of restitutionary remedies in his implied contract model. If the restitutionary remedies are now to be considered contractual, as he argues in his final section 'contractual remedies—what results from contract is contractual',[87] are they available in the same way as under the unjust enrichment model? Or, in the context of breach for example, along the lines of the R3R, which seeks to assimilate the restitutionary remedies into the traditional monetary contract remedies such as expectation or reliance damages? No attempt is made to answer these questions, especially in the context of the case involving breach or frustration. Hedley in this context appears comfortable to conclude that these remedies are contractual but are too disparate and variable for any synthesis. In light of this, it is hard to resist agreement with Burrows' observation that:

> it is arguable that some of [Hedley's] work adopts an approach to law that appears to reject, or to downplay, the importance of principles and principled reasoning . . . Coherence in the law is lost if categories and ideas are unprincipled.[88]

(3) Linked to (1) and (2), his approach to cases involving breach, frustration and rescission confirm the difficulties with his model. He describes these cases as a matter of contract, yet also concludes that the decisions 'are so radically

---

[85] See text to n 9 above.
[86] Hedley (n 4 above) 440.
[87] Hedley (n 4 above) 451 *et seq.*
[88] AS Burrows, *The Law of Restitution* (2nd edn, London, Butterworths, 2002) 14.

different, that no very precise theory can be adopted'.[89] If contract law is not 'very precise' (as it must be because it provides the theory for these cases on Hedley's model), and no guidance is given on the boundaries, then what is to say that an orthodox model of contract will not be adopted in disputes? If this is right then, as the historical overview has shown, the implied contract model can be an obstacle to justice by importing in questions of consent that are irrelevant.[90]

C. Jaffey

Jaffey's ambitious book maps out the law of restitution very differently to the orthodox account of the subject.[91] Like Hedley, he rejects the organising concept of unjust enrichment, arguing instead that the law of restitution is made up of distinct types of claims which are related to other established areas of law, without being part of them: (1) restitution for vitiated transfers, which is linked to the law of property; (2) imputed contract, which sees the court imposing an agreement on the parties in certain circumstances; and (3) disgorgement, which seeks to prevent profit-making from the wrongdoer.

The model of the law of restitution as made up of three distinct types of claim is predicated upon taking out of the province of restitution a number of claims arising in the contractual setting.[92] This includes the restitutionary awards, which follow on from a contract that is frustrated or terminated. Jaffey, like Hedley, argues that these types of cases should be dealt with by the law of contract. This, of course, requires some adjustment to the law of contract, which Jaffey outlines in the most radical terms. The starting point is that he adopts the reliance theory of contract in which the parties are responsible for the other's reliance, rather than the traditional model which understands a contract as entailing promises to perform.[93]

Contrary to what one would expect, this does not mean that the expectation measure of damages becomes redundant or only available in exceptional cases, as is the case with reliance damages under the classical model of contract. Instead, Jaffey states that the 'expectation measure is also generally appropriate as a measure of liability under the reliance theory', the main difference being that 'the expectation measure is appropriate as a proxy measure for the true, underlying reliance claim'.[94]

Within Jaffey's model, recovery of money paid or an award representing the value of the work done under a contract now terminated is not explained as a restitutionary remedy responding to unjust enrichment, but one which is compensating a party for its reliance losses under the law of contract.[95]

---

[89] Hedley (n 4 above) 455.
[90] See the discussion on history in section (ii) below.
[91] Jaffey (n 5 above), see ch 1 generally, esp 6–13.
[92] *Ibid* ch 2.
[93] *Ibid* 30.
[94] *Ibid* 37.
[95] *Ibid* 44–7, 56–8.

(i) Methodology

Whereas Hedley does not seek to overturn fully the classical model of contract but expand its reach, Jaffey argues that the classical model should be replaced by a reliance-based model of contract. As was pointed out in the introduction, Jaffey is still seeking to find an explanation for the cases. Certainly, when one looks at the details of his reliance model, one can see that its incorporation of expectation damages and restitutionary remedies enables him to fit the results of the cases in principle, although as will be shown in the section on fit below, it ultimately fails to do this successfully. Nevertheless, taking Jaffey's model on its own merits, it still represents a fundamental change in thinking about contract law: that contract law is about each contracting parties' responsibility for the others reliance interest rather than promises to perform. We are told that the reason for such a shift is that the restitutionary approach to claims following breach of contract (identified in this book as the dominant model) is problematic, partly because it is based on a 'faulty understanding of the law of contract, in the form of what will be referred to as the classical theory'.[96] This is why the switch to the reliance-based model was made.

However, it is not clear why the classical model of contract was misconceived. Where did the faulty understanding arise from? The closest we get to an explanation is the following passage:

> The implication is that, although the courts tend to speak in terms of promising (although contracting parties may not), they have tacitly understood and enforced agreements in terms of assumption of responsibility for reliance, and that this is a source of confusion and contradiction in the law.[97]

This is a very bold claim and one that Jaffey does not support with any authority.

Jaffey is on firmer ground when he argues that his reliance theory should be preferred because it provides a 'more coherent basis for a number of aspects of the law'.[98] This is a claim that the reliance model has distinct advantages over the classical model of contract. But even here, such a claim must be doubted because Jaffey admits that in relation to remedies for breach and frustration it is difficult to tell the two models apart, which is why he concludes 'it is not actually necessary to demonstrate that the reliance theory is superior to the classical theory and should displace it'.[99] In the next sentence he explains that 'at other points in the book it will be seen that only the reliance theory as an alternative to the classical theory will provide an adequate foundation for the law'.[100] Here, he points to disgorgement claims and those arising out of fiduciary duties.

---

[96] *Ibid* 30.
[97] *Ibid* 32.
[98] *Ibid* 32. Here he mentions cases involving economic duress, failure of consideration, quantum meruit, frustration.
[99] *Ibid* 33.
[100] *Ibid* 33.

However, it is submitted that not being able to show the improvement of the reliance model over the established classical model in the core types of claims—breach cases—raises serious questions over the necessity of the rejection of the classical model. This is not just because the switch is not seamless in these core types of cases, as will be shown in section on fit below. Even if there was a seamless transition between the two models, thinking about the law of contract in terms of primarily protecting reliance and not the performance interest represents a fundamental change in our conception of the law of contract. It is a questionable methodology to undergo an upheaval in the jurisprudential foundation of the law of contract on the basis of the gains (in terms of greater coherence) that may be made in the non-core cases, as Jaffey appears to argue.

As Jaffey does not make any historical claims about his model, it is possible to move on to the issue of fit.

(ii) Fit

The difficulties with Jaffey's model stem from the underlying problems of his shift to, and exposition of, the reliance theory of contract.

(1) Central to Jaffey's model is the fact that under his reliance theory of contract, breach is not required as a precondition for a contractual claim (eg damages or some other monetary claim).[101] It is essentially on this basis he argues that his model is able to deal more comfortably (than the classical model) with a number of cases, including those arising out of frustration and the fiduciary context (in both a breach is not necessary in order to bring a claim).[102] While it may be right to relegate the importance of breach in such cases, it leaves the serious problem of explaining the majority of cases where breach and termination are important. Indeed, throughout his discussion of cases of recovery for money paid or quantum meruit, termination for breach is assumed.[103] And here the reliance theory of contract faces a problem, because if it does not generate a duty to perform, 'how can non performance ever constitute "breach"?'.[104] It is not possible to get round this problem without giving primacy to the idea, contrary to Jaffey's objectives, that contracts are about performance.

(2) Trying to relegate the expectation measure of damage to the status of proxy fails to explain the cases adequately. In many of the cases in which the expectation measure is awarded, it is highly likely that it would have been possible to claim just the reliance loss, yet this was not done. If the reliance interest was to be protected directly, then this is the claim that should have been allowed. Yet the fact it was not suggests that it is the expectation measure which is the primary form of redress for breach of contract. The idea that the expectation measure is used to approximate

---

[101] Jaffey (n 5 above), see ch 1 generally, esp 31 n 11 and App 2.
[102] See text around n 100 above.
[103] Jaffey (n 5 above) 39–65. Also see K Barker, 'The Nature and Scope of Restitution ' (2001) 9 *RLR* 232, 234 n 16.
[104] Barker (n 103 above) 234.

to the reliance losses or to protect the reliance interest is simply not reflected in most of the cases.

(3) Linked to (1) above is the inability of the reliance theory to explain the rule that if a claim for reliance losses is used to escape a bad bargain, then it will be capped by the expectation measure: *C&P Haulage v Middleton.*[105] Here again, it seems that the expectation measure is employed not as a proxy but as the primary measure to determine the upper limit of recovery in such cases.

(4) The definition of reliance interest leaves more questions than it answers. If, in the context of a contract terminated for breach, the recovery of money is described as a reliance loss, why is the same return of money described as restitution in his category covering claims arising out of vitiated transfers?[106]

III. Conclusion

The previous chapter included but went beyond the immediate concern of this book, which is on restitution in the contractual context. This chapter has turned to that contractual context and specifically to restitution after breach. The important and influential work of Professor Kull has been particularly focussed on. His attempts, as well as those of Hedley and Jaffey, to reject the dominant model of an innocent party's right to restitution after breach, and to paint that area of the law as being based on contract and not unjust enrichment, have been analysed and found wanting. The historical message of Chapter 1 has been reinforced in this chapter in rejecting the historical and non-historical arguments put forward by these theorists.

It is therefore submitted that, at this point, we have established for the purposes of this book that the independent cause of action of unjust enrichment is a better explanation of restitution in the contractual context than is contract. However, a burning and topical question has so far been left open which it is convenient to address before again focussing specifically on restitution in the contractual context. That question is this: Is the cause of action of unjust enrichment best understood as applying an unjust factors or an absence of basis approach? That is the subject matter of the next chapter.

---

[105] [1983] 1 WLR 1461.
[106] Jaffey (n 5 above) ch 5 generally.

3

What is the Best Organisation for the Law of Unjust Enrichment: Unjust Factors or Absence of Basis?

I. Introduction

BEFORE BIRKS DECIDED to distance himself from it, his early work had done much to establish a framework for unjust enrichment claims in the common law.[1] Broadly, the common law approach requires the claimant to establish, among other elements, an 'unjust factor' (a term Birks coined)[2] in order to found his claim in unjust enrichment.[3] In contrast, the civilian approach to the unjust question asks if there is an absence of basis by inquiring into whether the '[e]nrichments are received with the purpose of discharging an obligation or, if without an obligation, to achieve some other objective as for instance the making of a gift, the satisfaction of a condition, or coming into being of a contract'.[4] The difference between the two approaches can be seen in the analysis of the swaps cases,[5] specifically in answering why the restitutionary claim founded in unjust enrichment was allowed. Those pursuing the common law approach focussed on

[1] As well as his many writings, this is best represented by his book-length treatments of the subject: P Birks, *An Introduction to the Law of Restitution* (Oxford, Clarendon, 1985) (a revised paperback edition was published in 1989) and P Birks and C Mitchell, 'Unjust Enrichment' in P Birks (ed), *English Private Law* (Oxford, OUP, 2000).

[2] The earliest and most detailed articulation came in Birks (1985) (n 1 above) 99–108.

[3] Broadly, the elements that need to be established in order to bring a claim in unjust enrichment are: (1) the defendant must have been enriched; (2) the enrichment must have been at the claimant's expense; and (3) the enrichment must have been *unjust*. This chapter focusses on the unjust question. These elements have been recognised as the foundation of an unjust enrichment claim in numerous dicta, including the House of Lords in *Banque Financiere de la Cite v Parc (Battersea) Ltd* [1999] 1 AC 221, 227 (Lord Steyn) and 234 (Lord Hoffmann).

[4] P Birks, *Unjust Enrichment* (2nd edn, Oxford, OUP, 2005) 102.

[5] These cases typically arose out of contracts between a local authority and a financial institution, usually a bank, in which one party would pay a fixed rate of interest on a notional sum, while the counterparty would pay interest on a floating basis (determined by the market rate). In many instances, the bank would pay money up front in anticipation of its interest liability, which had the effect that the local authority had a lump sum that would increase its liquid assets. These popular form of contracts were held to be ultra vires the local authorities and void by the House of Lords in *Hazell v Hammersmith and Fulham* [1992] 2 AC 1 (HL). There then followed a whole spate of cases in the 1990s in which parties tried to get restitution of the money (or its use value in a claim for interest) paid under the now void swaps contracts.

the unjust factors, such as failure of consideration or mistake of law,[6] as explaining the restitutionary award. German civilian scholars argued that the restitutionary award followed from the invalidity of the contract, as would be the case in civil law, rather than any unjust factor.[7] The inquiry into the intent of the parties, through the unjust factors, was irrelevant to the restitutionary award which followed because of the decision by the court that such contracts were void and their effect should be reversed.

These arguments were part of a wider thesis that the English law of unjust enrichment would do well to adopt the civilian absence of basis approach, seeking inspiration from the German model.[8] Recognising that the swaps cases lent much force to these arguments for the common law to adopt the German model, if it had not already, Krebs in an early work asked whether such a change was possible from within English law.[9] After a detailed overview he answered 'probably not'[10] because, in short, the infrastructure which enabled the German law to operate successfully its general enrichment action does not exist in English law.[11]

It is important to emphasise the implicit assumption in Krebs' conclusion because it provides a useful ground rule. This is that any change must as far as possible fit the cases, so that there is no major structural upheaval. There is a second assumption common to all involved in the debate about the correct approach to the unjust question, and this is that the two approaches are not reconcilable.[12] One cannot mix and match.

It is against this background that one can place Birks' new approach ('the new Birksian approach') in his last work, *Unjust Enrichment*,[13] in which he argued that the common law should adopt the civilian approach to the unjust question. He felt this change was necessitated by the swaps cases and, following the argument of

---

[6] Eg AS Burrows, *The Law of Restitution* (2nd edn, London, Butterworths, 2002) 386–401, esp 397–401.

[7] S Meier, 'Restitution after Executed Void Contracts' in P Birks and F Rose (eds), *Lessons from the Swaps Litigation* (London, Mansfield LLP, 2000) 168, 206–13; S Meier, 'Unjust Factors and Legal Grounds' in D Johnston and R Zimmermann (eds), *Unjustified Enrichment: Key Issues in Comparative Perspective* (Cambridge, CUP, 2002) 37, 67–75; and S Meier and R Zimmermann, 'Judicial Development of the Law, *Error Iuris* and the Law of Unjustified Enrichment' (1999) 115 *LQR* 556, 560–5.

[8] As well as the references in n 7 above, see to this effect R Zimmermann, 'Unjustified Enrichment' (1995) 15 *OJLS* 403, 414–16. A more recent example is JD Plessis, 'Toward a Rational Structure of Liability for Unjustified Enrichment: Thoughts from Two Mixed Jurisdictions' (2005) 122 *South African LJ* 142, 159–72. The early defenders of the unjust factors approach included M Chen-Wishart, 'In Defence of Unjust Factors: a Study of Rescission for Duress, Fraud and Exploitation' in D Johnston and R Zimmermann (eds), *Unjustified Enrichment: Key Issues in Comparative Perspective* (Cambridge, CUP, 2002) 159; and T Krebs, 'In Defence of Unjust Factors' in Johnston and Zimmermann, *ibid* 76

[9] T Krebs, *Restitution at the Crossroads* (London, Cavendish Press, 2000).

[10] *Ibid* 309.

[11] *Ibid* 309.

[12] As well as the works already mentioned see the most recent essays in AS Burrows and A Rodger (eds), *Mapping the Law: Essays in Honour of Peter Birks* (Oxford, OUP, 2006): AS Burrows, 'Absence of Basis: the New Birksian Scheme' (33); S Meier, 'No Basis: a Comparative View' (343); and G Dannemann, 'Absence of Basis: Can English Law Cope?' (363).

[13] Birks (n 4 above), the first edition came out in 2003.

German civilian scholars in particular, by the elegance that could be achieved from following the civilian approach.[14] It is noteworthy that the new framework Birks laid down for the unjust question would not, as far as one can tell at this early stage, cause an upheaval in the law. He has been able to reorient the inquiry into 'unjust' away from unjust factors to the civilian absence of basis approach, relatively smoothly. There are two reasons for this. The first is that Birks did not seek to import into English law any particular civilian model but sought to lay down 'an English version of the civilian sine causa approach'.[15] Secondly, we would do well to note the words of I Englard, whose early comparative study on a number of civilian systems and the common law led him to observe:

> systems may differ in their definition of causes and circumstances constituting failure of a transaction; they may equally differ in the details of restitution. But the basic principle of restitution remains common to all.[16]

As the most sophisticated and worked out argument for change, Birks' recent work will form the departure point for the present discussion on the correct approach to the unjust question. Part II will outline the key features of the new Birksian approach, and the differences between it and the German model it seeks inspiration from. This will set the contours of the ensuing debate by emphasising that it would be dangerous to align the new Birksian approach too closely with the German model. It will also enable us to perceive more clearly the similarities between the new Birksian approach and the unjust factors approach. As will be seen, Birks' new approach accommodates unjust factors in the form of what will be referred to as 'reasons for invalidity' within his pyramid view of unjust enrichment: reasons for invalidity (the base of the pyramid) explain absence of basis (the top layer of the pyramid). To this extent Birks thinks that his new approach can be reconciled with the unjust factors approach. Part III will defend Birks' pyramid on the basis that an ideal system of unjust enrichment will need to incorporate inquiries into reasons for invalidity and the absence of basis. The failure to combine the two has been at the root of some of the problems in the case law, which will be illustrated by examples. Birks' reconciliation means that many of the criticisms that are usually levelled at civilian absence of basis systems are less relevant. But three criticisms survive, namely that the new Birksian approach (1) finds it difficult to explain why a claim for restitution should not be able to capture by-benefits; (2) is a negative formulation, which creates difficulties of categorisation; and (3) would create a major upheaval in the law because it seeks to treat the termination of a contract as having, contrary to settled law, retrospective effect. These three criticisms will be examined in part IV.

---

[14] *Ibid* ch 5 is dedicated to making the case for change.

[15] *Ibid*, Preface, x.

[16] I Englard, 'Restitution of Benefits Conferred Without Obligation' ch 5 in *International Encyclopaedia of Comparative Law*, vol X *Restitution: Unjust Enrichment and Negotiorum Gestio* (Tèubingen/Dordrecht/Lancaster, JCB Mohr/Paul Siebeck/Martinus Nijhoff, 1991) para 5-1.

II. New Birksian Approach

The new Birksian approach organises the law around the principle of absence of basis, which, borrowing older terminology, he likens to a super unjust factor. By this he means: 'A single proposition covers every case: an enrichment at the expense of another is unjust when it is received without explanatory basis'.[17] How one decides whether there is an absence of basis or not depends on the way the enrichment was transferred in the facts at hand. Was the enrichment participatory or non-participatory? Participatory enrichments are sub-divided into 'obligatory' and 'voluntary' enrichments. If the enrichment was obligatory, the basis will fail if there was no obligation. In relation to voluntary enrichments, the basis is determined by the purpose to be achieved, which nearly always will be directed to bringing about a contract, trust or gift (in rare cases there may be another purpose). If this purpose is not achieved then the basis fails. In non-participatory enrichments (such as that created by theft), the assumption is that there is a failure of basis because the enrichment was acquired without the participation of the claimant.

It is an instructive exercise to see the differences between the new Birksian approach and the civilian system which influenced it the most, namely the German law of unjustified enrichment.[18] At a high level of generality there are three significant differences. The new Birksian approach (1) does not exclusively use an objective or subjective test for determining what is a basis; (2) arguably adopts a simpler, less complicated, notion of basis; and (3) is able to present a more unified law of unjust enrichment, without separating out certain fact situations, as is the case in Germany. Each of these will now be addressed in turn.

A. Objective and Subjective Tests of 'Basis'

Germany's general enrichment action is captured in s 812(1)(1) of the German Civil Code (BGB):

> A person who through an act performed by another, or in any other way, acquires something at the expense of that other person without legal ground, is bound to render restitution.[19]

This section is understood to have two limbs: (1) enrichment by transfer (*Leistungkondiktion*), and (2) enrichment in another way. It is the *Leistungkondiktion*

---

[17] Birks (n 4 above) 116.

[18] The primary sources used for the German law are Zimmermann (n 8 above); R Zimmermann and J Du Plessis, 'Basic Features of the German Law of Unjustified Enrichment' (1994) 2 *RLR* 14; Krebs (n 9 above) esp 13–30; and BS Markesinis, W Lorenz and G Dannemann, *The Law of Contracts and Restitution: a Comparative Introduction* (Oxford, Clarendon Press, 1997) vol I, ch 9.

[19] Translated in Zimmermann and Du Plessis (n 18 above) 14. See also Markesinis *et al* (n 18 above) 712.

that best characterises the German approach, which seeks to operate its enrichment law at a high level of generality and abstraction. The reasons for invalidity are not referred to in this section; indeed such matters are generally left to other areas of the law, leaving s 812 to step in once there is an absence of basis (or no legal ground, in German terminology). Despite this commitment to abstraction, it has been shown that reasons for invalidity do break through the surface and continue to be relevant within the enrichment provision.[20]

An important disagreement in German law is whether the legal ground for the purpose of the *Leistungkondiktion* is determined objectively or subjectively. An objective analysis defines the legal ground as a relationship of indebtedness, the purpose of the transaction being a discharge of the indebtedness. The more widely accepted subjective approach looks to the actual intention of the transferor, in order to determine whether the purpose of the performance has failed. Scott,[21] assessing the merits of the civilian (specifically German) approach against the unjust factors approach, illustrates the problem with each of the objective and subjective analyses.

The problem with the objective approach is its assumption that all payments are made to discharge a liability, even though this is not always the case. In recognition of this, those arguing for an objective analysis extend 'legal ground' to cover cases where there is a shared basis on which the enrichment is held, for example a gift or a compromise. But as Scott vividly illustrates, this extended version would still fail to explain the case where two parties are in dispute over money owed, say under a statute, which one of them (A) correctly believes is not due, but pays to the other (B) to end the matter. When it turns out that B's demands were ultra vires, A, in these circumstances, should be precluded from recovering since he knowingly paid to close the matter, accepting the risk he might have been right. Indeed, German law reaches this result through its knowledge defence (that the knowledge of the absence of legal ground bars restitution). But does the objective analysis reach this same result? Scott answers 'no' because the objective analysis cannot provide a basis on which B can keep the enrichment on the basis of a legal ground. It cannot be a compromise or a gift, because neither of these aims were *shared* by *both* parties, since B accepted the enrichment as his entitlement under the statute and not as a gift or compromise. The only way to get round the problem would be a subjective approach: A achieved his intention to close the matter and so there was a legal ground for keeping the enrichment

Scott argues, as part of her wider thesis, that the subjective approach is no more elegant than the unjust factors approach as the civilians claim; this is especially so when the purpose of the transfer is not clearly discernable. She also relies on an example to show where the subjective approach would fail. This is the case where M, a municipality, threatens to cut off L's supply if he does not pay the bill.

---

[20] For an example see Krebs (n 9 above) 155–8, more generally at 237.
[21] H Scott, 'Restitution of Extra-Contractual Transfers: Limits of the Absence of Legal Ground Analysis' [2006] 14 *RLR* 93, 98–103.

L (rightly) thinks the money is not due but pays to avert the harm. German law has a specific exception to allow restitution here (without it, the knowledge defence would prevent restitution, since L paid knowingly). The subjective approach cannot reach this result because ultimately L achieved his purpose (to avert harm).[22] Scott argues that the unjust factors approach would help here because it would focus on the voluntariness of L.

The new Birksian approach appears to sidestep these difficulties by adopting a mixed approach. It is generally objective when it comes to obligatory enrichments and subjective in relation to voluntary enrichments. Just as importantly, he does not discard unjust factors, as the German system seems to, but envisages their use as tools to indicate when a basis can fail. So in the case where L pays under threat from a municipality, an objective analysis would be applied under the new Birksian approach because the enrichment was obligatory (it was paid under a statute) and if the money was not due then the obligation and the basis would fail. But even on the subjective analysis the new Birksian approach would reach that result because it would take account of the impaired intent in deciding whether the basis failed or not. So it would seem the new Birksian approach is generally immune from Scott's criticisms.

B. Notion of Basis

The second significant difference between the German system and the new Birksian approach is the notion of basis. Aiming for a theoretical consistency, German law treats as a basis anything which justifies the retention of the enrichment in law. As well as the usual obligations under which enrichments pass and may be retained, this includes the recognition of unenforceable contracts, gifts, other gratuitous transfers, natural obligations and certain types of void contracts.[23]

A number of these bases need to be explained. In German law, a number of agreements are put on a par with contract, which would fall foul of the doctrine of consideration in English law.[24] Examples include gifts and agreements for gratuitous services. In relation to void contracts, German law uses the term to refer only to those cases in which restitution follows. Outside this category, the invalidity does not result in restitution and so forms a basis for the retention of the enrichment.

As Meier has shown, in English law restitution does not necessarily follow from invalidity.[25] In a number of situations enrichment passed under a void contract is

---

[22] Du Plessis uses a similar example to illustrate how the objective approach would reach the right result here: the involuntariness would result in the rescission of the contract, and so cause the lack of legal ground. J Du Plessis, 'Fraud, Duress and Unjustified Enrichment' in D Johnston and R Zimmermann (eds), *Unjustified Enrichment: Key Issues in Comparative Perspective* (Cambridge, CUP, 2002) 206.

[23] Markesinis *et al* (n 18 above) 726–7.

[24] For an argument that English law would need to consider the recognition of such agreements if it switched to an absence of basis approach, see Dannemann (n 12 above).

[25] Meier (2000) (n 7 above) 206.

not reversed. Unfortunately, English law does not use the term 'void' in a technical sense (in contrast to German law)[26] and indeed does not have a fully worked out strategy for when restitution should or should not follow. Nevertheless, it is highly likely that it is in cases where there is a minor invalidity (of form, say) rather than a major one, that parties should be able to retain the enrichments.[27] The core question, as in Germany, should be whether the invalidity necessitates a restitutionary award.

But how does Birks deal with void contracts under his new approach, as he must? He does not adopt the German approach, which would arguably sit very uncomfortably with English law because it would require the recognition of some void contracts as providing a valid basis. Instead, he uses as his starting point the tendency of English law to treat all void contracts as potentially yielding a restitutionary claim.[28] It is at the defences stage,[29] where the prima facie right to restitution is cut down effectively to those cases where the invalidity did not necessitate a restitutionary claim. For example, in some cases the failure to meet formal requirements renders the contract void. Despite this, a restitutitonary claim will not succeed, leaving one of the parties (or both) to retain the enrichment passed under the contract.[30] The net effect of this is to treat some void contracts as constituting valid bases, and commentators have argued that it may be better for this reason to adopt the more direct, less circuitous, German approach to achieve the same result. Accordingly, they argue that the cutting down should happen at the claim stage.[31] So for them in the informality example above, the retention of the enrichment is a result of the valid basis which survives the invalidity, rather than the defence which denies restitution of the enrichment.

There is some force to this criticism of the new Birksian approach, but it is not hard to see why effectively a technical notion of void contracts was not adopted. As mentioned already, Birks' strategy requires very little upheaval of the common law,[32] and broadly fits the decisions, without hampering the future development of a more sophisticated method to determine whether or not restitution should follow upon the invalidity of a contract. For the same reasons, he does not introduce into his definition of obligatory enrichments, agreements which are not recognised in English law, but which are treated on a par with contract in German law.[33] There is mention of gifts in his scheme, but importantly a gift is not legally treated like a valid obligation such as a contract because it does not come under the category of obligatory enrichments.

---

[26] Meier (n 12 above) 349; Krebs (n 9 above) 247–8

[27] Meier (2000) (n 7 above) 210.

[28] Birks (n 4 above) 113, 131–5.

[29] *Ibid* 240–58.

[30] *Tootal Clothing Ltd v Guinea Properties Ltd* (1991) 64 P & C R 455. The contract in this case fell foul of Law of Property (Miscellaneous Provisions) Act 1989, s 2, which states that unwritten contracts for the sale of land are void. See also D Sheehan, 'Natural Obligations in English Law' [2004] *LMCLQ* 172, 188–90.

[31] Meier (n 12 above) 349–51; and Dannemann (n 12 above) 368–9.

[32] See text to nn 14, 15 above.

[33] See text to n 24 above.

Ultimately there is nothing novel about the way the new Birksian approach comprehends the basis of an enrichment. Broadly, it will either be a valid obligation or a purpose which seeks to bring about a contract, trust or gift. At the outer edges are unenforceable contracts, but these tend to be recognised in English law as valid agreements, closer to enforceable contracts than not.

C. Greater Unity

A third major difference is the greater unity presented in the new Birksian approach, as compared with its German counterpart. The German law of unjust enrichment works most elegantly with the cases which come under the *Leistungkondiktion*.[34] Outside these transfer cases, German law finds it difficult to apply a straightforward absence of basis approach, which in turn has meant that a number of non-transfer cases are treated as discrete areas of unjust enrichment law. The fact situations which fall within this 'other' category include cases of the mistaken improver and claims arising out of the payment of another's debt.

Although the mistaken improver is not dealt with by Birks expressly, there is nothing to suggest that either this or the payment of another's debt cannot be dealt with under his absence of basis approach. Indeed, he is able to achieve this perhaps because (a) his system is not overly committed to defining basis by reference to transfer/performance,[35] and (b) unjust factors continue to play a role within his new approach. All this is not to deny the likelihood that specific principles would need to be developed for cases such as those involving a mistaken improver or the payment of another's debt (what are sometimes classified as indirect or non-participatory enrichment cases).[36] And the new Birksian approach could accommodate such a tailored approach to these cases, without sacrificing its unity.[37] Indeed, Smith has recently shown how a unified system of unjust enrichment, committed to the absence of basis approach, may tackle the particular problem posed by the indirect/non-participatory enrichment cases.[38]

These three significant differences outlined above go a long way to showing how the new Birksian approach has been able to adopt a civilian model for the common law without a major upheaval. This is partly because unjust factors continue to

---

[34] Meier (n 12 above) 354.

[35] MJ Schermaier, '"Performance-Based" and "Non Performance Based" Enrichment Claims: the German Pattern' [2006] *European Rev Private Law* 363 argues that the focus of German law on the idea of performance distorts the unity of enrichment law.

[36] The move to do this had already begun from within the unjust factors approach: P Birks, 'At the Expense of the Claimant: Direct and Indirect Enrichment in English Law' (2000) *Oxford U Comparative L Forum* 1, available at www.ouclf.iuscomp.org. Also see the detailed study by D Visser, 'Searches for Silver Bullets: Enrichment in Three-Party Situations' in D Johnston and R Zimmermann (eds), *Unjustified Enrichment: Key Issues in Comparative Perspective* (Cambridge, CUP, 2002).

[37] Although Sheehan is sceptical: D Sheehan, 'Unjust Factors or Restitution of Transfers *Sine Causa*' (2008) *Oxford U Comparative L Forum* 1, available at www.ouclf.iuscomp.org.

[38] L Smith, 'Demystifying Juristic Reasons' (2007) 45 *Canadian Business LJ* 281, 289–90, and more generally 294–9. Although he focusses on Canada, the suggestions are relevant to the English jurisdiction too.

play a role. The exact role they play will be investigated in the next section, which is devoted to defending the new Birksian approach.

III. The Pyramid

The new Birksian approach sees absence of basis sitting at the top of a pyramid at the bottom of which are reasons for invalidity (such as the unjust factors) reflecting the fact that:

> it will be true of every case in which an enrichment is received without any explanatory basis that its claimant will not have intended it to accrue to the defendant for in every case it will either have accrued absolutely without his consent, or, if with his consent, on a particular basis which has failed.[39]

The pyramid speaks of the law of unjust enrichment in which a restitution remedy is awarded when there exists a reason (the bottom layer) why the basis of the transfer fails (the top layer). For Birks, the pyramid represents a limited reconciliation between the unjust factors approach and his new approach. The main difference between the two approaches is the top layer of the pyramid, which raises the following question: Should we adjust our analysis to the unjust question so that it does not just look at reasons for invalidity (the bottom layer, and broadly the unjust factors approach) but also whether there has been an absence of basis (the top layer)? In other words is the pyramid a desirable model to adopt for our law of unjust enrichment? The short answer is that both layers of the pyramid—reasons and absence of basis—are essential to an ideal system of unjust enrichment.

The defence of the pyramid view of unjust enrichment will be undertaken through four case studies which will illustrate the following points:

(1) Relying primarily on reasons for invalidity (as the unjust factors approach does) generates a tendency to be claimant-focussed and often can result in:

    (a) the adoption of incorrect reasons to explain why restitution was awarded in a particular case;

    (b) insufficient attention being paid to existing obligations which unjust enrichment may clash with;

    (c) insufficient attention being paid to the basis of the enrichment, resulting in the risk of the assumption that a basis exists which in fact does not.

(2) Conversely, a primary focus on the absence of basis, especially one that suppresses reasons (as the German system does to a great extent), prevents a party from realising the freedom it has to choose when its obligation arises.

---

[39] Birks (n 4 above) 116.

A. Wrong Reasons: the Swaps Cases

The benefit and strength of the pyramid view is that it provides a focus and coherence to the various reasons for invalidity in the law. The top layer (absence of basis) guides and informs the role of reasons for invalidity: the reasons explain why there is an absence of basis. In this way, the top layer acts as an external controlling principle.

In contrast, the unjust factors approach without the top layer is not able to provide an external principle to guide its recognised reasons for invalidity (the unjust factors). The main negative effect of this lack of external principle is that the unjust factors approach has tended to seek some kind of coherence from within the unjust factors. And this, it is submitted, has resulted in a tendency for explaining most restitutionary awards through the intent-based family of unjust factors, which all speak of the non-voluntariness of the transfer.[40]

The problem with this tendency is that it results in the adoption of an analysis of a case in terms of the intent-based unjust factors even though the reason for invalidity is nothing to do with the non-voluntariness of the transfer. A clear example of this is the preference of those pursuing the unjust factors approach to explain the results in the swaps cases through the intent-based unjust factors.[41] As was hinted in the courts' language in some of the swaps cases (speaking of 'absence of consideration'), the reasons for invalidity in these cases had nothing to do with the non-voluntariness of the transfer. Instead, the reason for invalidity was the same reason that the contracts were declared void, namely that the contracts were concluded ultra vires the public authorities. Analysing the swaps cases in this way fits with English law's general approach to claims for restitution arising out of void contracts: the right to recover 'depend[s] on the reasons why the contract is defective'.[42] Moreover, if, as discussed earlier,[43] English law develops a more sophisticated approach to void contract cases by inquiring into whether the invalidity justifies a restitutionary award, it is possible that in some cases the claim for restitution will fail. This reinforces the point that the reasons for invalidity would be imposed (the court's decision of what the policy requires in the particular circumstances) rather than based on what the parties thought in transferring the enrichment.

It is also worth noting that it is less likely that a more sophisticated approach to restitutionary claims in the void contract context will develop from within the

---

[40] Eg mistake, duress and failure of consideration.

[41] P Birks, 'No Consideration: Restitution after Void Contracts' (1993) 23 *Univ Western Aus LR* 195, 206–8; Burrows (n 6 above) 386–401; Burrows (n 12 above) 38–9; AS Burrows, 'Swaps and the Friction Between Common Law and Equity' [1995] *RLR* 15, 16–17; and G Virgo, *The Principles of the Law of Restitution* (2nd edn, Oxford, OUP, 2006) 371, 386; although Virgo also recognises an alternative ground of restitution which he cites as being particularly useful in cases of fully executed swaps. Under this alternative ground, the award of restitution is founded on 'the reasons why the contract was void in the first place' (384).

[42] Meier (2000) (n 7 above) 206.

[43] See text to nn 25–37 above.

current system of unjust enrichment based on unjust factors. This is because the heart of the issue—does the invalidity of the contract in a particular case justify a restitutionary award—is predicated upon the acknowledgment that the justification, and therefore controlling factor, for the restitutionary award in the case of void contracts, is the particular invalidity involved (as the new Birksian approach would assume) rather than the deficiency of the parties' intent (as the unjust factors approach tends to assume). And the new Birksian approach, with its pyramid view of unjust enrichment, is able to assume this because the external principle of absence of basis guides it to the invalidity as the key feature in the void contract cases.

B. Wrong Basis: *CTN Cash and Carry v Gallaher*[44]

Focussing primarily on reasons can also result in insufficient attention being paid to the basis of the enrichment that was the subject of the restitutionary claim. In many cases this may not matter, but in some it may result in the adoption of the wrong basis. *CTN Cash and Carry v Gallaher* ('*CTN*') is a very good example. In this case, the claimant had ordered £17,000 worth of cigarettes from the defendants, who mistakenly made the delivery to the wrong warehouse. Unfortunately, before the defendant could redeliver the cigarettes, they were stolen. Subsequently, the defendant made a fresh delivery of cigarettes to the correct warehouse. However, the claimant was billed not just for the cigarettes which had been received but also those that were stolen, the defendant believing that the risk of loss under the sale contract was borne by the claimant. Despite their objections, the claimant paid for the stolen cigarettes because the defendant threatened to withdraw credit facilities it had provided to the claimant. It should be noted that there was nothing in the facts, as reported, to suggest that the payment was made as a kind of compromise.[45] The present action concerned the claim for restitution of the money the claimant had paid for the stolen cigarettes. The claimant argued that this payment had been vitiated by duress. Although the Court of Appeal recognised that there was no obligation under the contract to pay for the stolen cigarettes (the defendant had wrongly assumed this to be the case), the claim was dismissed.

At the heart of the problem in *CTN* was the Court of Appeal's failure to attach any significance to the fact that the payment was made under a non-existent obligation. Indeed, they assumed that it did not matter for the purposes of a duress claim whether the payment in question was made under a non-existent obligation or a valid obligation such as a contract.[46] Grouping the two together in this way created the risk that the standard of duress applied in the case would have the effect that the payment was treated as if it was made under a valid obligation rather than

---

[44] [1994] 4 All ER 714.
[45] Which distinguishes this case from the fact situation discussed earlier in the text following n 21.
[46] *CTN* (n 44 above) 717.

a non-existent one. It is hard to resist the impression that this is exactly what happened in the case. This is because one of the major reasons given for rejecting the duress claim in *CTN* only really makes sense if the payment was treated as if it was made under a valid obligation. Steyn LJ, who gave the leading judgment, argued that allowing a duress claim in the present case of commercial arms' length dealing, when the alleged threat came from someone who genuinely believed they were entitled to the sum, would 'introduce a substantial and undesirable element of uncertainty in the commercial bargaining process. Moreover, it will often enable bona fide settled accounts to be reopened when the parties to commercial dealings fall out'.[47] This mention of effecting 'bargains' or reopening 'settled accounts' is better suited to cases where the basis of the payment is a valid obligation.

The Court of Appeal's adoption of the wrong basis in this case is likely to have resulted in the wrong decision. This is because, contrary to the assumption made by the court, it should matter for the purpose of the duress claim whether the payment was made under an obligation or not. Although there are not many cases involving lawful act duress in the context of a non-existent obligation,[48] an instructive analogy may be made with the law of mistake where a higher level of mistake is required to reverse a transfer made pursuant to a valid obligation (fundamental) than one under a non-existent obligation (causative).[49] If such a variable approach is taken, then it is sensible to say that the law, as in cases of mistake, will take a more restrictive approach to setting aside for duress a transfer made pursuant to a valid obligation than one under a non-existent obligation. As we saw above, the court in *CTN* applied the standard of duress suitable to set aside a valid obligation. The evidence in the case was deemed not to satisfy this standard. However, as Dannemann has suggested, the evidence is likely to have satisfied a standard that would have been appropriate to the case in which the basis of the payment was not a valid obligation.[50] Indeed, the level of pressure and threat involved in the case was sufficient to make the court uncomfortable in the result it reached.[51] If this is right then the claim in *CTN* should have been successful.

As the analysis above illustrates, at the heart of the problem in *CTN* was the Court of Appeal's failure to incorporate into its analysis the fact that the payment

---

[47] *CTN* (n 44 above) 719.

[48] *Somes v British Empire Shipping Co* (1860) 8 HL Cas 338 may be an example.

[49] It could be argued that the better analogy would be with misrepresentation (which is after all an *induced* mistake) since duress involves an *induced* violation of consent. And if this is right then it would not be correct to suggest that, like the law of mistake, a stronger reason is needed to set aside an obligation, because in the law of misrepresentation there is no such idea of 'fundamental' or 'causative' misrepresentation. However, the reason why an analogy cannot be made with misrepresentation is that the approach of the courts to misrepresentation is more generous than mistake and duress: J Cartwright, *Misrepresentation, Mistake and Non-Disclosure* (London, Sweet & Maxwell, London) para 1-03. Crudely, it amounts to this: whereas the law does not tolerate any misrepresentations, it does tolerate certain levels of threats/pressure (lawful act, of course) and mistakes.

[50] G Dannemann, 'Unjust Enrichment by Transfer: Some Comparative Remarks' (2001) 79 *Tex L Rev* 1837, 1858–9; and *id* (n 12) 373–6.

[51] *CTN* (n 44 above) 719 (Steyn LJ) and 719–20 (Nicholls V-C).

was made under a non-existent obligation. Greater attention to this issue would have prevented the treatment of the payment as if it was made under a valid obligation. The new Birksian approach would have avoided this problem. This is because under this approach, the court would have at once paid more attention to the basis of the obligation.

The more controversial question is the reason that would be given for the absence of basis. So far it has been assumed that in a case like *CTN* the reason is duress. According to the new Birksian approach, where the party makes a transfer thinking there is an obligation when in fact there is none, the reason for invalidity is the proof that no such obligation existed. One need not go on and ask whether the transfer was non-voluntary (eg mistake or duress). So for Birks, the famous case of *Kelly v Solari*[52] need not be explained on the basis of mistake but simply by looking at the extent of the obligation.[53] The counter-argument to this is that mistake (a) figured in the court's reasoning in *Kelly v Solari*,[54] and (b) the mistake is relevant to the extent it shows that the transfer was not a gift, something which even the civilian approach must test for (indeed, this is why the condictio indebiti, on which the civilian approach is partially based, required that as well as showing that the money was not due, it also had to be shown that the claimant's transfer was mistaken).[55] All this is not to say that the reason identified by the new Birksian approach for the absence of basis in the *Kelly v Solari* type of case (which falls into the category of overperformance cases,[56] which all share the quality that the claimant is trying to claim back a performance he was not obliged to transfer) is far removed from the family of reasons to which mistake belongs (the intent-based unjust factors). One could argue that in the overperformance cases, there is an absence of intent to transfer because the extent of the claimant's intention is set by the obligation, and anything beyond (overperformance) is not due, and therefore is prima facie returnable. If this is right then the reason for invalidity in these cases falls into the conventional intent-based family of reasons.

It is important to note that the resolution of the question as to what is the reason for the absence of basis in these overperformance cases does not undermine the logic of the pyramid and the reality that in *CTN* the court's failure to pay any attention to the non-existent obligation led it unfairly to deny restitution.

---

[52] (1841) 9 M & W 54, 152 ER 24.

[53] Birks (n 4 above) 132.

[54] *Kelly v Solari* (n 52) 59.

[55] R Zimmermann, *The Law of Obligations: Roman Foundations of the Civilian Tradition* (paperback edn, Oxford, Clarendon Press, 1990) 848–51; Dannemann (n 50 above) 1848–9; and Meier and Zimmermann (n 7 above) 561.

[56] *Townsend v Crowdy* (1860) 8 CB (ns) 477, 141 ER 1251; and *Newall v Tomlinson* (1871) L R 6 C P 405. A number of the English and US cases are collected by Woodward in ch 11, 'Misreliance on a Supposed Requirement of a Valid Contract': FC Woodward, *The Law of Quasi Contracts* (Boston, Little, Brown, & Co, 1913).

C. Clashing Obligations: *Roxborough v Rothmans of Pall Mall Australia Ltd*[57]

Roxborough v Rothmans ('*Roxborough*') is discussed in greater detail in Chapter 6. For present purposes we need only note that the claim in this case was for the restitution of the tax element paid by Roxborough to Rothmans as part of the purchase price for tobacco products under the contract. The state-imposed tax was chargeable on the purchase of tobacco products. However, the High Court of Australia in another case held that states had no jurisdiction to charge such a tobacco tax, and this was the reason why Roxborough now sought to recover the part of the purchase price represented by the tax. By a majority the claim was allowed, broadly based on an expanded notion of failure of consideration: the tax element was paid to Rothmans who were then supposed to pay this over to the state, but as the tax was invalid, the purpose failed.

The noteworthy point for the present discussion is that the majority decision failed to explain how restitution could be allowed despite the presence of a valid contractual obligation calling for the payment of the tax. This is the reason why a number of authors have criticised the decision, and its result.[58] Another potential response has been to argue that this is one example of a case 'where restitution has been allowed despite the fact that the claimant's payment was made pursuant to a valid obligation'.[59]

As will be shown in Chapter 6, both responses go too far: the first response because it is committed to the termination precondition, which is not always necessary; and the second response, because it dangerously expands the scope of unjust enrichment, without any clear limitations. In this section, the point that needs to be emphasised is that the second response and the majority's decision illustrate an approach that focuses only on reasons for invalidity (in this case the presence of a qualified intent through the failure of basis unjust factor), without paying sufficient attention, if at all, to the absence of basis (in this case the contract obligation). The point is not academic in relation to a case such as *Roxborough* because by bringing into play absence of basis, as the pyramid would dictate, the burden of risks which may have been assumed under the contract are brought firmly into focus. As one commentator has observed, the court in *Roxborough* should have addressed, but did not, the important question whether 'the risk of constitutional invalidation of the Business Franchise Licenses (Tobacco) Act (NSW) was carried by the wholesaler or by the retailer'.[60]

---

[57] [2001] HCA 68; (2002) 76 AJLR 203 (HCA).

[58] J Beatson and G Virgo, 'Contract, Unjust Enrichment and Unconscionability' (2002) 118 *LQR* 352, 356. Burrows (n 6 above) 323 n 1.

[59] C Mitchell and J Edelman, 'Restitution' (2006) *All ER Rev* 337, 343.

[60] M Bryan, 'Unjust Enrichment and Unconcsionability in Australia ' in JW Neyers, M McInnes and SGA Pitel (eds), *Understanding Unjust Enrichment* (Oxford/Portland, Hart, 2004) 47, 64 n 82.

D. Enhancing Choice: *Deutsche Morgan Grenfell v Inland Revenue Commissioners*

The first three case studies above were designed to illustrate the problems caused by focussing primarily on reasons for invalidity without any attention to absence of basis. However, it is important to resist the temptation of primarily focussing on absence of basis, because reasons for invalidity continue to play a part. This last point will be reinforced in the present section by illustrating through *Deutsche Morgan Grenfell v Inland Revenue Commissioners* ('*DMG*') how a primary focus on absence of basis can prevent a party from realising the freedom it may have to choose when its obligation to pay, for example, arises. Failure to see this can result in the wrong result being reached.

The issue in *DMG* arose out of payments of advanced corporation tax (ACT) by the claimant (Deutsche) to the defendant (IRC). The UK tax regime allowed companies to defer their ACT liability, through a group election, to a later date, when they were due to pay their mainstream corporation tax (MCT). Crucially, this option to defer was not made available to companies in the position of Deutsche, whose parent company was based outside the United Kingdom. This discrimination was challenged successfully in the European Court of Justice and formed the background to *DMG*: Deutsche argued that had it been allowed the choice, it would have elected to defer its ACT liability to the later date. That it could not do this meant it lost out on the use of the money (quantified in terms of lost interest) between the time it actually paid and the time it could have paid had it been given the option to defer. Deutsche founded its interest claim in unjust enrichment, which succeeded at first instance in front of Park J[61] but was rejected in the Court of Appeal.[62] The subsequent appeal to the House of Lords succeeded,[63] and Park J's order was restored. The analysis which follows will focus on the first instance decision of Park J, as it best illustrates the point in this section.

On the assumption that a claim for interest can be founded in unjust enrichment,[64] the net effect of Park J's reasoning at first instance was that the claimant was entitled to restitution because it had mistaken its ability to make an election, which it would have done and paid tax at a later date. So he did not think the tax was not due or that the obligation ultimately to pay that tax had been set aside, simply that the claimant mistakenly paid earlier. Birks felt this decision was wrong, because it allowed recovery of money which was due.[65] This resembles the objective German approach, discussed and criticised earlier,[66] one which focusses on whether the money was *ultimately* owed, without any attention being paid to the

---

[61] [2003] EWHC 1779, [2003] 4 All ER 645 (Ch).

[62] [2005] EWCA Civ 78; [2006] 2 WLR 103.

[63] [2007] 1 AC 558.

[64] For the argument that the parties were wrong to assume this, see TA Baloch, 'Disguised and Outlawed Interest Claims in Unjust Enrichment' [2006] *RLR* 115.

[65] Birks (n 4 above) 138–9, describing the first instance decision as reaching 'an indefensible result'.

[66] See part II, section A.

non-voluntariness of the transfer.[67] However, this approach proves to be too simplistic and reaches the wrong result in *DMG* as analysed by Park J because it ignores consideration of the way in which Deutsche would have exercised its choice voluntarily. This would have shown that Deutsche would have elected to defer its ACT liability to the later date. Importantly, this deferral would mean there was then no basis for the ACT payment at the time it was made and accordingly, as Park J held, it would be recoverable;[68] or in reality, since it would have to be paid at the later date, it was the use value which Deutsche lost by being denied its choice to defer. Unless we say that recovering the use value is not important (something which would be difficult to justify in a commercial market), then the above analysis of *DMG* provides a good lesson of the dangers of pursuing an approach which looks to ultimate liability, because its effect is to prevent a party from taking advantage of the freedom it had to choose the time at which its obligation (= basis) to pay arose.

Birks' disagreement with Park J does not, I suggest, undermine the argument made here, that Birks' new approach is preferable. With respect, he failed to apply his analysis in the way required by the pyramid: more attention was paid to the basis of the transfer than the reasons for invalidity, which in this case would have led to greater consideration of the non-voluntariness involved and its impact on the obligation to pay.[69] This point can be reinforced by testing the result reached by the unjust factors approach. Under this approach, the focus on reasons for invalidity (mistake) would certainly mean that more attention would be paid to the non-voluntariness involved and its impact on the obligation to pay. However, the problem arises because the inquiry into absence of basis is not part of the unjust enrichment claim under the unjust factors approach. This is the reason why an unfortunate feature of the *DMG* litigation is that the question as to the basis of the payment was inadequately investigated.[70]

---

[67] Under this approach, as long as a legal ground is ultimately found for a payment then there is legal ground to retain it even though the 'transferor's purpose may not have been achieved': Du Plessis (n 8 above) 173.

[68] This is one of the ways Edelman presents Park J's reasoning: J Edelman, 'Limitation Periods and the Theory of Unjust Enrichment' (2005) 68 *MLR* 848, 856; and J Edelman, 'The Meaning of "Unjust" in the English Law of Unjust Enrichment' (2006) *European Rev Private Law* 309, 325.

[69] This perhaps underlines that one needs to be careful in applying the new Birksian approach because it does not commit to one uniform definition of basis as being either subjectively or objectively determined. As was discussed earlier (see part II, section A), this is the strength of Birks' new approach, but it can also be its weakness if care is not taken in determining the right basis, and eg determining the basis objectively when it is the subjective perspective which is relevant. This is what is likely to have happened in *DMG*.

[70] One example of this is the debate over whether the effect of the ECJ decision was that the tax was not due at the time it was paid. Burrows thinks that the Court of Appeal in *DMG* were right to treat the tax as not being due: AS Burrows, 'Restitution in respect of Mistakenly Paid Tax' (2005) 121 *LQR* 540, 545. Stevens disagrees with the Court of Appeal's conclusion on this, his points emphasising the kind of factors that the Court of Appeal should have considered to strengthen their argument: R Stevens, 'Justified Enrichment' (2005) 5 *OUCLJ* 141, 143. This is beside the argument indorsed here that without even considering the ECJ decision, Deutsche's 'valid obligation to pay coupled with its power to elect not to pay meant that there was no binding obligation at the time of payment': Edelman (2005) (n 68 above) 856.

IV. Three Criticisms of The New Birksian Approach

The reconciliation between the absence of basis approach and the unjust factors approach achieved by Birks takes care of some of the criticisms aimed at attempts to reorient English law to the absence of basis approach.[71] However, three criticisms still survive. These are that the new Birksian approach (1) fails to deal adequately with by-benefits;[72] (2) is a negative formulation, which creates difficulty of categorisation;[73] and (3) would cause a major upheaval in the law because it effectively treats the termination of a contract as having, contrary to settled law, retrospective effect.[74]

A. By-Benefits

The issue here can be illustrated through examples. Consider the case where Tom improves his land which results in increasing the value of his neighbour, John's, property; or if Tom's heating system benefits John because he lives above Tom and heat rises. Both the absence of basis and unjust factors approach agree that Tom should not in either example be able to recover the benefit which John enjoys. However, it is argued that the unjust factors approach reaches this result neatly because quite simply there is no unjust factor involved. The civilian absence of basis approach cannot reach this result because prima facie, it can be said that John's enrichment is without basis and therefore recoverable. For that reason, exceptions need to be added to prevent restitution.[75] For example, in the new Birksian approach by-benefits are not recoverable because they are treated like gifts.[76]

---

[71] Eg the argument in defence of the common law approach that unjust factors continue to matter because their identity influences details of the restitutionary response: Chen-Wishart (n 8 above); and R Stevens, 'The New Birksian Approach to Unjust Enrichment' [2004] *RLR* 270, 271. This argument is predicated on a vision of an absence of basis approach which does not investigate unjust factors. However, as has been shown, the new Birksian approach, with its pyramid view of unjust enrichment, keeps such matters firmly within its analysis through its consideration of the reasons for restitution. Another criticism of the absence of basis approach has been that it would reverse the burden of proof because the burden of proving the necessary element of the claim (that the enrichment had a basis) would end up being on the defendant rather than the claimant, who brings the action. However, this view was never correct from the perspective of the pure absence of basis approach because it is the claimant who continues to have the burden to prove his claim: Meier (n 12 above) 350–1. Even if it were true, there is nothing to prevent the new Birksian approach from placing the burden of proving the absence of basis on the claimant: Burrows (n 12 above) 45.

[72] Burrows (n 12 above) 44 and 46; and Edelman (2006) (n 68 above) 319–21; and Sheehan (n 37 above) pt 3(A)(i).

[73] L Smith, 'Unjust Enrichment: Big or Small' in S Degeling and J Edelman (eds), *Unjust Enrichment in Commercial Law* (Sydney, Thomson LLP, 2008) 49.

[74] Sheehan (n 37 above) pt 3(C).

[75] Meier (n 12 above) 355–66.

[76] Birks (n 4 above) 158.

It is submitted that it is not so clear that there is no unjust factor that could be employed in the by-benefits case: why not ignorance or mistake? But even if it is right that the unjust factors approach is better at dealing with by-benefits, it is still worth sacrificing the greater elegance achieved in such cases for the more coherent picture which the absence of basis approach outlined here is able to achieve in the cases discussed above.

B. Negative Formulation

In a series of characteristically lucid papers, Lionel Smith has examined the challenges thrown up by the absence of basis model.[77] It is important to be clear that he has not expressly defended the unjust factors approach as being better necessarily. His main message is that there is very little between them.[78] However, in one respect his observations can be seen as a criticism which may persuade some not to accept the new Birksian approach defended here. In his most recent paper he argues that the absence of basis idea 'is an entirely negative formulation', and 'it is hard to define a category of analysis by saying what it does not have'. He argues that 'it does not tell you why the defendant is liable'.[79]

It is not clear why this observation is necessarily true, or whether it is even a fatal objection, especially in light of what Smith goes onto say. If we start by understanding that having a negative definition creates difficulties because no guidance is given on the boundaries or the content of a category of law, then the same can be said about the final formulation Smith gives for what he considers to be the principle underlying the law of unjust enrichment, namely that it is about defective transfers. And transfers are defective because of some involuntariness or 'other reasons'.[80] Both of these reasons provide the normative foundation for the law of unjust enrichment. But how is the 'other' category any easier to define for the purposes of analysis? The truth is that there is no perfect definition, but the commonality[81] of absence of basis across the board at least enables us to ask the right question. Moreover, with reasons for invalidity at the bottom of the pyramid, we are also taking advantage of the positives from the unjust factors approach. In short, it seems that the best way to realise Smith's analysis is the pyramid of Birks: absence of basis (defective transfer) = defect of consent (unjust factors) or other reasons such as ultra vires (other normative reasons which explain why the transfer is defective).

---

[77] L Smith, 'The Mystery of "Juristic Reason"' (2000) 12 *Supreme Court L Rev* (2d) 211; *id* (n 38) and *id* (n 73).

[78] Note his opening points relevant to the merits of each system: in the end 'the two approaches are not that different after all . . . the underlying principles that make enrichment just or unjust do not change': Smith (n 38) 284. He says that when he looked at question in 2000 he 'did not think either approach was better or worse as a matter of abstract justice' (283).

[79] Smith (n 73 above) 49.

[80] *Ibid* 52.

[81] This is the theme of Stevens' recent paper: R Stevens, 'Is There a Law of Unjust Enrichment' in S Degeling and J Edelman (eds), *Unjust Enrichment in Commercial Law* (Sydney, Thomson, 2008).

C. Retrospectivity of Termination

The objection here is that Birks' explanation of how his model operated in the context of a restitutionary claim following a contract terminated for breach, effectively treated termination as having retrospective effect. It is certainly true that Birks aligns terminated contracts with contracts which are void and voidable (describing all of them as invalidated). This is in contrast to settled law that termination has prospective effect.

This objection is valid and adopting Birks' approach, without more, would cause a major upheaval. However, the objection is not fatal and the new Birksian approach can be adapted, without importing the approach to termination which Birks suggested. The key is not to focus on termination but the condition attached to the transfer of the benefit under a contract. This is something that is best understood once the failure of condition model, proposed in this book, is laid out in Chapter 6. That chapter will then show how the focus on the conditionality of a transfer of a benefit enables the new Birksian approach to operate, consistently with the current law, without treating termination as necessarily having retrospective effect.[82]

V. Conclusion

This chapter sought to defend the new Birksian approach, which argues for and shows how the English law of unjust enrichment should switch from its current unjust factors approach to the civilian absence of basis approach. More broadly, the arguments in this chapter illustrate that the law does not have to be confined to its historical shape. Although the historical discussion in Chapter 1 provided some support for the unjust factors approach,[83] this chapter argued that an ideal system of unjust enrichment needs to go beyond unjust factors and test for absence of basis as well. This was the lesson learnt from looking at modern case law, when the unjust factors approach has been tested in the courts and has shown itself to be defective in a number of ways.

The chapter began by emphasising the uniqueness of the new Birksian approach and the way in which it differs from the German absence of basis approach, from which it seeks inspiration. As Birks put it, his approach sought to lay down 'an English version of the civilian sine causa approach'. One of the key ways he achieved this was through the pyramid model for the law of unjust enrichment: at the bottom of the pyramid are reasons for invalidity which can show when there is an absence of basis, the top layer of the pyramid. By incorporating reasons for invalidity (which include the unjust factors), the pyramid also represents a reconciliation between the

---

[82] See Chapter 6, part V.
[83] Chapter 1, text from n 195 onwards.

absence of basis approach and the unjust factors approach, all of which also insure (as far as we can tell at this stage) that adopting Birks' model would not cause a major upheaval in the law.

The chapter then went on to vindicate the new Birksian approach by showing, through case law examples, why an ideal system of unjust enrichment should investigate reasons for invalidity and absence of basis. For example, it was shown that focussing on reasons for invalidity only, as the current unjust factors approach does, creates problems including (a) the adoption of wrong reasons being given to explain the restitution award in a particular case, and (b) insufficient attention being paid to the basis (eg contract or other type of obligation) of the enrichment, resulting in the risk of the assumption that a basis exists which in fact does not.

In the final part, we saw that the reconciliation Birks achieved in his model meant that many of the criticisms normally aimed at the absence of basis approach do not apply to the new Birksian approach. Three remaining criticisms were then examined, two of which were shown not to be fundamental, especially in light of the benefits achieved under the new Birksian approach. The third criticism, concerning the way Birks envisaged that the operation of his approach required termination of the contract to have retrospective effect, was potentially a serious objection. However, this criticism need not be fatal since the new Birksian approach can be adopted without treating termination as necessarily having retrospective effect. This point will become clear once the new model introduced in this book is laid out in Chapter 6. For this reason, this third criticism will be revisited in Chapter 6.[84]

Chapters 1 to 3 have concerned themselves with the existence, foundation and exposition of the law of unjust enrichment. More specifically, the chapters vindicate one aspect of the dominant model: the innocent party's restitutionary claim, which follows when the contract is terminated, is founded on unjust enrichment, rather than the law of contract or some equitable notion of unconcientiousness. Where this book departs from the dominant model is in endorsing the absence of basis approach, rather than the unjust factors approach. With the best approach to unjust enrichment decided, we can now move on to the heart of the thesis in this book. In the final three chapters, the dominant model will be rejected and a new model proposed that applies across the contractual context, which has been defined as concerning contracts which are (a) terminated for breach, (b) subsisting and (c) unenforceable. Under the new model, it will be argued that the resolution of two questions will decide whether a party may be able to claim the restitution of the value of a benefit transferred under a contract: (1) Was the transfer of the benefit conditional? (2) Has there been a qualifying failure of condition?

Finally, a point should be flagged at this stage about the new model and its relationship to the discussion in this chapter. This is that the new model is consistent with both the unjust factors approach and the absence of basis approach, defended in this chapter.

---

[84] See Chapter 6, part V.

4

The Role of Unjust Enrichment in the Contractual Context: an Introduction to Chapters 5 and 6

I. Background

T HIS SHORT CHAPTER introduces the next two chapters, which work towards mapping out the role of unjust enrichment in the contractual context.

We have seen in earlier chapters that, as regards an innocent party's right to restitution after breach, the dominant model is that it is only upon termination[1] that a party can elect to claim for the restitution of the value of the benefits transferred under the contract, instead of his or her expectation damages. This is said to be a claim outside the contract founded upon unjust enrichment for (total or partial) failure of consideration. Although the law strictly requires there to be a *total* failure of consideration, it is agreed amongst the majority of writers that this requirement should be jettisoned.[2] More recently there has emerged a body of opinion which argues that termination should not be a necessary precondition for the unjust enrichment claim in the contractual context.[3] The dominant model, and these variations on it, raise a number of problems which will form the basis of the discussion in the two chapters which follow.

(1) The dominant model is influenced by and focusses almost exclusively on the role of unjust enrichment when the *contract* (or its main performance) fails. This has meant that insufficient attention has been paid to lessons that can be learnt from examining how unjust enrichment can be employed to recover an apportioned part

---

[1] As to the choice of this term and others adopted in this chapter, see the discussion below in part II.

[2] Representative examples are AS Burrows, *The Law of Restitution* (2nd edn, London, Butterworths, 2002) 333–6; G Virgo, *The Principles of the Law of Restitution* (2nd edn, Oxford, OUP, 2006) 323–6; P Birks, *Unjust Enrichment* (2nd edn, Oxford, OUP, 2005) 119–12; and RGB Goff of Chieveley and GH Jones, *The Law of Restitution* (7th edn, London, Sweet & Maxwell, 2007) para 19-009.

[3] SA Smith, 'Concurrent Liability in Contract and Unjust Enrichment' (1999) 115 *LQR* 245; J Beatson, 'Restitution and Contract: Non-Cumul?' (2000) 1 *Theoretical Inquiries in Law* 83; A Tettenborn, 'Subsisting Contracts and Failure of Consideration: a Little Scepticism' (2002) *RLR* 1; M Bryan, 'Rescission, Restitution and Contractual Ordering: the Plaintiff Election' in A Robertson (ed), *The Law of Obligations: Connections and Boundaries* (London, UCL, 2004); and J Edelman and E Bant, *Unjust Enrichment in Australia* (Melbourne, OUP, 2006) 266–7.

of a contract.[4] The most important lesson is that recovery in this context reveals a longstanding error at the heart of many of the models, namely that a contract must be terminated before a claim for unjust enrichment can be made for *any* benefits passed under the contract. This is because termination of the contract has never been a precondition to recover, for example, money paid under an instalment. This raises a number of questions. Why is it that termination is not required in the apportioned contract context? Does this mean that the termination precondition can be jettisoned completely? If not, what is its role today? These last two questions are not straightforward because even those who have argued against it[5] do not go as far as proposing the total abandonment of the termination precondition.

(2) Whether one lays down termination as a precondition or holds that unjust enrichment should be available upon any breach, the focus on breach is problematic. This is because it implies that unjust enrichment is only concerned with benefits passed under a contract in consideration of a contractually promised counter-performance: it is only in these circumstances that failure of consideration will coincide with breach (failure of the counter-performance is a failure to perform the contractual promise). While this may be the most common example of the claim, failure of consideration does not have to coincide with breach of a promise, since consideration for the promise may be a contingent event (eg the act of a third party or an act of nature) whose occurrence is not promised by either party. Although these cases are not very common, it will be shown that a claim founded upon unjust enrichment enables the recovery of the value of the benefit when the contingent event fails, without the necessity of terminating the contract.

(3) The language of partial and total failure in many of the texts can be inaccurate and liable to mislead. Two examples illustrate this:

(a) Not clarifying whether there is a total or partial failure can lead to problems in cases where recovery has been allowed in the context of apportioned contracts. For example, if one measures each instalment against the whole contract, then recovery in respect of that instalment is an example of a partial failure. As was pointed out in (1) above, there is a tendency to view recovery in this context in this way because it can be employed as another example of the courts recognising partial failure of consideration. As Virgo puts it:

> An alternative mechanism to avoid the strict rigours of the requirement that the consideration must have totally failed before it can constitute a ground of restitution is to apportion the consideration.[6]

Yet the courts have in a number of leading cases considered recovery in apportioned contract cases as being founded on *total* failure of consideration.[7] Moreover, recovery in this context has always been allowed, without in any way being considered an exception to the total failure rule. By being considered more

---

[4] The main exception being the treatment of the subject in Edelman and Bant (n 3 above) ch 4.
[5] See n 3 above.
[6] Virgo (n 2 above) 320.
[7] *Goss v Chilcott* [1996] AC 788 and *Stocznia Gdanska SA v Latvian Shipping* [1998] 1 WLR 574.

like an exception, the significance of recovery in the apportioned contract context is once again underplayed.

(b) The termination precondition insulates those arguing against the need for the failure to be total from having to address directly a key question: if not total failure, then should every failure of consideration generate a claim in unjust enrichment? Without answering this question precisely (ie what is a qualifying partial failure?), retaining the termination precondition means that the failure of consideration cannot be too small, otherwise it is unlikely to qualify as a termination. But this is a rather uncertain mechanism to rely on to avoid the aforementioned question. Yet the existence of the mechanism hints at the possibility that, contrary to some authors' views, failure of consideration and termination are linked in some way. Indeed, the historical discussion in Chapter 5 will reinforce this view, and illustrate that the idea of failure of consideration is the foundation not only of the unjust enrichment claim but also of the principles determining when a contract can be terminated.

(4) It is a mantra amongst many scholars that money and non-money benefits should be treated alike. They admit that this is a controversial position because the law has not generally used failure of consideration language in dealing with non-money benefits. But the argument has been that symmetry dictates that the two should be dealt with in the same way by the law. Burrows, McKendrick and Edelman have recently and powerfully restated the case for this unified treatment of all benefits:

> a more vigorous analytical approach, which seeks to build a logical symmetrical body of law, will wish to sweep away the old division and erect in their place a unified law based on the recovery of benefits conferred on consideration which happens to fail.[8]

Admirable though the case for symmetry may be, it is submitted that the distinction between the two should be kept in mind throughout any analysis to the extent that money and money benefits are *returnable*, and the non-money benefits dealt with in Chapters 5 and 6 (ie for work done) are *non-returnable*. This is because it is only in relation to the restitution of non-returnable benefits that certain difficult issues arise, including the following.

(a) In claiming restitution of the value of the benefit transferred under a contract, a claimant will be obliged to give counter-restitution of any benefits received. Is this counter-restitution requirement flexible so that in relation to non-returnable benefits, a monetary equivalent can be given instead? The difficulty arises because the counter-restitution of non-returnable benefits appears to apportion the contract for the parties, something which the law is reluctant to do.[9] Note that the restitution of the value of money (as an example of a returnable benefit) does not run into the same problem, because the effect of such an award will never appear to apportion the contract.

---

[8] AS Burrows, E McKendrick and J Edelman, *Cases and Materials on the Law of Restitution* (2nd edn, Oxford, OUP, 2006) 250; Virgo (n 2 above) esp 125–6; and Birks (n 2 above) 49–55.

[9] To the extent that the parties are left in a position in which a discrete portion of the contract is being valued in a way which had not initially been agreed by the parties.

(b) To what extent can a party in breach of an entire contract claim for any beneficial part performance enjoyed by the innocent party? Again, if the part performance was a returnable benefit (such as money) no problem arises: a claim for the restitution of its value can be made. It is only when the part performance is non-returnable that there is an issue, because restitution in these circumstances appears to be inconsistent with the entire contracts rule that remuneration will only be given for full, not part, performance of the contract.

Essentially, the difficulty is that the restitution of non-returnable benefits appears to clash with (1) the objective that the law should not apportion the contract for the parties, and (2) the entire contracts rule. An account committed to symmetry from the start does not acknowledge this potential clash and the difficulties posed in resolving it. This is the main reason why the analysis throughout the following chapters will be sensitive to the distinction between returnable and non-returnable benefits.

(5) Very little, if any, time is spent by many leading works in explaining the relationship between accrued rights to receive performance and the claim in unjust enrichment. One reason for this could be the fact that termination for breach is prospective and not retrospective. And since accrued rights precede termination, allowing unjust enrichment to interfere with these rights in some way would be to apply termination retrospectively. However, the problem with this explanation is that termination combined with unjust enrichment does have a retrospective effect. For example, money paid before termination can be recovered. Moreover, relying on the mechanism of termination for breach shifts the focus away from the fact that the accrual of a right is something quite independent of the fact of breach.

(6) The lack of attention paid to the relationship between accrued rights and the unjust enrichment claim may be the product of another problem at the heart of the traditional accounts of the law in this area. As with much of the framework of the law of unjust enrichment, the law in relation to unjust enrichment in the contractual context is built upon older cases. In relation to the termination precondition, this can create problems, because this requirement is founded on cases in which the rules on discharge are said to have operated differently to today: upon breach, the innocent party would rescind the contract ab initio. Under these circumstances, one need not worry about accrued rights, because they would be set aside too. In contrast, termination in the modern analysis is not to have this effect. It is to operate primarily prospectively. If it is right that the older cases required rescission ab initio, then their utility for the modern discussion comes under question. This tension has not really been resolved openly in the discussions. Chapter 5 will address this problem by showing, through a historical analysis, that the older cases remain relevant because their casual use of the term 'rescission' disguises the fact that their understanding of the process was not too different from the modern law of contractual discharge. Moreover, even if they did understand breach to allow rescission ab initio, it was not perceived as a precondition for an unjust enrichment claim. Recovery in the apportioned contract cases is evidence of this.

II. The Model Proposed in this Book

The key to determining whether unjust enrichment can be employed to claim the restitution of the value of the benefit transferred under a contract depends on whether that transfer of the benefit was unconditional or conditional. If the transfer of the benefit is conditional then prima facie the failure of that condition may allow the transferor to claim restitution of the value of the benefit transferred under the law of unjust enrichment. Although the principle may be simply stated, it constitutes an important but novel departure from orthodoxy; and the law surrounding it is complex, not least because the terminology has not been used consistently or precisely. For this reason the following three situations will be used as a focus for the detailed arguments in Chapters 5 and 6, as well as the terminology that will be employed:

(1) A enters into a contract for the purchase of B's house. A makes an advance payment of £18,000. On the set date, B refuses to transfer the property. A wishes to claim back his part payment.

(2) A enters into a contract with B in which B will deliver 1 tonne of cement every month for two years, commencing 15 January 2007. A is to pay after physical receipt of the cement every month. In July 2007, A contacts B to tell him the February delivery was defective, since it was not in accordance with certain quality conditions in the contract. B does not dispute this and the time for curing the defective delivery has passed. A now wishes to claim back the price paid for the February delivery.

(3) Same facts as (1) except that the contract between A and B is now that money is paid subject to approval by B's landlord. B is ready to transfer, but B's landlord refuses to approve A's purchase. A wants to claim his money back.

In each of the three cases it is submitted that two questions will determine whether a right to restitution prima facie arises. Was the transfer of the benefit conditional (transferred upon a 'basis' or for a 'consideration')? Has there been a qualifying failure of condition (in *some*, but not all, cases this is described as 'termination' or 'discharge' or 'rescission')?

In the parentheses, the alternative terms used to describe the operative fact in each question are stated. Whether a payment is conditional has historically been described as a payment upon a consideration or, more recently, upon a 'basis'. The criticisms of the term consideration are well catalogued and persuasive; essentially consideration tends to focus the mind too much on a contractually promised counter-performance.[10] As example (3) shows, sometimes the payment is conditional upon a contingent event (something which neither party has promised will come about). 'Basis' is a term increasingly preferred by authors.[11] This term is

---

[10] Many of the references are collected in F Maher, 'A New Conception of Failure of Basis' (2005) *RLR* 96, n 5, 97–100 generally.

[11] As well as Maher, see Birks (n 2 above) 119.

useful and will still be used, but primarily to illustrate how the present ground of recovery in the contractual context fits within the overall model of unjust enrichment defended in this book, and what in Chapter 3 was called the 'new Birksian approach'. The language of 'condition' or 'conditional' is preferred because it captures more quickly and elegantly the nature of the transfers of benefits upon which unjust enrichment focuses (eg rather than say payment upon a basis or payment upon a consideration, one can just say conditional payment). More importantly, it also connects to the long-established principles which have developed around the law relating to conditions.

The answer to the second question, above, what is a 'qualifying failure of condition' depends on the circumstances. There is a variety of terminology used in the first of those circumstances, namely where the condition is a contractual counter-performance (promissory condition) of an unapportioned contract (in contrast with a contingent condition (case 3) or a promissory condition to an apportioned contract (case 2)). Here, the qualifying failure is one which requires the contract to be 'terminated' or 'discharged' or 'rescinded'. All three terms have been used to describe when certain breaches discharge both parties from their prospective obligations, with accrued rights still surviving. This is in contrast to rescission ab initio, which avoids the contract for all purposes, retrospectively and prospectively. This book prefers to use the terms 'termination' and 'discharge' in the following way: upon a fundamental breach of contract, the parties can *terminate* the contract, which will *discharge* them from their prospective obligations.

There is much to be said for Treitel's use of the term 'rescission' (in the first 11 editions of his textbook, *The Law of Contract*) especially since, as will be shown, it provides a link with the older cases. However, overall his use of the term is not helpful (and the abandonment of it by the new editor of Treitel's work, Edwin Peel, is justified) because it refers to a collection of remedies, namely (1) the refusal to perform by the innocent party, and (2) claiming restitution of the value of the benefit transferred.[12] The second remedy is one which is referred to in this chapter, and more generally in this book, as one for restitution founded on unjust enrichment. Indeed, in a later chapter this is how Treitel himself referred to this remedy.[13] It is submitted that it is only likely to cause further confusion by employing two terms for one remedy.

With the primary terms fixed we can now turn to an overview of the next two (and final) chapters.

---

[12] G Treitel, *The Law of Contract* (11th edn, London, Sweet & Maxwell, 2003) 759–60.
[13] *Ibid* 1049–56.

III. Overview of Chapters 5 and 6

Chapter 5 examines the historical foundations of the claim for unjust enrichment in the contractual context. It will illustrate, amongst other things, how the conditionality or unconditionality, and more commonly the law relating to performance of contractual obligations, has been at the root of the relationship between unjust enrichment and contract. One of the effects of the model proposed in this book is that it draws a very close relationship between the laws of unjust enrichment and contract. The dependency of unjust enrichment on contract becomes very clear, because how one understands the conditionality of a transfer of a benefit depends, as we will see, on the construction of the contract. This could generate criticism that the independence of the unjust enrichment claim is being eroded and the claim being *mutated* into contract; and the primary basis for such an argument will be the older law. However, such a criticism will be resisted, because one of the benefits of the historical analysis in Chapter 5 will be to show that the model proposed here best reflects the older law.

Chapter 6 will set out the general principles relevant to the unjust enrichment claim in the contractual context. This chapter elaborates on the model outlined above. The substance of the discussion is split into five parts. Part II will define the meaning of 'condition' and sets out what is a 'qualifying failure of condition'. This part will also discuss the meaning and impact of accrued rights on the right to restitution, as well as the principle of prevention. Part III is dedicated to illustrating the distinctiveness of the quantum meruit claim. At the root of the distinctiveness is the non-returnability of the benefit. Part IV explains how the model operates when the claimant is the party in breach and when the restitutionary claim arises in the context of unenforceable contracts. Part V will then address how the model presented in this chapter fits into the new Birksian approach defended in Chapter 3. Finally, part VI will examine and reject the main objection to the model put forward in this book. This is that restitution upon failure of condition is, or should be, a contractual claim, rather than one founded on unjust enrichment. It is worth noting that, in recognition of the criticism of the dominant model made above,[14] throughout the chapters the analyses will be sensitive to the distinction between apportioned and unapportioned contracts and returnable and non-returnable benefits.

---

[14] See part I above.

5

Historical Foundations of the Modern Law of Unjust Enrichment in the Contractual Context

I. Introduction

T HIS CHAPTER WILL analyse the historical foundations of the modern law. Part II, which will be the largest, will track and understand the evolution of what has been referred to throughout this book as 'the dominant model'. It will examine the establishment of the requirement that only certain failures of contractual performance enable a party to rescind (that is, to terminate) the contract before it can rely on claims that today fall within the modern law of unjust enrichment. Part III will investigate the meaning of the term 'rescission', as used by the older cases, and the total failure requirement. Part IV will focus on the quantum meruit claim and the extent to which a money had and received (MHR) claim can be employed in the context of an apportioned contract.

II. Evolution of the Dominant Model

We have seen that, as regards an innocent party's right to restitution after breach, the dominant model is that the innocent party after termination is entitled to restitution for (total or partial) failure of consideration. While most commentators regard the traditional insistence on a total failure as unnecessary, the key requirement of termination remains. In this part, I will therefore focus on that termination requirement.

At its very simplest, the underlying assumption made by the dominant model is that failure of performance by one party (A) can justify the refusal to perform by the other party (B) (giving him the right to terminate the contract). This refusal is only justified because each party's performances are *dependent* on each other in some way: A's performance is a condition precedent or is a concurrent condition to B's performance (we are in this sense talking about promissory conditions). It is almost second nature to contract lawyers to think that most promises (and their performance) in a contract are dependent. This indeed is one of the features of the modern law of contract: I give a performance on the basis that I will get something in return.

However, this presumption in favour of dependency was not always the norm in English law, which for a long time proceeded on the basis that contractual promises were independent. This meant that each party could bring an action for the failure of performance of the other, even though they were incapable of fulfilling their own promise. This presumption of independency is said by many accounts to have been transformed in the latter part of the eighteenth century by Lord Mansfield in *Kingston v Preston* (1772) ('*Kingston*')[1] and *Boone v Eyre* (1778) ('*Boone*'),[2] where the modern rules on termination and dependency of contractual promises are said to have been laid down.

Both these cases are of central importance and did greatly influence the modern law. However, in order to understand these cases better (which will be the subject of sections B and C), some background on the law relating to performance is required (section A). This will enable us to understand the principles laid down in these cases, as well as assessing the extent of their innovation: did they depart from existing law[3] or, as others argue, recognise what was already in the law before?[4] Against this background, we will then be in a position to track the establishment of the dominant model (section D).

A. Background: Independency

With the rise of assumpsit and the promissory basis of contract (certainly by the end of the sixteenth century until well into the eighteenth century),[5] contractual promises were considered independent unless there were express words to make the promises dependent.[6] It could be said that, in contrast to today, there was a

---

[1] (1772) cited in argument in *Jones v Barkley* (1781) 2 Doug 684, 689; 99 ER 434.

[2] (1778) cited in argument in *Duke of St Albans v Shore* 1 H Bl 270, 273; 126 ER 160.

[3] CC Langdell, *A Summary of the Law of Contracts* (2nd edn, Boston, Little Brown & Co., 1880) s 143, 183–6; TA Street, *The Foundations of Legal Liability: a Presentation of the Theory and Development of the Common Law* (New York E Thompson, 1906) 137 *et seq*; S Williston, *The Law of Contracts* (1st edn, New York, Baker, Voorhis & Co, 1920) vol II, ss 816–17, 1565–7; and AL Corbin, *A Comprehensive Treatise on the Rules of Contract Law* (St Paul, West Publishing, 1960), vol III, s 654, 138 (n 6) and 140.

[4] S Stoljar, 'Dependent and Independent Promises' (1956–58) 2 *Sydney L Rev* 217; and W McGovern, 'Dependent Promises in the History of Leases and other Contracts' (1977–78) 52 *Tul L Rev* 659.

[5] How far into the eighteenth century is not an easy question to resolve, because it is difficult to track when the presumption as to dependency exactly occurred. Nevertheless, as will be argued below, the temptation to see a sudden change during Lord Mansfield's time should be resisted: see part II, section B(i) and (ii) below.

[6] Although these questions arose mostly in the context of covenant claims, the same principles applied in regular assumpsit claims too: for an example see *Peeters v Opie* (1671) 2 Wms Saund 350, 85 ER 1144 ('*Peeters*'). The principles on contractual performance laid down by Serjeant Williams in his notes to *Pordage v Cole* (1669) 1 Wms Saund 219, 85 ER 449 ('*Pordage*'), were understood by him, despite being expressed in the language of covenants, as being consistent with the decision in *Peeters*: ibid 352, n 3. Also the leading case of *Thorp v Thorp* (1701) 12 Mod 455, 88 ER 1448 (for the pleadings see 3 Ld Raym 341, 92 ER 722) was an action upon the case and not an action on a covenant (see text around n 44 below).

presumption in favour of independent promises. The result of treating promises in this way was that each party could sue the other without any performance being rendered. A typical and often quoted example from the period is *Nichols v Raynbred* (1615) ('*Nichols*').[7] In this case the claimant was allowed to sue for the price of a cow, without offering to deliver it. It is important not to dismiss cases such as *Nichols* as representing a primitive law that simply did not appreciate the importance of performance to a contract. The law applied in that case needs to be put in context as follows.

(1) The independency presumption needs to be seen in light of the prevailing theory of contract enforcement at the time, namely that since a promise for a promise was sufficient consideration, one need only then go on to show there was a breach to bring an action of assumpsit. Simpson has summarised the message emerging from many cases in the following way: 'Why should performance be averred; the plaintiff has satisfied the requirement in assumpsit by showing the promise, consideration and breach: what else is needed?'[8]

Also, proceeding in this way would not have been unusual from the perspective of other contractual actions such as covenant and debt, which were conceptualised as unilateral (the action only considered one party's undertaking), leaving the parties to defend their claims through a cross-action.

(2) The presumption in favour of independency did not mean dependency was not recognised. The view appears to have been that parties were free to use words to make their promises expressly dependent. As Lord Holt put it in *Thorp v Thorp* (1701) ('*Thorp*') (after recognising the danger that a construction of independency poses to the parties): 'If he make a bargain, and rely on the other's covenant or promise to have what he would have done to him, it is his own fault'.[9]

Given that the rules on when promises were considered dependent were clear, this kind of system was arguably as certain and respectful of commercial realities as the modern law, which starts from the presumption that promises are dependent. Moreover, the clarity of the rules could have encouraged negotiation and settlement.

(3) Construing promises as independent also allowed just results in some of the cases, and so should not necessarily be seen as the courts failing to recognise or appreciate the performance interest. A good example here is *Ughtred's Case*,[10] in which the claimant argued that the defendant's father had granted him an annuity which the defendant had failed to pay for 11 years. The defendant argued that the claimant had failed to aver the performance he was to give in return for the annuity, namely that he (the claimant) would maintain a castle, appoint a master

---

[7] (1615) Hob 88, 80 ER 238.

[8] AW Simpson, *A History of the Common Law of Contract* (Oxford, OUP, 1975) 463.

[9] (1701) 12 Mod 455, 464; 88 ER 1448. The other reports (in which the case is known as *Thorpe v Thorpe*) are not as detailed: 1 Salk 171, 91 ER 157; Holt KB 28, 90 ER 913; Holt KB 96, 90 ER 951; and 1 Ld Raym 662, 91 ER 1341.

[10] (1591) 7 Co Rep 96, 77 ER 425. Although an action on an annuity it was considered relevant for contractual actions: Stoljar (n 4 above) 221.

gunner and six soldiers. If the defendant's argument had been allowed, it would have barred the claimant's action (as would be the case here if their promises were seen as dependent), resulting in a possible injustice. Since the claimant was not able to amend his pleadings, allowing the defendant's plea would mean that, even if the claimant had given due performance, his action would have been forever barred.[11] Alternatively, even if he had averred performance it may be that there was a small shortfall. In light of the defendant's argument, such a shortfall would be fatal since it would represent a failure of a condition precedent and therefore excuse the defendant from his obligation to pay. In both of the above scenarios, the defendant would be unjustly enriched. And so to get round this, the court construed the promises as independent, giving the claimant some redress and leaving the defendant to his cross-action.[12]

(4) In a number of cases (although this is not always obvious from the reports), the claimant had in fact performed but the question in the case was simply about the technicality of the way the performance had been pleaded.[13]

The approach to independency and dependency outlined above was perceived to have created a not easily reconcilable body of law, something which was noted throughout the eighteenth century.[14] The difficulty in the cases is likely to have been created by three types of tension within the courts' approach: (1) the importance of the wording to assess the dependency of the promises, a requirement that was bound to attract criticism of overtechnicality, especially if it frustrated (2) the plain intentions of the parties, which the courts sought to protect,[15] and (3) reaching just results in cases where a dependent construction would leave one of the parties unjustly enriched.[16]

One way out of the difficulties was to adopt a more flexible approach, coupled with a clear statement as to the factors determining whether a promise was dependent or independent. Both these solutions are said to have been first laid down by Lord Mansfield in *Kingston* and *Boone*.[17]

B. Antecedents of *Kingston* and *Boone*

Kingston concerned an agreement in which the defendant would ultimately transfer his business to the claimant. The dispute came down to whether the defendant's

---

[11] He could not bring a claim again because of res judicata or estoppel on record: *ibid* 222.

[12] *Ibid* 221–2 and 229–32.

[13] *Beany v Turner* (1670) 1 Lev 293, 83 ER 413; and there was also an argument about the ill averment of the performance in *Thorp* (n 6 above).

[14] *Thorp* (n 6 above); *Thomas v Cadawallader* (1744) Willes 496, 125 ER 1286; and *Goodisson v Nunn* (1792) 4 TR 761, 100 ER 1288.

[15] 'And therefore such a construction would entirely defeat the intention of the parties': *Hunlocke v Blacklowe* (1670) 2 Wms Saund 156, 157; 85 ER 893. Lord Holt's judgment reported in *Thorp* (n 6 above) also shows the importance of the parties' intention to the law. Also see Stoljar (n 4 above) 238, n 162.

[16] See text around n 12 above.

[17] See references in n 3 above.

obligation to transfer his business was dependent on the claimant's payment of a security deposit. The specific facts of the case are less important than Lord Mansfield's approach to determining the performance obligation in question. After articulating the different types of performance obligations (independent, condition precedent and concurrent) he is reported to have said that the 'dependence, or independence of covenants was to be collected from the evident sense and meaning of the parties'.[18] This indicated that the key factor in determining the order of performance was the parties' intention, not some verbal formula. However, another important question remained: was strict performance always required to fulfil one's dependent obligation? If the answer was 'yes' then, as was discussed earlier in relation to *Ughtred's Case*, there was a strong possibility that a minor breach would result in unjust enrichment of one of the parties.[19] *Boone* vividly illustrates the problem and the approach Lord Mansfield adopted to solve it.

In *Boone*, the claimant had transferred to the defendant a plantation in the West Indies together with a stock of slaves, promising that he had good title to both. The defendant agreed to pay £500 plus £160 as an annuity for the claimant's lifetime. In an action for non-payment of the annuity, the defendant said that the claimant had never had possession of the slaves legally and so did not have title. Judgment was given for the claimant, on the basis that here the mutual covenants went to only a part, and not the whole, of the consideration. Accordingly, the covenants were not a condition precedent to each other, leaving the breach to be remedied by damages. It was said that if the defendant's pleas were to be allowed it would mean that the absence of one slave would bar the claimant's claim. Lord Mansfield is reported to have said:

> The distinction is very clear, where mutual covenants go to the whole of the consideration on both sides, they are mutual conditions, the one precedent for the other. But where they go only to a part, where a breach may be paid for in damages, there the defendant has a remedy on his covenant, and shall not plead it as a condition precedent.[20]

To what extent did *Kingston* and *Boone* create new law? Two factors make it difficult to answer this question. The first, as discussed in Chapter 1, is the poverty of the legal literature covering (in particular) the first half of the eighteenth century, which makes it difficult to track the development of the law in that period.[21] Secondly, we do not have a full report on either case; indeed, the judgments relied upon come down to us in the form of extracts in other reported cases.

Does the paucity of reports suggest that the cases were not that innovative after all? This would be an unsafe assumption simply because the law publishing market was not so organised as to interpret the lack of reports as indicating the unimportance of the decision. After all, the main reporter of Lord Mansfield's decisions,

[18] *Kingston* (n 1 above) 692.
[19] See text around n 12 above.
[20] *Boone* (n 2 above) 273.
[21] See Chapter 1, n 88.

Sir James Burrow, had initially compiled his reports for his 'own private use, and not for public inspection'.[22] Moreover, they do not claim to record every decision of Lord Mansfield. Furthermore, the immediate importance given to these decisions shows that they were recognised as important in their time.

Some clue as to the extent of the innovation arises from the surviving papers that were put before the judges in both cases,[23] as well as detailed MS reports on the cases that contain the argument of counsel on each side, with references to the cases that were cited.[24] Although the arguments noted are probably incomplete, what is noted sheds more light than any of the printed reports of either decision.

(i) Kingston

The importance accorded to the parties' intention in *Kingston* was not so novel, as similar statements can be found in earlier cases.[25] *Kingston* is seen as important for it appeared to prioritise the parties' intention over the technical verbal formula that had previously dominated discussion of the dependence and independence of promises. The MS papers show that, except for one case relied on by both parties, their arguments are consistent with the cases in which the wording is determinative of the order of performance.[26] However, there is a sense in which the arguments that were founded on these cases were not debating the technicality of the words since we see each side talking about the 'import of the whole deed',[27] 'from the nature'[28] of the deed and the 'construction of the articles',[29] all of which are indicative of the more modern approach and consistent with Lord Mansfield's reported judgment. Moreover, we also see specific arguments on each side which under an approach committed to verbal formulae would have been rejected. One argument relied on by Francis Buller, for the claimant, was that 'the subject matter of the [claimant's] covenant is such that it could not be performed before the [defendant's] covenant was performed'.[30] So that even if the covenants were dependent, it would have been no bar to the claimant's present claim that he had

---

[22] J Burrow, *Reports of Cases Argued and Adjudged in the Court of King's Bench during the time of Lord Mansfield's presiding . . . from . . . 1756, to . . . 1772* (4th edn, London, E & R Brooke, 1790) iii (Preface).

[23] The judges' papers are primarily made up of the case stated: LI Dampier MS APB 17 (*Kingston*) and LI Dampier MS APB 41 (*Boone*). The brief note of the arguments, in a rushed hand, appear consistent with the greater detail of the arguments noted in MS (see n 24 below). Both sets of papers are likely to belong to Ashurst J.

[24] These appear in a separate manuscript in each case: LI Hill MS 11, ff 380–1 (*Boone*) and LI Hill MS 10, ff 180–6 (*Kingston*).

[25] See n 15 above.

[26] The cases appear in the note of Francis Buller's argument (LI Hill MS 10, f 181) on behalf of the claimant: *Cole v Shallet* (1682) 3 Lev 41, 83 ER 567; *Trench Executor of Squire v Trewin* (1696) 1 Ld Raym 124, 91 ER 980; *Blackwell v Nash* (1722)1 Str 535, 93 ER 684; and *Dawson et UX v Myer Mil'* (1726) 2 Str 712, 93 ER 801. The one exception referred to was the case of *Staples v Alden* (1678), 2 Mod 309, 86 ER 1091, in which the focus appears to be on the 'intent of the parties' (*ibid* 310). Nash Grose, defendant's counsel, 'admitted the law to be as laid down by Mr Buller': LI Hill MS 10 f 184.

[27] LI Hill MS 10 f 182.

[28] *Ibid* f 183.

[29] *Ibid* f 184.

[30] *Ibid* f 181.

not performed. Similarly, Nash Grose for the defendant relied on an argument that, if the covenants were not dependent, the defendant would be left to rely on the security of the claimant who was 'not worth a farthing',[31] an argument that Lord Mansfield was clearly persuaded by in the published report of the case.[32]

Without a full account of the argument it is difficult to tell whether the extracts quoted above were representative or were a small part of the overall argument that was dominated by a debate on whether certain verbal formulae had been used in the deed. It is also at this stage worth noting that the cases are unlikely to have been the only sources for the arguments. For example, Buller cites '[Fletcher] 2 MS Notes 142' for his argument that the subject matter of the covenant was such that the claimant would not be able to perform before the defendant performed his covenant.[33] I have not been able to trace this source, which as the title of it suggests is a reference to a manuscript, not published at the time.

The likely interpretation is that, despite the case law,[34] practice (based perhaps on literature that was not necessarily published) had moved on from prioritising verbal formulae to a more commercial reading of the contracts, which was led by what the parties intended in their agreements. This is captured in Lord Mansfield's judgment and to that extent he was following what was being argued by counsel. If this is right, then the novelty of his judgment is not so great. However, his judgment did not make absolutely clear the position of the older cases; indeed, it could be said the parties' intention can be consistent with the close reading of the agreement. This is perhaps why the older cases, which were relied upon by counsel in *Kingston*, continued to be cited. In *Goodisson v Nunn* (1792) (*'Goodisson'*),[35] the judges tried to emphasise the message in *Kingston* and clearly signal that the older cases were no longer representative of the courts' approach.[36] In this case the claimant had agreed to sell his land to the defendant for £210 before 2 September. Each party also agreed that failure to perform their obligation would require the other to pay £21. The claimant bought an action of debt for this sum based on the

---

[31] *Ibid* f 185.

[32] *Kingston* (n 1 above) 691.

[33] LI Hill MS 10 f 182.

[34] Which cuts off at 1726. And note that these cases from the 1720s appear in Strange's reports, which were not published until 1755. That is not to say they were not available in manuscript form before then. However, it would be wrong to assume that reports were necessarily available in manuscript form before publication, especially when they concerned judges' reports of their own arguments ('judgments' in modern terms). A good example is Willes CJ's report of *Thomas v Cadwallader* (1744) Willes 496, 125 ER 1286, which Grose J implied he did not know about at the time he was counsel in *Kingston*: 'I have since found that that was not the first case [*Kingston*] where those sentiments began to be entertained; for it appears from a late publication of reports from the manuscripts of Lord Chief Justice Willis, that in a case of *Thomas v Cadawallader*, his lordship . . . seemed very desirous that the governing rules should be so to construe such covenants as that the real intention of the parties should be carried into effect. This was afterwards done in *Kingston v Preston*': *Glazebrook v Woodrow* (1799) 8 TR 366, 371–1; 101 ER 1436. In assessing these comments one must also keep in mind the interest of Grose J in emphasising the novelty of *Kingston*, a case in which his arguments had been accepted. See also Chapter 1, n 88.

[35] (1792) 4 TR 761, 100 ER 1288.

[36] That the message was not so clear because in other decisions the older cases continued to be cited, see text from n 63 onwards.

defendant's failure to perform. The defendant tried to argue that the claimant's obligation to transfer the land was a condition precedent to his obligation to pay the consideration. The argument resisting this construction was driven by the older cases such as *Pordage*[37] and *Blackwell v Nash*,[38] which were employed to show how the particular wording of the contract made the covenants independent rather than dependent. Lord Kenyon's rejection of this argument and approach is clear, as is his opinion on the older cases:

> The old cases, cited by plaintiff's counsel, have been accurately stated; but the determinations in them outrage common sense. I admit the principle on which they profess to go; but I think that the judges misapplied that principle . . .
>
> I am glad to find that the old cases have been over-ruled; and that we are now warranted by precedent as well as by principle to say this action cannot be maintained.[39]

(ii) Boone

In relation to the principle in *Boone*, Stoljar observed that 'however important the decision, it was part and parcel of a continuing development, it was not (as is sometimes thought) a suddenly inspired creation'.[40] He cites some early cases and a number from the seventeenth century, in which there is implicit or explicit recognition of the idea indorsed in *Boone*, that the materiality of the breach will influence the construction a court gives to the promises at hand.[41] Certainly, the MS papers show that the claimant, whose argument was eventually accepted, relied on one of the cases which Stoljar cites as applying a similar principle to *Boone*.[42]

But for three reasons, it is important not to overestimate the influence of the decisions Stoljar cites as echoing the principle in *Boone*: first, because those cases do not confidently or expressly speak of the kind of principle Lord Mansfield laid down. Secondly, if we focus on the case law alone, there was, as Stoljar's own work shows, a conflict in the cases.[43] The defendant's submission shows this, since the cases he placed reliance on focussed on the words in the deed.[44] Indeed, one of the cases relied on was *Thorp*,[45] a leading decision from the early eighteenth century in which Holt CJ sought to lay down general principles on when a promise or covenant is independent or dependent. In the fullest report of the case there is no principle outlined which resembles that which Lord Mansfield applied in *Boone*. And this is unsurprising, because at the heart of Holt CJ's principle in *Thorp* is the assumption that unless express words say so, promises are independent.[46] A

---

[37] See n 6 above.

[38] See n 26 above.

[39] *Goodisson* (n 35 above) 764–5.

[40] Stoljar (n 4 above) 243.

[41] *Ibid* 229–32. The cases include *Hunlocke v Blacklowe* (1670) 2 Wms Saund 156, 85 ER 893; and *Hayes v Bickerstaff* (1675) Freem KB 194, 89 ER 138.

[42] *Cole v Shallet* (n 26 above): LI Dampier MS APB 41 f 1v; and LI Hill MS 10 f 180.

[43] Stoljar (n 4 above) 232–4.

[44] *Brocas' Case* (1588) 3 Leonard 219, 74 ER 644; and *Thorp* (n 6 above).

[45] See n 9 above.

[46] See text to n 9 above.

principle driven by verbal formulae would not have sat comfortably with the flexibility of Lord Mansfield's formula in *Boone*, which allows the court to ignore the words of a deed or agreement depending on the materiality of the breach. Thirdly, we must not underestimate the way in which Lord Mansfield's judgment is recorded. The MS papers also contain what is most likely to be a summary of Ashurst J's conclusion in the case: 'Whether precedent or subsequent must depend on the nature of the case. This is in its nature must be considered as mutual and party takes mutual remedies'.[47] Had this been the surviving judgment in the case, it is submitted that it would not have quite captured the flexibility and full range of the principle laid down by Lord Mansfield in *Boone*.

The gap between the cases Stoljar cites and the *Boone* principle leaves the question as to the source of the principle. It is difficult to answer the question definitively since it is possible that, as with *Kingston*, the reported decisions relied on by Stoljar had been overtaken by contemporary thought which presented a principle closer to that applied by Lord Mansfield in *Boone*.[48] One potential source of the *Boone* principle may have been the practice of chancery, which had developed a body of law that resembles closely the *Boone* principle. In the *Treatise of Equity* published in 1737, the following appears in the section on 'Where Equity will relieve the want of performance of a condition':

> And some say, that in all cases that lie in compensation, equity will relieve; for where they can make compensation no harm is done. So that altho' an express time be appointed for the performance of a condition, the judge may, after the day is past, allow a reasonable space to the party, making reparation for the damage, if the damage be not very great, nor the substance of the covenant destroy'd by it.[49]

Although the point in the extract is made tentatively ('And some say'), the majority of works before and after express it more confidently: 'The substantial distinction which governs the interference of courts of equity in cases of conditions broken, is not whether the condition be precedent or subsequent, but whether compensation can or cannot be made'.[50] We can be confident that Lord Mansfield was aware of this particular area of law, not just because of his own successful chancery practice but also because of his likely involvement (as a chancery junior) in one of the more important cases on the law relating to conditions during the eighteenth century.[51]

---

[47] LI Dampier Mss APB 41 f 1v.

[48] See text to n 20 above.

[49] [Ballow], *A Treatise of Equity* (London, D Browne & J Shuckburgh 1737) 43.

[50] J Fonblanque (ed), *A Treatise of Equity* (2nd edn, London, W Clarke & Son, 1799) 399 n k. See also Anon, *A General Abridgment of Cases in Equity* (2nd edn, London, J Shuckburgh, 1734) 108 (n (a)); and G Gilbert, *The History and Practice of the High Court of Chancery* (London, J Worrall and W Owen, 1758) 339. See also *Alexander Popham v Bampfeild and Al* (1682) 1 Vern 80, 23 ER 325. In so far as this case expresses the materiality of the distinction between conditions subsequent and precedent, this was less important during the eighteenth century: see the quotation from Fonblanque above as an example.

[51] *Hervey and others v Aston and others* (1737–38) West T Hard 350, 25 ER 975. At 379, the list of counsel who appeared at the hearing for the petition for appeal included a 'Mr Murray', which is likely to be William Murray, the future Lord Mansfield. William Murray was called to the Bar in 1730: J Oldham, 'Murray, William, first earl of Mansfield (1705–93) in *Oxford Dictionary of National Biography* (Oxford, OUP, 2004).

Overall then, it is likely that Stoljar was correct to conclude that *Boone* was not as novel as some authors have argued. However, the source of the principle was less likely to be the older cases from the seventeenth century (to which Stoljar refers) and more likely to be the body of law that had developed in equity and/or the practice in the courts of law in the period before Lord Mansfield during the eighteenth century.

C. The *Boone* Principle in Detail

This section will prepare the way for a discussion in the next section (D) on the reception of the *Boone* principle and its role in the establishment of the dominant model. In order to do this, it is important to analyse *Boone* in greater detail.

(1) It is not immediately clear what is meant by 'mutual' in the first sentence.[52] In a number of contemporary eighteenth century discussions 'mutual' is used as short form for the fact that each promise is independent and performance need not be averred.[53] However, such a construction would make the first sentence meaningless for two reasons: first, because conditions by their nature are dependent and so it is difficult to understand how they could then be independent (if mutual in 'mutual conditions' is a reference to such an independence). Secondly, even if this was the case, then the first sentence would be empty of content because there would not be a difference between mutual covenants and mutual conditions, since both would be expressing that the promises are independent and performance need not be averred. And this would be inconsistent with the purpose of the sentence which seeks to equate mutual conditions with dependent promises, specifically one that 'is precedent to another'.

The most likely meaning of mutual here is as to quantity (*two* conditions or *two* covenants). Mutual covenants are by their very nature unilateral and independent, whereas mutual conditions are dependent. And so the meaning of the first sentence is that two promises will be considered as being dependent, one precedent on another, if they go to 'the whole of the consideration on both sides'.

(2) *Boone* itself does not give any evidence as to what could be considered 'whole' or 'part' of a consideration, a problem compounded by a lack of clarity over different types of situation in which the *Boone* principle could apply. Two situations suggest themselves:[54] first, when A covenants to do two or more things and B covenants, in return consideration, to do one thing in return. If A fails to perform one of the promises, it would technically go to part of the consideration

---

[52] For ease of reference the material extract from the case is: 'The distinction is very clear, where mutual covenants go to the whole of the consideration on both sides, they are mutual conditions, the one precedent for the other. But where they go only to a part, where a breach may be paid for in damages, there the defendant has a remedy on his covenant, and shall not plead it as a condition precedent' (n 20).

[53] Eg Francis Buller's argument in *Kingston* (Ll Hill MS 10 ff 181–3); *Thorp* (n 6 above); and *Cole v Shallet* (n 26 above).

[54] Williston (n 3 above), vol II, s 822, 1573–4.

and would not prevent (if the *Boone* principle is to be followed literally) A from enforcing B's return covenant. However, it is clear, as was suggested by *Boone* and later cases, that the comparative importance of the broken promise to that which is fulfilled is material to whether B's covenant is enforced (looking at it from a different perspective, B is excused from performing). This first situation is one which follows the fact pattern of *Boone*. However, the logic in the principle is also applicable to a second situation. Here, A has partly performed a single covenant, but defaults part way through. His ability to recover on B's counter-promise depends on the extent of the part performance and materiality of the breach. Again the key is to compare the importance of what he has not performed with what he has.

There is another, incorrect way, of understanding the 'whole' and 'part' distinction. This alternative reading would focus on the first sentence, and would infer from the word 'whole' that only a total failure of consideration would prevent A from enforcing B's return promise or that B would only be excused from performing its promise in these circumstances. However, such a reading would be counter-intuitive, ignoring the second sentence and the case law which applied the *Boone* principle, all of which state the inquiry in terms of the importance of what was performed to what was not (what I will refer to as substantial/non-substantial performance).

As it reinforces the point earlier, it is worth pointing out that the relative ease with which later case law understood the whole/part distinction perhaps indicates a pre-existing familiarity with the principle enunciated in *Boone*.[55]

(3) The context of the *Boone* principle was, as the first sentence shows, a case where one performance was a condition precedent to another. It is in these circumstances that, employing the example in (2) above, B may say that 'your failure to perform (since it was a condition precedent to my performance) excuses my obligation to perform'. *Boone* shows that B's ability to make this argument depends on the quality of A's failure because if it is non-substantial then the court responds to B's argument by treating the contractual promises as independent. Two points can be made against this background:

(a) Is the *Boone* principle limited to the context where one's party's performance is a condition precedent to the other party's performance or where each party is to perform concurrently (concurrent conditions) as well (together 'dependent promises')? Despite the wording of the *Boone* principle, its applicability to dependent promises generally appears to have been uncontroversial because, as we shall see later, it was in sales cases (a common example of concurrent conditions) that the appearance of the *Boone* principle was crystallised in the form we know it today.[56] That *Boone* should apply to cases of condition precedent and concurrent conditions rather than just the former makes sense since the 'requirements for a plaintiff whose right is subject to a concurrent condition are qualified in the

---

[55] See part II, section B(ii) above.
[56] See part II, section D(ii) below. It may be a telling fact that when Serjeant Williams replicated the *Boone* principle in rules 3 and 4 of his notes to *Pordage*, the words condition precedent are omitted: see text to n 65 below.

same way as the requirements of one whose rights are subject to a condition precedent'.[57]

(b) The *Boone* principle relied on the laws relating to conditions and performance generally for its operation. Against the background of dependent promises, any failure by A would usually have justified B's refusal to perform its dependent promise. But the *Boone* principle intervened to deny B any justification by treating the promises of A and B as independent. However, if A had failed to perform substantially then the promises would be treated as dependent and B would then be justified in his refusal to perform.

(4) The *Boone* principle was not fully compatible with the idea of fidelity to the parties' intentions, for it operated to ignore these intentions depending on the effect of the breach (ie when the contract was executed (full or partial)). This tension was inevitable, as our previous discussion showed, otherwise one party would have unfairly benefited with part performance without having to pay.[58]

However, the *Boone* principle appeared to assume that some sort of performance had occurred. What would happen if the contract had not yet been performed, if it had remained predominantly executory? The answer came in *St Albans v Shore* ('*St Albans*'),[59] where the court applied the *Boone* principle to this stage (executory) as well: did the term in question go to the whole of the consideration or only part? If it went to the whole then the parties intended it to be a dependent obligation.[60]

There was a further problem, because the line between executed and executory contracts was not always clear. For example, if in an executory contract there was information as to the type of future breach, should it be taken into account when determining the type of term and its impact?[61] The answer became clearer when, in the course of the nineteenth century, the courts exclusively adopted the a priori approach exemplified in *St Albans*, so that the type of breach (the ex post facto approach illustrated in *Boone*) was no longer a relevant consideration. This was made possible by a clearer vocabulary, in the form of conditions and warranties, which made the parties' intentions easier to ascertain.[62]

(5) The main motivation for the *Boone* principle is helpfully summarised by Serjeant Williams in his influential notes to *Pordage*:

---

[57] Williston (n 3 above) vol II, s 832, 1588.

[58] See text to n 12 above.

[59] (1789) 1 H.Bl 270, 126 ER 158.

[60] With no performance actually rendered, the courts at this stage of the enquiry would usually consider terms that were 'important', 'chief inducements', 'material', 'Pith or essence' or 'essential' as ones that went to the whole of the consideration: see, eg *St Albans* (n 59 above); *Campbell v Jones* (1796) 6 TR 570, 573;110 ER 708; *Ellen v Topp* (1851) 6 Exch 424, 442; 155 ER 609; and *Graves v Legg* (1854) 9 Exch 709, 712; 156 ER 304 (counsel's comments are based on the older cases).

[61] *Hoare v Rennie* (1859) 5 H & N 19, 157 ER 1083, answered this question 'no', laying down that only if the performance was accepted could the contract begin to be considered as executed. In the meantime, the materiality of the breach would be ignored. This was a distinction not without its problems: see *Honck v Muller* (1881) 7 QBD 92, where the criticisms of *Hoare v Rennie* are discussed.

[62] See part II, section D(ii) below.

Hence it appears that the reason of the decision in these and other similar cases, besides the inequality of damages, seems to be, that where a person has received a *part* of the consideration for which he entered into the agreement, it would be unjust that because he has not had the *whole*, he should therefore be permitted to enjoy that part without either paying or doing anything for it.[63]

The reference to the inequality of damages was that if A was not allowed to claim B's return performance because of a non-substantial failure of consideration, then an inequality would arise: B would benefit from a substantial performance without payment, which would cause hardship to A; and this hardship was greater overall than B's hardship in not receiving perfect performance (especially if a solution could be found to remedy the shortfall in damages).

In the previous discussion we saw that it would be wrong to emphasise the novelty of *Boone*.[64] Similarly, it would be wrong to treat *Boone* and *Kingston* as providing a clean break from the older law and setting up some sort of new regime on the law relating to performance. That is, of course, not to undermine the importance of the cases, which represented a definite shift by the end of the eighteenth century in which the dependence of the promises were more readily assumed and a more transparent formula used to adjust for the otherwise unfair results that would arise in cases of dependent promises.

However, the older cases continued to play a role, even though it could be said, at the very least, that a shift in thinking required the courts to revisit the reasoning and relevance of those decisions. However, such a conscious streamlining of an important body of law did not take place during the eighteenth century (indeed it would be difficult to achieve something like it today). All this may explain the very influential set of rules that Serjeant Williams laid down at the end of the eighteenth century to deduce when promises were independent or dependent. His five famous rules sought to synthesise a whole body of law, including many of the older cases which had arguably been taken over:

1. If a day be appointed for payment of money, or part of it, or for doing any other act, and the day is to happen, or *may* happen, *before* the thing which is the consideration of the money, or other act, is to be performed, an action may be brought for the money, or for not doing such other act *before* performance; for it appears that the party relied upon his *remedy*, and did not intend to make the *performance* a condition precedent . . .

2. When a day is appointed for the payment of money, &c, and the day is to happen *after* the thing which is the consideration of the money, &c is to be performed, no action can be maintained for the money, &c before performance . . .

3. Where a covenant goes only to a *part* of the consideration on both sides, and a breach of such covenant may be paid for in damages, it is an independent covenant, and an action may be maintained for a breach of the covenant on the part of the defendant, without averring performance in the declaration . . .

[63] *Pordage* (n 6 above) 320 n 4.
[64] Part II, section B(ii).

4. But where mutual covenants go to the *whole consideration* on both sides, they are mutual conditions, and performance must be averred . . .

5. Where two acts are to be done at the *same time*, as where A covenants to convey an estate to B on such a day, and in consideration thereof B covenants to pay A a sum of money on the *same day*, neither can maintain an action without shewing performance of, or an offer to perform, his part, though it is not certain which of them is obliged to do the first act; and this particularly applied to all cases of sale.[65]

Each rule was supplemented by commentary and illustrations. Rules 3 and 4 were extracted from *Boone*. Williams' rules were extremely influential in the nineteenth century. In many ways, it could be argued that Williams' work had a greater impact on contract law, in terms of style of work and presentation and substance, than the first book published on contract law nine years before Williams' notes.[66] Williams' notes have been criticised by scholars, who argue that Williams' rules were not internally consistent, which in turn created oddities in the law which remain today.[67] It is worth illustrating one of these as it touches on an area with which we are concerned.

Consider rules 3 and 2 and their potential clash: which agreements were adjustable under rule 3 and which were caught by rule 2? The importance of this question lies in the fact that in many contracts, including those relating to building, charterparties and sea carriage, payment was postponed until after performance. If performance was to be strict under rule 2 (so that payment could only be claimed if *perfect* performance was rendered), this caused a potential clash with rule 3, which would apply to allow payment even where the performance was not perfect. In a persuasive account, Stoljar points out that the law's (and indeed Williams') failure to reconcile these two rules gave rise to a number of glosses traceable in the law today.[68] For example, a part-performing servant had to look at quantum meruit for this claim (outside contract), while for a part-performing builder there was greater leeway to claim under the contract. In charterparties, rule 3 intervened to enable freight money to be claimed where carriage had been delayed or was of insufficient quantity; whereas in the same context rule 2 intervened to create a principle that contractual payment would be denied if there was short delivery. More generally, these examples were the source of the principle of pleading which Stoljar described thus:

> where the rendered performance was merely bad or faulty, the claimant could still aver performance and thus recover payment, although his deficiency gave rise to an action or counterclaim against him; but where his performance was short, i.e. terminated prematurely, he was unable to aver performance and therefore remained without a contractual action.[69]

[65] *Pordage* (n 6 above) 320 n 4.

[66] JJ Powell, *Essay upon the Law of Contracts and Agreements* (London, J Johnson and T Whieldon, 1790)

[67] Williston (n 3 above) vol II, s 823; Stoljar (n 4 above) 245–52; and M Bridge, 'Discharge for Breach' (1982–83) 28 *McGill LJ* 867, 877.

[68] Stoljar (n 4 above) 248–50.

[69] *Ibid* 249.

However, the criticism of Williams' rules should be tempered by the reality that to some extent the underlying law itself was communicating mixed messages. As well as criticising the older cases,[70] there were decisions also illustrating the limits of *Boone* and the need to recognise that in some circumstances the specifications of time, and the facts of the case, meant that strict performance was necessary and that any failure should not be adjusted under the *Boone* principle; and to this extent some of the older cases appeared consistent with this goal.[71] The short point is that it would be harsh to blame Williams for the inconsistency in the law.

D. Reception of *Boone* and Establishment of the Dominant Model

It is worth emphasising point (5) in the previous section that,[72] contrary to the way it is presented today or the significance it was to assume, the *Boone* principle was not laid down as an illustration of when a party's performance obligations were discharged. Nevertheless, the seeds for such a development were present, because the effect of the *Boone* principle was to say that a substantial failure of consideration would excuse counter-performance. Although not used in *Boone* itself, the term 'rescission' came to be used to describe the position when the innocent party accepted the substantial failure and discharged the performance obligation on each side. In short, the term rescission assumed a substantial failure of consideration.[73] And it was at this stage that a party could bring an indebitatus assumpsit claim for MHR or quantum meruit.[74] If we replace the term rescission with termination, then what has been described begins to resemble what this book refers to as the dominant model. How we reach this stage will be tracked in this section.

The dominant model did not emerge straight away, something which is less surprising when we consider that the *Boone* principle was competing, as Serjeant Williams' rules showed, with other conflicting rules on performance, which appeared to operate differently depending on the type of contract in question.[75]

---

[70] Eg *Goodisson* (n 35 above), see text to nn 35–9 above.

[71] *Glazebrook v Woodrow* (1799) 8 TR 366, 101 ER 1436. If *Boone* had exclusively defined the province of the law relating to performance, it would have effectively undermined the utility of a condition precedent in certain circumstances, since non-substantial performance would always be tolerated and adjusted for through a damages award.

[72] Beginning at text to n 63 above.

[73] The term 'rescission' is discussed in greater detail in part III, section B.

[74] See Chapter 1, n 1. The fluidity of the definition should be noted. Certainly, by the nineteenth century, indebitatus claims came to encompass the quantum meruit, even though strictly there was no sum certain on which a debt could arise: JH Baker, 'The Use of Assumpsit for Restitutionary Money Claims 1600–1800' in E Schrage (ed), *Unjust Enrichment: the Comparative Legal History of the Law of Restitution* (2nd edn, Berlin, Duncker & Humbolt, 1999) 34, n 13. For present purposes, this fluidity ultimately is not fatal because (1) in so far as they are relevant, the distinctive features of the quantum meruit will be kept in mind throughout the historical discussion; indeed, the quantum meruit is the subject of a separate section; and (2) quantum meruit and indebitatus claims were both considered *at the time* to be non-contractual (distinct from special assumpsit and the requirement for an express promise). See part IV, section B and Chapter 6, part III.

[75] See the paragraph following text to n 67 above.

That the *Boone* principle was able to emerge from such a situation is in large part due to the dominance of sales cases in the nineteenth century, which, as we shall see, provided the arena in which there was a clash between the MHR claim and the special assumpsit claim (part of the general and special counts respectively).[76] It was out of this clash that the dominant model emerged, as a way of explaining the extent to which the MHR claim was subsidiary to the special assumpsit claim. These cases also crystallised the distinction between conditions and warranties, which persists today. The second part of this section will track this development.

Part (i) will look at the pool of cases which are usually cited as best illustrating the subsidiarity of the general counts to the special counts. The aim of this part will be to put these cases into context because, within the broader picture of common law development, they are misleading, unreliable or motivated by concerns unrelated to the inquiry. At best they may communicate the message that the contract must be 'at an end', 'gotten rid of' or 'set aside'. But without an explanation of why this should be so, our understanding is not really aided. Some of the cases could easily be interpreted as going further: the presence of the contract outlaws a claim under the general counts.

(i) Early Forms of Subsidiarity

Two groups of cases fall to be discussed in this part. The first and main group commonly cited are what I will refer to in this section and the rest of the chapter as the 'horse warranty cases'.[77] Representative of the second group are the cases collected in the much quoted article on the difference between rescission and termination for breach in which Shea[78] argues that the contract had to 'go' before the general counts could be used.[79]

In the horse warranty cases, the buyer was claiming back the return of the price he had paid for the horse(s) which turned out to be unsound, in breach of the seller's warranty. The cases then tell us that the claim for MHR can only be successful if the contract has been 'rescinded' or at 'an end'. Where the contract is 'open', the buyer is confined to his claim for damages on the contract. Stated in such compelling terms, one can see why these cases attract so much attention and are seen as laying down the relationship between the MHR and special assumpsit

---

[76] To rely on the special assumpsit required the pleading of the whole contract: Chapter 1, part II, section B. To rely on such a claim would entail the party declaring specially. For indebitatus or quantum meruit claims, a party would be making a general declaration. On the distinction between *special* and *general* declaration, see E Lawes, *A Practical Treatise on Pleading in Assumpsit* (London, W Reed, 1810) 1–2.

[77] *Power v Wells* (1778) 2 Cowp 818, 98 ER 1379; *Weston v Downes* (1778) 1 Doug 21, 99 ER 19; *Towers v Barrrett* (1786) 1 TR 133, 99 ER 1014; and *Payne v Whale* (1806) 7 East 274, 103 ER 105. Out of the modern account reference to them can be found in JH Baker, *An Introduction to Legal History* (4th edn, London, Butterworths, 2002) 373; DJ Ibbetson, *A Historical Introduction to the Law of Obligations* (Oxford, OUP, 1999) 279; and W Swain, 'Cutter v Powell and the Pleading of Claims in Unjust Enrichment' [2003] *RLR* 46, 51.

[78] AM Shea, 'Discharge from Performance of Contracts by Failure of Condition' (1979) 42 *MLR* 623.

[79] *Ibid* 628.

claims. However, the results of the cases are couched in terms which suggest that they were motivated by a procedural concern; the courts were not laying down any definitive principles of subsidiarity. Furthermore, the terms 'open' and 'rescinded' were used loosely and did not correspond to the way they came to be used at the time or subsequently.

Once it had been decided that assumpsit could be used in an action for breach of warranty,[80] as opposed to the more usual way of claiming in deceit, it was unsurprising that the question arose of whether the buyer, instead of claiming damages, could reject the horse and use the general count for MHR to claim the purchase price back. *Power v Wells* (1778) held that 'the money had and received [claim], with no other count was an improper action to try the warranty'.[81] This point is further explained in the oft cited *Weston v Downes* (1778) ('*Weston*') in the same year. Here again, the buyer sought to reject the horse and claim his money. It was proved at trial that the warranty had been given and that the seller had promised to take back the horse if disapproved of and returned within a month. Indeed, the seller had allowed the buyer to return two previous pairs he had taken under this contract, and it was only when the buyer attempted to return the third pair that he refused. The court denied the buyer the remedy of MHR. After declaring himself to be a 'great friend'[82] to this action, Lord Mansfield explained that in the present case it should not be allowed because the seller would then have no notice of the claim against him.[83] For this reason, it was held, the most appropriate way to proceed was to declare specially on the contract. Buller J hints at another distinction by introducing us to the term 'open' contracts: he says that the action would have been allowed if the seller had accepted the goods back for then there was no question of trying the warranty; and since he had not accepted the horse back, the contract would be considered 'open'.[84]

The full extent of this notice requirement is articulated in *Towers v Barrett* (1786), where the term 'open' is contrasted with 'rescinded', a distinction which was to become very influential. In this case the buyer was deemed to have taken the horses back, and so the claim for MHR was allowed. Nevertheless, the judges took the opportunity to explain why the MHR claim was not always the appropriate form of action to take for breach of warranty. In Lord Mansfield's words:

> I said in the case of *Weston v Downes*, that I would guard against all inconveniences which might arise from it, particularly a surprise on the defendant; as where the demand arises

---

[80] *Stuart v Wilkins* (1778) 1 Doug 18, 99 ER 15. See also Swain (n 77 above) 51. M Lobban, 'Contractual Fraud in Law and Equity, c1750–c1850' (1997) 17 *OJLS* 441, 460 (n 116) points out that the practice of employing assumpsit in warranty cases was established earlier. He cites a case from 20 years before *Stuart*, which appears in Sir Dudley Ryder's notebook. This same source, as we saw in Chapter 1 (see text to nn 88–97), showed that much of the famous list enumerated by Lord Mansfield in *Moses v Macferlan* (1760) 2 Burr 1005, 97 ER 676, also reflected earlier case law.

[81] *Power v Wells* (n 77) 819.

[82] *Weston v Downes* (n 77) 24.

[83] Another motivation may have been restricting the expansion of MHR: see Chapter 1, text to nn 166–7.

[84] *Weston v Downes* (n 77) 24–5.

on a special contract, it should be put on record. But I have gone further than that; for if the parties come on trial on another ground, though there happen to be a general count for money had and received, I never suffer the defendant to be surprised by it, unless he has had notice from the plaintiff that he means to rely on that as well as the other ground.[85]

In the case there is a continuation of the use of the term 'open' to describe the fact that the question of the warranty still had to be tried. Unfortunately, the judges used 'rescinded' as a description for when the seller had accepted the goods back under the contract. They further confounded this mistake by talking about it as 'ending the contract'.[86] The contract could hardly be said to be at an end or rescinded, since it was never understood to be discharged retrospectively or prospectively (quite the opposite was true: the contract was closer to being discharged by performance, since the parties had done all that was required of them under the contract). Further, rescission was not necessarily a prerequisite for if, as Lord Mansfield explains in the quotation above, the seller had notice, then the claim for MHR could be brought regardless of whether the horse was accepted back or not.

The important point to note about these cases is that it is clear from the courts' approach that their primary aim was to prevent surprise on the defendant because the declaration for the MHR count (and the indebitatus claims generally) did not reveal the specific basis of the claimant's claim.[87] It was a procedural concern unrelated to any general principle of subsidiarity. As we will see in the next section, in the course of the nineteenth century, as the MHR claim was increasingly employed in the contractual context, the courts became less nervous about the surprise element. This signalled the diminishing influence of the reasoning behind the horse warranty cases. And indeed this is why later decisions were influenced by the vocabulary and the end results of these cases, rather than their reasoning. All this is reflected in the path taken by the law of warranty in the nineteenth century, and the confusing way in which the term rescission was applied and came to be understood.[88]

In relation to the second group of cases, Shea argues that the essential principle of subsidiarity was captured in phrases like 'Where there is an express promise, another promise cannot be implied'[89] or 'Promises in law only exist where there is no express stipulation between the parties'.[90] More generally, he suggests that this

---

[85] *Towers v Barrett* (n 77) 134.

[86] *Ibid* 135.

[87] A discussion from slightly later shows that the scope of the warranty and whether it was breached was by no means an easy question: Anon, 'On the Sale and Warranty of Horses' (1828–29) 1 *Law Mag Quart Rev Juris* 318. As is the case now, the involvement of experts and conflicting precedents as to what made a horse sound or unsound complicated the evidential burden of the parties (329). Also see the cases collected under the heading 'breach of warranty' in the chapter on 'Warranty of a Horse' in H Roscoe, *A Digest of the Law of Evidence on the Trial of Actions at Nisi Prius* (London, Butterworth, 1827) 156.

[88] See part II, section D(ii) and rescission is discussed in part III, section B.

[89] *Chater v Beckett* (1797) 7 TR 201, 205; 101 ER 931.

[90] *Toussaint v Martinnant* (1787) 2 TR 100, 105; 110 ER 55.

is what is meant by the tag, *Expressum facit cessare tacitum,* for which he cites a whole raft of cases. The danger with adopting any of these rationalisations is that they could easily be interpreted as outlawing the MHR claim, or the general counts generally, wherever the initial relationship arises from a contract, something which does not represent the law as we understand it today. This on its own is not critical, but it makes it important to look at the cases he cites in support of his principle. A large number of the cases do not refer to the Latin tag or any variation of it. Taking the horse warranty cases as a typical example of the majority of the cases he mentions, none of them go as far as outlawing the MHR claim where a contract exists.

Looking at the cases which specifically raise the issue, we see that on closer analysis they are more likely to be anomalies than representative of the way the courts viewed the relationship between the two types of counts. *Chater v Beckett* (1797) arose out of the following facts: C claimed that D promised to pay H's debt and C's costs of litigating against H to date if C would stop proceedings. When C stopped proceedings, D paid the debt but not the costs. C's claim for the costs under the contract was rejected by the court on the basis that (a) the (performed) promise to pay the debt was a guarantee within the Statute of Frauds, and (b) the whole contract was 'entire' so that invalidity of the promise to pay the debt also invalidated the promise to pay the costs. C then sought to rely on the general count for money paid to the defendant's use[91] to recover his costs. It was whilst rejecting this claim that Lord Kenyon is said to have spoken the words, quoted above.[92] However, this was not the reason used by the majority (Grose and Lawrence JJ), who had no objection on the general count being raised (they thought it was not proven). Keeping the context of the case in mind, it is likely that what Lord Kenyon meant by his words was that, as the agreement in this case was held void (it is assumed this was intended to mean unenforceable) under the Statute of Frauds, one could not get round this via an implied promise, otherwise the purpose of the statute would be undermined.

In *Toussaint v Martinnant* (1787) ('*Toussaint*') the claimant was trying to enforce a security bond against the defendant. As the defendant had been declared bankrupt, the claimant thought the special count on the bond would fail, and so pleaded generally to recover the pleaded debt. The claim failed, the court holding that as the claimant had an existing security, an implied promise would not be raised to secure another remedy. Buller J went further and stated the principle that 'Promises in law only exist where there is no express stipulation between the parties'.[93] Looking at the cases in which this decision is cited, it seems that its significance lies in the realms of securities and bonds, rather than some broader reflection of when the claimant can or cannot declare generally.[94] Indeed, the only time it appears outside this context,

---

[91] Initially the MHR claim had been pleaded also.

[92] See text to n 89 above.

[93] *Toussaint v Martinnant* (n 90 above) 105.

[94] To take three: *Martin v Court* (1788) 2 TR 640, 100 ER 344; *Howis v Wiggins* (1792) 4 TR 714, 100 ER 1261; and *Peck v Wood* (1793) 5 TR 130, 101 ER 75. Specifically, *Toussaint* had become a leading case on the right of a surety to prove his counter-security against the principal debtor, even though the circumstances were such that the counter-security could not have been enforced on its own terms at

it is used in relation to whether a contract can be implied to cover certain losses. Perhaps the best explanation of *Toussaint* can be found in those cases in which it has been held that, once the contract contains the required remedy, the court will not imply another promise replicating the same remedy.[95]

Other cases cited for the support of the same principle are older and can be interpreted as outlawing the general counts when a special one is available.[96] Ibbetson rightly argues that these cases are more accurately perceived as representing a 'clear—and wholly sensible—rule that a party to an express contract could not simply discard it and sue on an implied contract'.[97] Where the contract could be set aside (eg for breach), the implied contract could be relied upon (in the form of the general counts).[98] This brings us to the best way in which to understand the principle summed up in the Latin tag: 'So long as the express contract continues unexecuted, the maxim is expressum facit cessare tacitum'.[99]

(ii) Establishment of the Dominant Model

Today, one of the most common ways in which the court conducts its enquiry into whether a party's performance obligation has been discharged or not (which in turn provides a gateway for the claim in unjust enrichment) is through the language of conditions and warranties. The distinction between conditions and warranties is in large part due to the jurisprudence that grew up around sales of goods transactions in the nineteenth century, and was later collected and codified in statute. Its enduring legacy was that it provided the most eloquent and simple way of applying the *Boone* principle.

As has been discussed, the only issue in the early warranty cases was whether the MHR count would be a surprise on the defendant or not. This procedural concern was not so extraordinary when one considers that it was still considered unusual

that date (this is because the principal debtor became bankrupt before the counter-security was payable and the surety had yet to pay the creditor). The reasoning was that the counter-security was payable absolutely and could be treated as an existing debt at law (even though the right to enforce it would arise at a future date). On this and the later developments which overturned *Toussaint*, see E Deacon, *The Law and Practice of Bankruptcy* (London, J and WT Clarke, 1827) 289–90; and *Young v Taylor* (1818) 8 Taunt 315, 322; 129 ER 404.

[95] See, eg *Schlencker v Moxsy* (1825) 3 B & C 789, 792; 107 ER 926. *Baber v Harris* (1839) 9 Ad & E 532, 535; 112 ER 1313. In *Toussaint*, the bond would have performed the same function as the indebitatus claim. In the background to this case is the fact that, usually, attempts to make indebitatus do the work of debts on a bond were rejected on the forms of actions grounds and on the basis of the division between specialties and parol contracts. However, the judges did not reject the claimant's argument on the basis that he employed an improper form of action to enforce the debt on a bond. Rather, they achieved the same result by laying down a principle that if a remedy exists, indebitatus assumpsit cannot be resorted to. On relying on general counts to enforce bonds, see *Fenner v Meares* (1746–79) 2 Black W 1269, 96 ER 746. For criticism of this development, and the impropriety of employing general money counts in this context, see *Johnson v Collings* (1800) 1 East 98, 104; 102 ER 40.

[96] *Duncomb v Tickridge* (1648) Aleyn 94, 82 ER 933; *Jacob v Allen* 1 Salk 27, 91 ER 26; and *Weaver v Boroughs* (1725) 1 Str 648, 93 ER 757.

[97] Ibbetson (n 77 above) 279.

[98] *Ibid.*

[99] Lawes (n 76 above) 8.

to declare generally upon a warranty.[100] As the action became more established, the concern with the surprise element disappeared. Indeed, there were a number of cases in the first quarter of the nineteenth century which envisaged that a buyer may reject a chattel for breach of warranty and, as one of his remedies, claim back the price.[101]

An excellent snapshot of the law at the time is given in this quotation from an article on the 'Sale and Warranty of Horses':

> Let us now consider how the rights of the parties are affected by the horse being unsound at the time of the warranty. The contract thus being broken on the part of the seller, it is at the buyer's option either to treat it as a nullity, and release the horse, or to retain him notwithstanding, and bring an action on the warranty. In the former case, the price paid is the measure of damages which he will be entitled to recover in an action, in the latter, the difference between that price and his real value. If he offers to rescind the contract, and return the horse, he may also recover the expenses of his keep, but, in order to [do] this, a positive tender is needed.[102]

As can be seen, by 1829, the buyer as one of his options could rescind and recover the purchase price. There are two points to note about the law at this time. The first is that the *Boone* principle is not traceable at this stage in these contracts, for they were simple sale transactions where the types of breaches did not raise the question about the substantiality of the failure of consideration. The subjects of litigation were obviously substantial failures that would justify excusing performance, and a claim for MHR. The second point to note is the decreasing significance of the horse warranty cases, since the notice requirement was no longer considered a bar to the MHR claim on a breach of warranty.

All this was to change with the decision in 1832 of *Street v Blay* (1831) ('*Street*').[103] In an action by the seller for the price, the buyer resisted on the basis that he could and did reject the horse as it was unsound. It was proved at trial that the horse was unsound at the point of sale and that rather than rejecting it straightaway the buyer had engaged in transactions involving the horse. The court, consistently with the law at the time, as described above, could have found for the seller, treating the buyer's subsequent actions as an acceptance of the horse. Instead, the court took the step of denying the buyer's right of rejection, where the property in the goods had passed. They admitted this principle was contrary to

---

[100] How unusual depends on how well the practice had been established before *Stuart*: see n 80 above. Part of the reason for the uncertainty over allowing assumpsit in this context was the idea that a warranty was a separate undertaking from the main transaction: see S Stoljar, 'Conditions, Warranties and Descriptions of Quality in Sale of Goods (Pt 1)' (1952) 15 *MLR* 425, 425–32, where he also discusses the confusing way in which warranty was defined both as an agreement collateral to, and a representation in, the main contract. Part 2 of the article is in S Stoljar, 'Conditions, Warranties and Descriptions of Quality in Sale of Goods (Pt 2)' (1953) 16 *MLR* 174.

[101] *Curtis v Hannay* (1799, 1801, 1819) 3 Esp 82, 170 ER 546; *Caswell v Coare* (1809) 1 Taunt 567, 127 ER 954; *Parker v Palmer* (1821) 4 B & A 387, 106 ER 978. Many of the cases are collected in Stoljar, (Pt 1) (n 100 above) 436 (see esp n 68). Also see S Williston, 'Rescission for Breach of Warranty' (1903) 16 *Harv L Rev* 465.

[102] See (n 87 above) 332.

[103] (1831) 2 B & Ad 456, 109 ER 1212.

previous cases, but they rationalised this by referring to cases that they felt were more persuasive, namely the horse warranty cases.[104] The court held that these decisions laid down the rule that:

> where the property in the specific chattel has passed to the vendee, and the price has been paid, he has no right, upon the breach of the warranty, to return the article and revest the property in the vendor, and recover the price as money paid on consideration which has failed, but must sue upon a warranty, unless there has been a condition in the contract authorising the return, or the vendor has received back the chattel, and has thereby consented to rescind the contract, or has been guilty of fraud, which destroys the contract all together.[105]

This was a remarkable rationalisation of the horse warranty cases, since nowhere in those decisions is there any mention of the right of rejection and recovery being denied because the property has passed and cannot now be revested. The reason for denying the claim in those cases, as discussed, was a practical concern for a lack of notice; there was no theoretical objection to such a claim, indeed Lord Mansfield envisaged its availability if notice was provided.[106] Moreover, the requirement for notice was no longer a prerequisite. The effect of *Street* was to propertise a distinction of practice and in the end radically change the remedies available to a buyer for a breach of warranty.

The rule laid down in relation to specific goods was extremely influential,[107] but had the potential, despite its exceptions,[108] for harshness in denying the right to reject where it was most needed. Lord Abinger's judgment in *Chanter v Hopkins* (1838) expressed the frustration most memorably:

> A good deal of confusion has arisen in many of the cases on this subject, from the unfortunate use made of the word 'warranty'. Two things have been confounded together. A warranty is an expressed or implied statement of something which the party undertakes shall be part of a contract; and though part of the contract, yet collateral to the express object of it. But in many cases, some of which have been referred to, the circumstance of a party selling a particular thing by its proper description, has been called a warranty; and the breach of such a contract, a breach of warranty; but it would be better to distinguish

---

[104] See n 77 above.

[105] *Street* (n 103 above) 962.

[106] See especially text to n 85 above.

[107] As is evident in s 11(1)(c) of the first Sale of Goods Act 1893: 'Where the contract is not severable, and the buyer has accepted the goods, or part thereof, or *where the contract is for specific goods, the property in which has passed to the buyer, the breach of any condition to be fulfilled by the seller can only be treated as a breach of warranty, and not as ground for rejecting the goods and treating the contract as repudiated, unless there be a term of the contract, express or implied, to that effect*' (emphasis added). The awkward assumption that in a sale for specific goods the parties always intend to pass title immediately (as well as the aforementioned clause see s 18, r 1 of the 1893 Act) was dispensed with in the Sale of Goods Act 1979 (see ss 11(4) and 17(1)).

[108] In *Street* the court held that the principle was confined to sales for specific goods and not (1) 'executory contracts, where an article, for instance, is ordered from a manufacturer, who contracts that it shall be of a certain quality, or fit for a certain purpose' ((n 103) 463); (2) sales where the buyer has the option to test the goods, and must return them as soon as he discovers the defect; and (3) sample sales.

such cases as a non compliance with a contract which a party has engaged to fulfil; as, if a man offers to buy peas of another, and he sends him beans, he does not perform his contract; but that is not a warranty; there is no warranty that he should sell him peas; the contract is to sell him peas, and if he sends them anything else in their stead, it is a non performance of it.[109]

Along with *Barr v Gibson* (1838),[110] this case became the leading authority for the exception to the principle of *Street*: a sale of a chattel by description implied a warranty that it will be of that description. If this warranty is breached, the party will be able to reject the goods and claim the return of the price paid on a consideration which has failed.

The contrasting remedies available in the defective performance of sales concerning specific goods and those sold by description came to be expressed by the terms 'warranties' and 'conditions' respectively.[111] But this was a distinction based on a classification which was not watertight and did not always reflect the commercial realities of a sale contract.[112] Its appeal and enduring quality rested on the explanation the courts began to adopt for the distinction:

> But with respect to statements in a contract descriptive of the subject matter of it, or of some material incident thereof, the true doctrine, established by principle as well as authority, appears to be, generally speaking, that if such descriptive statement was intended to be a substantive part of the contract, it is to be regarded as a warranty, that is to say, a condition on the failure or non performance of which the other party may, if he is so minded, repudiate the contract in toto, and so be relieved from performing his part of it, provided it has not been partially executed in his favour. If, indeed, he has received the whole or any substantial part of the consideration for the promise on his part, the warranty loses the character of a condition, or, so to speak perhaps more properly, ceases to be available as a condition, and becomes a warranty in the narrower sense of the word—viz., stipulation by way of agreement, for the breach of which a compensation must be sought by damages (see *Ellen v Topp* (6 Exch 424–441), *Graves v Legg* (9 Exch 709–716); adopting the observations of Serj. Williams on the case of *Boone v Eyre* (1 H.Bl 273 note (a)), in 1 Saund. 320. d., 6th ed; *Eliot v Von Glehn* (13 Q.B. 632)). Accordingly if a specific thing has been sold, with a warranty of its quality, under such circumstances that the property passes by the sale, the vendee having been thus benefited

---

[109] (1838) 4 M & W 399, 404; 150 ER 1484.

[110] (1838) 3 M & N 390, 150 ER 1196.

[111] Stoljar (Pt 1) (n 100) 436–8.

[112] See Stoljar (Pt 2) (n 100) 174–7, where he shows that the courts adopted flexible definitions of 'specific goods' and 'sales by description' so that the same contract could fall into either category. The reality was that the buyer wanted a remedy for a defective performance, and the idea that his remedial options would depend on the classification of the sale was not popular in the United States: see the early criticism of W Story, *A Treatise on the Law of Sales of Personal Property* (2nd edn, Boston, Little, Brown & Co, 1853) 439 onwards. A number of states had decided not to follow *Street*, and allowed the buyer a right to reject for a breach of warranty. By the beginning of the twentieth century, Williston ((1903) 16 *Harv L Rev* 465; (1904) 4 *Colum L Rev* 195) and Burdick ((1904) 4 *Colum L Rev* 1; (1904) 4 *Colum L Rev* 265) were arguing over what was the predominant rule, if any, across the United States. Williston was arguing that it was a draw, that as many states allowed the right of rejection for breach of warranty as those that did not. In any event, he felt that the rule allowing rejection had the most intrinsic merit, and was the one that he adopted in the US Uniform Sales Act.

by the partial execution of the contract, and become the proprietor of the thing sold, cannot treat the failure of the warranty as a condition broken; (see *Bannerman v White* (10 C.B.N.S 844)); but must have recourse to an action for damages in respect of the breach of warranty. But in cases where the thing sold is not specific, and the property has not passed by the sale, the vendee may refuse to receive the thing proferred to him in performance of the contract, on the ground that it does not correspond with the descriptive statement, or in other words, that the condition expressed in the contract has not been performed. Still if he receives the thing sold, and has the enjoyment of it, he cannot afterwards treat the descriptive statement as a condition, but only as an agreement, for a breach of which he may bring an action to recover damages.[113]

This kind of explanation was far from the minds of the judges who had laid down the distinction in the first place. But it was one which was popular not just within the sales of goods context,[114] indicating the appeal of the condition/warranty distinction for contracts in general.

To repeat, this explanation of the distinction, one which continues today, was that the condition represented substantial failure, thereby justifying rescission and the claim for MHR which followed, whereas a warranty represented a non-substantial failure that would only sound in damages. The extracts nevertheless still imply a more flexible standard to classifying terms and breaches, one which allows the court to allocate different results depending on whether the contract is, broadly speaking, executory or executed. So, in terms of conditions and warranties, the court, it would appear, was free to treat a condition as a warranty if, after execution, it appeared that the breach was minor. This flexible approach was the net effect of *Boone* and *St Albans v Shore,* as discussed earlier.[115] But a number of factors caused the law to discard this flexible approach in favour of one which sought to follow strictly the intention of the parties at the time of the contract, rather than looking at the impact of the breach. This became easier when parties began to express themselves by using the terminology of conditions and warranties.

The first factor was the increasing reference to and applicability of the will theory that made parties' intentions and courts' non-intervention sacrosanct.[116] The second factor was the encouragement given to de facto classification, regardless of the consequences of breach, in sales law, codified in the first Sale of Goods Act.[117]

---

[113] *Behn v Burness* (1863) 3 B & S 751, 755–6; 122 ER 281. See the rather different approach, but one that is nevertheless consistent with *Boone,* in *Lord Gilbert Kennedy v Panama, New Zealand and Autralian Royal Mail Co* (1867) LR 2 QB 580. For an early example see the rationalisation in Dodd, 'Rescission' (1837) 13 *Leg Obs* 241, 244.

[114] Eg neither *Behn v Burness* (n 113 above) and *Lord Gilbert Kennedy v Panama, New Zealand and Australian Royal Mail Co* (n 113 above) were sales of goods cases.

[115] In part II, section B.

[116] Although *Ellen v Topp* (n 60 above) described the flexible rule as 'sound' the following comment by Pollock CB suggests that overriding the parties' intentions was not a step that the courts were entirely comfortable with: 'it is remarkable that, according to this rule, the construction of the instrument may be varied by matter ex post facto, and that which is a condition precedent when the deed is executed may cease to be so by the subsequent conduct of the covenantee in accepting less as in the cases referred to' (441).

[117] See Sale of Goods Act 1893, s 11(1)(c) (sale of specific goods) and s 13 (sale of goods by description).

The third was the convention to treat certain common terms in contracts in the same way.[118]

This approach to classification of terms and discharge continues today.[119] It has attracted criticism, particularly since it outlaws the consideration of the consequences of breach, something that would allow (arguably at the cost of certainty) more justice in cases where there has been a minor breach of a condition.[120] But this shift to delegating the task of defining the terms of the contract to the parties' intentions, as discoverable from the relevant and admissible evidence, to the exclusion of the consequences of the breach, does not diminish, it is submitted, the continuing influence and relevance of the principle laid down in *Boone*.

It is still the case that only breach of a condition (substantial failure) will allow the termination of the performance obligation.[121] The principles of contract represent the idea (primarily through the terminology of conditions and warranties) that only a substantial failure should excuse performance. The fact that *what* constitutes a substantial failure, and at *what* point it should be assessed, can vary from case to case, should not detract from this commitment.

The account above has focussed on sales cases and the MHR claim, but the model which emerged was of general application, as the section on quantum meruit will show. Indebitatus claims in the context of unenforceable contracts under the Statute of Frauds followed the same pattern: the defendant's failure discharged the claimant's performance obligation, allowing him (the claimant) to claim on the general counts.[122] Importantly, by following the same pattern in the context of unenforceable contracts as when the contracts were enforceable, this group of cases show us that the claims therein are truly independent of the contractual claim under the special counts and that it is not the enforceability of the

---

[118] Most commonly in charterparty cases: *Behn v Burness* (n 113 above); *Bentsen v Taylor* [1893] 2 QB 274 (CA); *Maredelanto Compania Naviera SA v Bergbau-Handel Gmbh (The Mihailos Angelos)* [1971] 1 QB 164.

[119] G Treitel, *The Law of Contract* (11th edn, London, Sweet & Maxwell, 2003) 788; and J Beatson, *Anson's Law of Contract* (28th edn, Oxford, OUP, 2002) 134.

[120] For the limits to the strictly a priori approach and possible solutions, see Lord Devlin, 'The Treatment of Breach of Contract' (1966) *CLJ* 192; and G Treitel, 'Some Problems of Breach of Contract' (1967) 30 *MLR* 139. Bridge (n 67 above) 886 *et seq* discusses some of the ways in which the more flexible approach has crept its way into the modern law. More recently, some concession has been made by way of amendments to the Sale of Goods Act 1979: s 15A (added by Sale and Supply of Goods Act 1994, s 4) denies the right of rejection in non-consumer cases where the breach of the condition is 'so slight that it would be unreasonable for him to reject them'.

[121] This point and its source in *Boone* is most clearly expressed in Treitel (n 119 above) 759 and 770.

[122] These cases related to a claimant recovering money paid if the defendant did not show good title (*Adams v Fairbain* (1817) 2 Stark 277, 171 ER 845; and *Gosbell v Archer* (1835) 2 Ad & El 500, 111 ER 193); or where the claimant recovers for services rendered (*Pulbrook v Lawes* (1876) 1 QBD 284; *Scarisbrick v Parkinson* (1869) 20 LT 175; in *Snelling v Lord Huntingfield* (1834) 1 CM & R 20, 149 ER 976, the claim for the work done was conceded) or goods delivered (*Mavor v Pyne* (1825) 3 Bing 285, 130 ER 522).

contract which is 'analytically relevant'[123] but the type of performance given which determined when the general counts could be relied upon.[124]

In conclusion, part II began by showing how the shift to a presumption that contractual performances were dependent posed a challenge for the law: *any* failure by one contracting party (A) would excuse the other contracting party (B) from performing its obligations. Moreover, B could keep the performance A had rendered to B. The *Boone* principle most famously intervened to provide a solution: only a substantial failure of consideration (performance) would justify B's refusal to give counter-performance. Importantly, the *Boone* principle did this through the application of the laws relating to performance and conditions: a substantial failure justifies the refusal to perform because the promises are treated as dependent (one is a condition for the other); a non-substantial failure does not justify refusal because the promises are treated as independent (not conditional upon each other). Although *Boone* itself was not directed to the question, sales cases in particular transformed it into an illustration of the subsidiarity of the MHR claim to the claim on the contract (special assumpsit): only upon a breach of condition, which represented a substantial failure of consideration (allowing what came to be known as rescission), could a party bring a claim for MHR. If we replace the term rescission with termination, then what has been described begins to resemble what this book refers to as the dominant model.

III. Rescission and Total Failure of Consideration

This part will analyse the requirements in the case law that an innocent party's MHR claim would not succeed until (a) the contract was rescinded ab initio, and (b) there was a total failure of consideration. To what extent, if any, did these two requirements represent the law's view of the subsidiarity of the MHR claim to the special assumpsit claim? The importance of this issue lies in the fact that both requirements are potentially inconsistent with the view outlined above, that it is the substantial failure (and hence the laws relating to conditions and performance) which best represents the law's view of the subsidiarity of the MHR claim to the special assumpsit claim, rather than the setting aside of the contract ab intio (rescission) or total failure of consideration.

---

[123] D Ibbetson, 'Implied Contracts and Restitution: History in the High Court of Australia' (1988) 8 *OJLS* 312, 322.

[124] 'The fact that the contract might have been unenforceable in the first place is analytically irrelevant, and in truth this line of cases stands on all fours with such decisions as *Planche v Colburn*': Ibbetson (n 123 above) 322.

A. Total Failure of Consideration

In the absence of an account of the foundation of what today is called the termination precondition, there is a suspicion that perhaps the total failure requirement protected the sanctity and primacy of contract.[125] However, we can now see that the foundation of the termination requirement is failure of consideration and it is aimed at instructing us when the parties are discharged from their performance obligations, leaving the way open for a MHR claim to be made. In this way, the sanctity of the contract is protected; and importantly, it only requires a substantial failure of consideration. So what more is achieved by insisting on the total failure requirement? An answer to this question emerges by looking at the case which is said to have established the total failure requirement.

In *Hunt v Silk* (1804) ('*Hunt*'),[126] the claimant rented a house from the defendant, putting down a £10 deposit, and paying an annual rent of £90. The defendant further agreed to make certain repairs and alterations at his own expense within 10 days of the claimant taking over the lease. Despite a number of requests, the defendant failed to fulfil this repairing obligation and the claimant left the house and brought a claim for MHR to recover the deposit, which was refused. There were at least two[127] concerns which lead to this decision and may tell us something about the total failure requirement: (1) if the claimant's argument were allowed there would be nothing to stop him from trying to rescind after 12 months; and (2) rescission was impossible because the parties could not be put in statu quo.

This first concern replicates that which was addressed by *Boone*, namely that it would be unfair to deprive the defendant of the whole benefit of the lease because of his incomplete performance. Without the judges expressing themselves as such, the court in *Hunt* was simply carrying out the exercise of determining whether the claimant could be excused from his counter-performance by the defendant's failure. Even so, the question of returning the parties in statu quo remains. The inability or reluctance of the law to see beyond the actual return of the thing itself (it would not be possible to return the 10 days enjoyed by the claimant) meant that the decision might be justified: on the logic applied in the case, allowing the claim would have left the claimant with a profit (ie the 10 day stay). As we will see in Chapter 6, as the law of unjust enrichment developed, the requirement of total failure was either ignored or applied to situations where it was difficult to maintain that there was ever a total failure.[128] There are indeed early cases of around the

---

[125] E McKendrick, 'Total Failure of Consideration and Counter-Restitution: Two Issues or One?' in P Birks (ed), *Laundering and Receipt* (Oxford, Clarendon Press, 1995).

[126] (1804) 5 East 449, 102 ER 1142.

[127] I do not focus on the third possible reason of waiver of the breach by the claimant: the contract did not oblige the claimant to pay until the repairs had been done; his subsequent payment was arguably a waiver of the breach.

[128] See Chapter 6, part II, section B(ii). Some relevant examples are collected in AS Burrows, *The Law of Restitution* (2nd edn, London, Butterworths, 2002) 338 *et seq.*

same time which show that the commitment to total failure was not consistent.[129] This leaves the way open to argue that if the courts are more flexible about valuing benefits, the requirement of total failure can be shed.[130]

Nevertheless, the analysis so far shows that, in so far as *Hunt* stood for the requirement of total failure of consideration, its raison d'etre was not protecting the sanctity of contract (the principle in *Boone* took care of this) but the court's commitment to literal restitution. This last point is reinforced when we see that in quantum meruit claims, which were considered part of the same family as indebitatus claims, a total failure requirement never emerged.

B. Rescission

The general assumption of scholars trying to explain the reason why the relationship between contract and unjust enrichment has caused difficulties is that the old cases, such as *Hunt*, proceeded on the basis that discharge for breach operated retrospectively, so that a claim in unjust enrichment could only be brought once the contract was rescinded ab initio.[131] Accordingly then, what is important is not the failure of performance (imported into the law by the *Boone* principle) but the absence of the contract. If this is right then it could cause problems of fit with the modern law where it has been repeatedly held that discharge operates prospectively. As McKendrick put it:

> So, if discharge acts prospectively only, how can a claim be brought the aim of which is to restore both parties to their pre-contractual position? Restitutio in integrum, it can be argued, is a principle which finds its home when a contract is set aside ab initio, for example, in cases of undue influence or misrepresentation, and so cannot be applied where the contract is set aside prospectively.[132]

This problem is said to have been resolved by *Fibrosa Spolka Ackcynja v Fairbairn Lawson Coombe Barbour Ltd* ('*Fibrosa*'),[133] which held that the unjust enrichment claim was not confined to contracts set aside ab initio. This view of the cases and their resolution contradicts the argument in this chapter that it was certain failures of performance, rather than the wiping away of the contract, which best represent the subsidiarity of the MHR claim to the special assumpsit claim; the contract being wiped away literally was not a necessary precondition. This point will be illustrated in the apportioned contract context, where the MHR claim could be

---

[129] In *Beed v Blandford* (1828) 2 Y & J 278, 148 ER 924, the intermediate possession of the property sold was held to defeat the claim for the deposit, whereas the same factor was ignored in *Wright v Newton* (1835) 2 CrM & R 124, 150 ER 53.

[130] An argument considered in detail in Chapter 6, part II, section B(ii).

[131] The following list is not exhaustive: RM Jackson, *History of Quasi Contract* (Cambridge, CUP, 1936) 86; W Holdsworth, *History of English Law* (London, Methuen, 1922–66) vol xii, 520; McKendrick (n 125 above) 225–6; and R Goff of Chieveley and GH Jones, *The Law of Restitution* (7th edn, London, Sweet & Maxwell, 2007) 509 and 511.

[132] McKendrick (n 125 above) 226.

[133] [1943] AC 32.

relied upon to recover an apportioned part of a contract without setting aside the contract ab initio.[134] This part will focus on examples which show that when it mattered, the court did not understand rescission or discharge to be retrospective.

The starting point are the horse warranty cases, which laid down the language of open and rescinded contracts, that was to prove so popular, and which we have encountered already. Here we see the first misuse of the word 'rescission'. As was discussed above,[135] the term rescission in those cases was used to describe the moment when the party returned the horse to the seller and he accepted it back. And as the right to return arose under the contract, this was effectively discharge by performance and not wiping away the contract ab initio, as the terminology implies. Further, this use of the term rescission told us nothing about whether the contract was discharged retrospectively or prospectively.

The best way to test the necessity of whether a contract needed to be rescinded ab intio for a claim on the general counts would have been to identify those cases where, despite a successful claim for MHR, a counterclaim was also allowed. Such cases are extremely rare, but there is a suggestion that courts, faced with such a situation, would not have denied the counterclaim. In *Palmer v Temple* (1839) ('*Palmer*'),[136] a defaulting purchaser of land sought to recover his deposit, fully aware that the defendant would have a cross-claim for the breach of contract. The court appears entirely comfortable with this and allows the purchaser to recover the part payment as MHR, with the following direction as regards the defendant's damages claim:

> But, as the defendant may have his cross action against the plaintiff on the clause in the agreement before cited, the reasonable course would be to refer to arbitration the question whether the damages should be reduced, and to what amount, or whether the defendant is entitled to recover more than 300l. for breach of his contract, giving the arbitrator power to award accordingly.[137]

The argument in the case and the criticism[138] of the decision offered at the time by Sugden,[139] focusses on the question of whether a party in default should be allowed to rely on its own breach to recover, rather than the equally forceful argument (had it been valid at the time) that a MHR claim requires the contract to be rescinded ab initio, which would mean that the innocent party cannot rely on the same contract for its damages claim. It is likely that any such argument would not have been entertained by the court. Nevertheless, the rarity of such actions and the specific facts of the case (no general principle was laid down; the court decided the case on its interpretation of the contract and what it had to say about forfeiture of

---

[134] In part IV, section B.
[135] See text to nn 86–7 above.
[136] (1839) 9 Ad & E 508, 112 ER 1304.
[137] *Ibid* 521.
[138] *Ibid* 513–19.
[139] E Sugden, *Practical Treatise of the Law of Vendors and Purchasers of Estates* (11th edn, London, Brooke & Clarke, 1846) 41.

the deposit) mean that other examples should be looked at to reinforce the argument that discharge was not necessarily considered to be retrospective.

Part of the problem in *Palmer* was the absence of a resale condition in the contract, of which a typical example would be:

> full liberty to rescind the contract, and resell the lot either by public or private sale, without the necessity of previously tendering a conveyance thereof to the defaulter; and the deficiency, if any, by the second sale, together with all charges attending the same made good by the defaulter.[140]

As the earliest edition of the influential book by Sugden on the sale and purchase of estates shows, such terms were much encouraged in contracts.[141] Of more relevance is the content and what it implies: that the rescission of the contract does not avoid the contract ab initio, otherwise the term governing resale and the losses claimed thereunder would go too. Yet, as countless cases illustrate, this is not the case.[142] These cases also show the loose terminology, going from describing the first contract as 'annulled', 'conditional' to 'void',[143] yet none of these tags are accurate because the resale clause and damages shortfall is still recoverable on the contract.

This becomes clearer in the leading case of *Maclean v Dunn* (1828),[144] which concerned the right of resale, when there was no express stipulation for it in the contract. Interestingly, here the defendant tried to resist the claimant's claim for the resale loss on the basis that 'the resale rescinded the contract at all events, and deprived the plaintiff of any right to sue'.[145] Best CJ disagreed, holding that this was inconsistent with the practice of the trade which was 'founded on good sense, to make resale of a disputed article, and to hold the original contractor responsible for the difference'.[146] Although the term rescission continued to be used,[147] this case was seen as a leading decision on the point: on default, the right to resale did not rescind the contract ab initio, rather the resale was evidence of the performance obligation being discharged, leaving the innocent party free to claim its resale loss, if any, on the contract.[148]

---

[140] *Icely v Grew* (1836) 6 Nev & Man 467, 469. This series of reports was not included in the English Reports for editorial reasons (a decision was taken not to include collateral reports) rather than quality: see G Williams, 'Addendum to the Table of English Reports' (1941) 7 *CLJ* 261.

[141] E Sugden, *Practical Treatise of the Law of Vendors and Purchasers of Estates* (1st edn, London, Brooke & Clarke/Butterworth, 1805) 25, advises that such a condition 'should never be omitted'. He cites decisions from the eighteenth and early nineteenth centuries as examples of cases where the court has enforced this condition.

[142] The leading examples are *Hagedorn v Laing* (1815) 6 Taunt 163, 128 ER 996; and *Lamond v Davall* (1847) 9 QB 1030, 115 ER 1569.

[143] All of these expressions can be found in Lord Denman's judgment in *Lamond v Davall* (n 142 above) 1031–2.

[144] (1828) 4 Bing 722, 130 ER 947.

[145] *Ibid* 726.

[146] *Ibid* 728.

[147] This is the reason why Chalmers incorporated the term in the resale provision (s 48) of the Sale of Goods Act 1893.

[148] Diplock LJ provides an excellent summary of the right to rescission in a case involving the resale provisions in the 1893 Act: 'Rescission of a contract discharges both parties from any further liability to perform their respective primary obligations under the contract, that is to say, to do thereafter those

The next set of cases concern the question of the recoverability of interest on a MHR claim. Cases of the period show as established law that upon a claim for MHR, interest could only be recovered if it was stipulated in the contract.[149] If the MHR claim really required the contract to be wiped away, then the contract term allowing interest would be wiped away too, which as these decisions show was not the case.

The final set of cases concern arbitration clauses. If rescission for breach was genuinely retrospective, then these clauses would be considered void as well. Yet by the leading accounts no such rule existed at the time and even fraud was not treated as definitively undermining the arbitration clause in the contract.[150] Indeed, one of the leading cases on the effect of fraud on an arbitration clause[151] arose from a claim for MHR, yet at no stage was it suggested that since the MHR claim required rescission this would wipe out the contract and the arbitration clause with it.[152]

Perhaps the most accurate depiction of the principles in this area is best captured by Treitel's observation that, since practical considerations dictated many of the results in the courts' decisions, it would be unwise to explain them 'by reference to any single theory of retrospective or prospective effect'.[153] Although

---

things which by their contract they had stipulated they would do. Where rescission occurs as a result of one party exercising his right to treat a breach by the other party of a stipulation in the contract as a repudiation of the contract, this gives rise to a secondary obligation of the party in breach to compensate the other party for the loss occasioned to him as a consequence of the rescission' (*Ward v Bignall* [1967] 1 QB 534, 548).

[149] *De Havilland v Bowerbank* (1807) 1 Camp 50; 170 ER 872; *De Bernales v Fuller* (1810) 2 Camp 426; 170 ER 1206; *Fruhling v Schroeder* (1835) 2 Bing NC 77; 132 ER 31; and *London, Chatham and Dover Railway Co v South Eastern Railway Co* [1893] AC 429, where the House of Lords considered many of the cases and approved the principle in *De Havilland v Bowerbank*: 'I think we ought not to depart from the long established rule that interest is not due on money secured by a written instrument unless it appears on the face of the instrument that interest was intended to be paid, or unless it be implied from the usage of trade, as in the case of mercantile instruments' (per Lord Herschell at 440).

[150] The following accounts say nothing that would suggest that when the contract is void so is the arbitration clause; indeed, it seems that the arbitration clause was capable of covering most disputes: S Kyd, *A Treatise on the Law of Awards* (1st edn, London, S Crowder, 1791) 31 *et seq*; A Hammond, *Comyns' A Digest of the Law of England* (5th edn, London, J Butterworth *et al*, 1822) 651 *et seq*; J Caldwell, *A Treatise of the Law of Arbitration* (1st edn, London, J Butterworth, 1817) 1 *et seq*; and F Russell, *A Treatise on the Power and Duty of an Arbitrator* (1st edn, London, W Benning & Co, 1849) 3 *et seq*. The one exception may have been fraud, but even here the leading authority at the time did not rule out the issue of fraud being referred to the arbitrator if the parties so intended: *Wallis v Hirsch* (1856) 1 CB NS 316, 321; 140 ER 131. This echoed the approach of the modern law, which has in the main not viewed the allegation of fraud as automatically knocking out the arbitration clause: *Russell v Russell* (1880) 14 Ch D 471; *Camilla Cotton v Granadex* [1976] 2 Lloyd's Rep 10; *Cunningham v Buchanan Jardine* [1988] 1 WLR 678 (CA). This has been further refined as the law has articulated and become committed to the doctrine of separability (see *Harbour Assurance v Kansa General Insurance* [1993] 1 QB 701). Indeed, the Arbitration Act 1996, unlike its predecessor, omits any express power of the court to revoke the arbitrator's authority or to say that this clause will cease to have effect when there is an allegation of fraud involved. Unless, of course, the fraud vitiates the arbitration agreement itself: see the discussion in D Sutton and J Gill, *Russell on Arbitration* (22nd edn, London, Sweet & Maxwell, 2003) 304.

[151] *Wallis v Hirsch* (n 150 above).

[152] It is suggested that had the court in *Wallis v Hirsch*, *ibid*, in 1856, been faced with the facts of *Heyman v Darwin* [1942] AC 536, they would have reached the same conclusion.

[153] G Treitel, *Remedies for Breach of Contract: a Comparative Account* (Oxford, OUP, 1989) 383.

he is likely to have had recent cases in mind when he made this observation, perhaps the best illustration of it are the older cases considered and referred to above. It is highly likely that the main source for the impression that rescission is *always* retrospective was Cyprian Williams' interpretation of *Henty v Schroeder*.[154]

IV. Apportioned Contracts and Quantum Meruit

This section will look at the MHR claim in the apportioned contract context and the quantum meruit claim in the contractual context.

A. Apportioned Contracts

The dominant model is based on the case when the contract is rescinded. However, there was also the possibility of bringing a claim for MHR for an apportioned part of a contract, without the overall contract being set aside. Although there are fewer instances of such cases, one clear and early example from Lord Mansfield's time is the case of *Stevenson v Snow* (1761) ('*Stevenson*'),[155] in which the claimant, who had been insured, claimed back in an action for MHR part of the premium paid to the defendant insurer. The defendant had insured the claimant's voyage, and the part of the premium claimed related to that part of the voyage that had not been completed. The defendant resisted the claimant's claim on the basis that the contract was entire and the risks of the voyage had blended together such that they could not now be treated as divisible. The claimant argued that the voyage (and necessarily the consideration) was divisible, and in so far as the voyage was incomplete 'part of the consideration fails'.[156] Lord Mansfield allowed recovery, holding that the 'insured received no consideration for this proportion of this premium. And then this case is within the general principle of actions for monies had and received to the plaintiff's use'.[157] The key point in the case was that the voyage was divisible and therefore the voyage could be apportioned accordingly.

The logic at work in *Stevenson* can be seen from a different perspective in cases where there had been a short delivery of goods, which the buyer accepted.

---

[154] (1879) 12 Ch D 666. M Albery, 'Mr Cyprian Williams' Great Heresy' (1975) 91 *LQR* 337, traces how Mr Williams' interpretation of *Henty v Schroder* (1879) 12 Ch D 666, in his popular textbook on the sale of lands, influenced the idea that discharge was retrospective. On the face of it *Henty v Schroder* seems to support this view, but H Walker, 'Rescission of Contracts for Sale of Land' (1932) 6 *ALJ* 49, persuasively argues that the reason for the decision was that 'no damages were claimed in the bill' (50) rather than any principle that a contract was void ab initio upon breach. Perhaps the judge had simply expressed himself casually, like those before him.

[155] (1761) 3 Burr 1237, 97 ER 808.

[156] *Ibid* 1239.

[157] *Ibid* 1240.

Although these cases are in the main about the claim for the price of the goods accepted,[158] the decisions show that had the price for the contracted-for quantity been paid in advance, the buyer would have been able to claim back that part of the price which correlated to the goods not delivered.[159]

The important point to note about the MHR claim in the apportioned contract context is that the contract itself stays on foot; there is no need for or mention of rescission.[160] Overall contract performance need not be discharged. Instead, the right to restitution, as is the case with the dominant model,[161] is best understood in the following way: the transfer of the benefit was conditional on the performance which has failed; or to put it differently, there has been a failure of consideration of an apportioned part of a contract.

B. Quantum Meruit

In assessing the history of this claim during the period when explanations of its basis become more visible,[162] specifically its relationship to special assumpsit, it is important to keep four points in mind.

(1) The first is the meaning of the term quantum meruit:

> Quantum meruit, is a certain action of the case, brought where one employs a person to do a piece of work for him, without making any agreement about the same; in this case it is by law implied, that he must pay for the work as much as shall be reasonably demanded; that is to say, so much as he has deserved.[163]

From a modern perspective, the definition does not lend itself easily to a restitutionary or contractual analysis. For example, it cannot easily be said that an award of what is 'reasonable' will always reverse an unjust enrichment. All this takes us into modern debates on the definition of benefit in unjust enrichment.[164] Its

---

[158] *Oxendale v Wetherell* (1829) 9 B & C 386, 109 ER 143. See also *Shipton v Casson* (1826) 5 B & C 378, 108 ER 141; and *Richardson v Dunn* (1841) 2 QB 218, 114 ER 85. These are further discussed in Chapter 6, part II, section B(i).

[159] This is implied in the cases above and see also *Devaux v Conolly* (1849) 8 CB 640; *Whincup v Hughes* (1871) 24 LT 76, 81; and *Behrend & Co v Produce Brokers Co* [1920] 3 QB 530. See the section 'On Apportionment' in M Pothier, *A Treatise on the Law of Obligations* (Philadelphia, R Small, 1826), vol II, 39, esp 42.

[160] See Chapter 6, part II, section B(ii), esp n 23.

[161] See especially part II, section D(ii).

[162] Baker (n 74 above) 38. Baker, *ibid* 36, explains that generally the action was common form by the time of James I (1603–).

[163] G Jacob, *A Law Grammar; or, rudiments of the law* (1st edn, London, A Ward, 1744) 132. Similar definitions are to be found in the entries on quantum meruit in (there are no page numbers) T Blount, *Nomo-Lexikon, a Law Dictionary, interpreting such difficult and obscure words and terms as are found in our common or statute, ancient or modern lawes* (London, J Martin and H Herringman, 1670); E Coles, *An English Dictionary, explaining difficult terms that are used in divinity, husbandry* (London, R Bonwick et al, 1717); T Cunningham, *A New and Complete Law Dictionary; or, general abridgment of the law* (1st edn, London, W Flexney et al, 1771) vol II. The promise mentioned in these entries is one that was imposed by the courts, as is made clearer in the quotation from Giles, on which also see J Impey, *The Modern Pleader, containing several forms of declarations in all actions* (London, J Butterworth, 1794) 208.

[164] See part (iii) of this section and in Chapter 6, part III.

relevance to the historical discussion arises because the case of *Planche v Colburn* (1831) ('*Planche*')[165] is at the centre of some of the afore-mentioned debates and understanding the definition of benefit, as we will see, provides a helpful starting point to put this case in context.

(2) Connected to (1) above is the fact that one needs to be sensitive to how the quantum meruit was perceived in the older law and now by modern scholarship. It is not uncommon for modern historical scholarship to perceive the quantum meruit as follows: 'When explanations of the doctrine were proferred in the eighteenth century, the general assumption seems to be that *quantum meruit* is not fictitious or restitutionary but is based on contract implied in fact'.[166]

However, this view is predicated upon modern boundaries of contract, which are not exclusively and strictly defined by the express factual promise (as was the case for the eighteenth century and part of the nineteenth century). From the older perspective the quantum meruit was non-contractual,[167] which is why it was generally grouped with the indebitatus claims as an action based on a promise implied in law.[168] When the implied contract language became more commonplace, the quantum meruit was grouped in the same way too.[169] As an example of the contrast between the two perspectives, consider the cases where the quantum meruit was given where a contract clearly existed but the price was not fixed. Like the action for the agreed sum,[170] the quantum meruit in this context is today most likely to be considered a contractual claim.

(3) Thirdly, and perhaps less emphasised in the literature, is that there were a number of neighbouring actions covering the same ground as the quantum meruit, without always being clearly distinguished. Two such claims will be considered below.

The first action for the indebitatus assumpsit could be employed for work and labour if there was a fixed sum, in contrast with the quantum meruit, where the claim was for a reasonable sum.[171] The differences between the actions can be illustrated by the way they would be pleaded: the former would be directed to

---

[165] (1831) 5 Car & P 57, 172 ER 876; (1831) 8 Bing 14, 131 ER 305.

[166] Baker (n 74 above) 38; and Ibbetson (n 123 above) 315–16. See also Barton, who says that contemporary references to the quantum meruit count being implied in law translate in 'our terminology' to an implication of fact: J Barton, 'Contract and Quantum Meruit: the Antecedents of *Cutter v Powell*' (1987) 8 *J Leg Hist* 48, 57.

[167] See n 74 above.

[168] A good example is J Mallory, *Modern Entries, in English; being a select collection of pleadings in the Court's of King's Bench, Common Pleas and Exchequer* (London, R Gosling, 1734–35) vol 1, 299–300 (see para 5). Also see the following where quantum meruit is perceived as based on a promise implied in law: *Pilkington v Peach* (1680) 2 Show KB 135, 89 ER 841; and *Buckley v Collier* (1692) 1 Salk 113, 91 ER 406. See Chapter 1, part II, section A and part III, section A, for references showing that indebitatus claims were based on implied promises in law.

[169] Impey (n 163 above) 160–1 and 208.

[170] See Chapter 1, paragraph following text to n 29.

[171] Determination would be in the hands of the jury, which did not give them the freedom this implies to set any sum, especially as we progress through the eighteenth century: Swain (n 77 above) 51. For the control over juries during the eighteenth century more generally, see Chapter 1, part II section B, text to n 39 onwards.

claiming a fixed sum, whereas the latter would claim 'so much money as he reasonably deserved to have'.[172]

The second action is that relating to wages, which is more difficult to distinguish from a quantum meruit. Nevertheless, the wages claim was more like an indebitatus claim for a fixed sum and was likely to arise in set, familiar employment situations such as those involving 'servants, clerks, and agents'.[173] More pertinently, this claim was considered distinct from a quantum meruit in terms of the amount that could be claimed in certain situations. One large difference was that prevention by the employer would allow a party to claim his whole wages, while a party confined to the quantum meruit was restricted to the reasonable value of what he had done in the same circumstances.[174]

(4) Fourthly, the role of policy should be noted since it plays such a prominent role in the leading cases on quantum meruit. This is because in mariners' contracts the question of when a claim for part performance could be made had wider policy repercussions than in other types of contracts. For example, if the sailors were confident that their part performance would attract an award of a quantum meruit, it was felt that there would be a greater risk of abandonment and a lack of an incentive to save the ship: 'if a ship do not return, but is lost by tempest, enemies, fire, &c the mariners shall lose their wages; *for otherwise they will not use their best endeavours, nor hazard their lives to save the ship*'.[175]

It is against this background that we can begin to understand how the relationship between the quantum meruit and the special assumpsit claim worked. The earliest and most visible passage which is referred to in relation to the subsidiarity of the quantum meruit to the special assumpsit is this passage from the popular book, *An Introduction to the Law relative to Trials at Nisi Prius* ('*LNP*'):

> If a man declare upon a special agreement, and likewise upon a quantum meruit, and at the trial prove a special agreement, but different from what is laid, he cannot recover on either count, not on the first because of the variance, nor on the second because there was a special agreement. But if he prove a special agreement and the work done, but not pursuant to such agreement, he shall recover upon a quantum meruit, for otherwise he would not be able to recover at all: as if in a quantum meruit for work and labour, the plaintiff proved he had built a house for the defendant, though the defendant should afterward prove that there was a special agreement about the building of it, viz that it should be built at such a time and in such a manner, and that the plaintiff had not performed the agreement, yet the plaintiff would recover upon the quantum meruit,

[172] As an example of a declaration containing both claims, see Impey (n 163 above) 212–13.

[173] J Smith, *A Selection of Leading Cases* (London, 2nd edn, A Maxwell, 1841–42) vol II, 20–1.

[174] *Ibid* 19–21. Although Smith does express this option with 'hesitation' (*Goodman v Pocock* (1850) 15 QB 576, 582; 117 ER 577). See also *Smith v Hayward* (1837) 7 Ad & E 544, 112 ER 575. Certainly, works from the eighteenth century treated wages in the mariners' context as a distinct category; no doubt because the claim for work depended on whether freight was earnt by the shipowners: Impey (n 163 above) 261 *et seq*; and C Viner, *A General Abridgment of Law and Equity, alphabetically digested under proper titles with notes and references to the whole* (C Viner, Aldershot, 1742–57) vol XV, 234.

[175] Viner (n 174 above) vol XV, 235–6 (emphasis added). Also see quotation from *Hulle v Heightman*, text to n 187 below.

though doubtless such proof on the part of the defendant might be proper to lessen the quantum of damages.[176]

This rather ambiguous passage raises more questions than it answers. Is the first proposition (contained in the first sentence) indicative of some view of the subsidiarity between the quantum meruit and the claim on contract or, as some appear to argue, a pleading point not responding to this issue but later glossed for this purpose (at the end of the eighteenth century and beginning of the nineteenth)?[177] Consistent with the idea that the proposition was probably expressing a pleading rule, and that at this time the relationship between the two types of claim was not fully worked out, is the confusion caused when we consider the second proposition (contained in the second sentence). Here it is not immediately clear what is the difference between the situations envisaged in each proposition, such that a quantum meruit is outlawed by the special agreement in the first proposition, but not in the second.

It is submitted that the passage was expressing (awkwardly) the subsidiarity of the quantum meruit claim to that for special assumpsit. Taking this passage as its starting point, the ensuing discussion will illustrate the relationship between the two counts in three sections. The first section will show that there is likely to have been an appreciation of the subsidiarity of the quantum meruit to the special assumpsit when the passage was written (albeit that it was not clearly expressed in the passage). It will then track how that subsidiarity developed through the eighteenth and early nineteenth centuries. The second section aims to understand a series of cases which appear to be less concerned with subsidiarity and more concerned with identifying a beneficial performance, before awarding a quantum meruit. The aim of this section is to show that these cases are not inconsistent with those analysed in the first section. Indeed, they are examples of the kind of cases envisaged in the second proposition in the *LNP* quotation above. The final section looks at *Planche*, and what this case tells use about the nature of the quantum meruit.

(i) Subsidiarity

The first proposition in the *LNP* quotation above[178] reflected the idea that a quantum meruit, without more, would undermine the contractual bargain for the same

---

[176] (London, C Bathurst, 1767) 129–30. This first edition was published anonymously, but was 'supposedly' written by Lord (Henry) Bathurst, who was Francis Buller's uncle: Baker (n 77 above) 414. Buller *may* have done much of the research for this work: J Oldham, 'Buller, Sir Francis, first Baronet (1746–1800)' in *Oxford Dictionary of National Biography* (Oxford, OUP, 2004). Subsequent editions were published under Buller's name. In relation to the quotation, the margin of the text cites *Weaver v Boroughs* (1725) and *Keck's Case* (1744) for the propositions in the first and second sentences, respectively. Neither of the reports relied upon were published, and have not been found in MS form: Barton (n 166 above) 54 *et seq.*

[177] Barton (n 166 above) 59–60; Swain (n 77 above) 51–2 does not talk about the passage being glossed, but nevertheless argues that a principle of subsidiarity only really emerged at the end of the eighteenth century; the main architect, according to him, was Lord Kenyon.

[178] See text to n 176 above.

work. In this way the quantum meruit claim had to be subsidiary to the claim on the contract. Although it is difficult to find express discussion of this issue until much later in the late eighteenth and early nineteenth centuries, a good starting point is to return to part of the passage cited earlier from Giles Jacob's *Law Grammar* (1744): 'Quantum meruit, is a certain action of the case, brought where one employs a person to do a piece of work for him, without making any agreement *about the same*'.[179]

This quote hints at the fact that a quantum meruit claim was in some way subsidiary to the special assumpsit claim: if the contract covers the work you have done then you cannot opt to claim on a quantum meruit for the same work; or as Lord Kenyon put it in *Cutter v Powell* (1795) ('*Cutter*'): 'That where the parties have come to an express contract none can be implied *has prevailed so long* to be reduced to an axiom in law'.[180]

Of course, without more this statement may suggest that a quantum meruit would never be possible in the context where an express contract formed the basis of the relationship between the parties. However, such an impression should be resisted because it was understood that in some circumstances a part performing party under a contract could rely on a quantum meruit. Many of these circumstances were recited by counsel on both sides in *Cutter*. For example, the death of a common servant midway through a year's hire did not prevent his estate from claiming his wages; or, in the most common and established set of examples, mariners' cases where the sailor would generally be able to claim wages without full performance where 'the voyage is lost by the fault of the owners, as if one ship be seised for a debt of the owners, or on account of having contraband goods'.[181] Broadly speaking, it was possible to say, as the discussion in Viner's section shows, any prevention or disablement by the sailor's employer would excuse the sailor's obligation to perform fully.[182] This much was well settled by the time of *Cutter*, which is why Dockray rightly points out that there was nothing novel about the case at all.[183]

The most high profile example of a case of prevention was *Hulle v Heightman*.[184] This case arose out of the claimant sailor's claim that the defendant had prevented

---

[179] Jacob (n 163 above) 132 (emphasis added). That the province of quantum meruit is in cases where there is no agreement is also apparent in these early cases: *Pierson v Atkinson* (1672) Freem KB 70, 89 ER 52 and *Lovett v Hobbs* (1679) 2 Show KB 127, 89 ER 836.

[180] (1795) 6 TR 320, 324; 101 ER 573 (emphasis added).

[181] *Ibid* 321. Although note that debates were still possible as to whether some events would excuse full performance. See eg the suggestion in *Curling v Long* (1797) 1 Bos & Pul 634, 637; 126 ER 1104, that capture and recapture of a ship would discharge the sailor, who could then bring a claim for his full wages; this point was debated in the *Beale v Thompson* litigation: (1803) 3 Bos & Pul 405, 127 ER 221; 4 East 546, 102 ER 940.

[182] Viner (n 174 above) vol XV, 235. This is the section relied on for the proposition quoted from *Cutter*, above.

[183] In fact he thinks it is a mystery why it attracted as much attention as it did: M Dockray, '*Cutter v Powell*: a Trip outside the Text' (2001) 117 *LQR* 664.

[184] (1802) 4 Esp 75, 170 ER 647. Subsequent proceedings where Le Blanc J's decision is upheld can be found at (1802) 2 East 145, 102 ER 324.

the voyage from being completed and the claimant from therefore earning his wages. The question for the court was whether the claimant could rely on 'common counts for work and labour'[185] in order to recover money for work he had done on the voyage before the defendant's prevention. Le Blanc J applied the language that had been inspired by *Weston*:[186] was the contract open or rescinded? If it was open, the defendant could not rely on the general counts and would be confined to a claim on the contract. Le Blanc J held that the contract was open and rejected the claim based on the general counts. The reason given echoes the policy decisions which dominated these types of cases:

> That he could see many dangerous consequences from allowing sailors, upon any dis-agreement with the captain to leave the ship; and though the captain afterwards offered to take them back, to hold the contract so completely rescinded, that the sailor should be allowed to proceed generally for work and labour.[187]

Le Blanc J did not think the defendant's actions amounted to the rescission of the contract. There are two points to note about the case. First, the language and approach of the judge to the availability of the claims for work and labour aligned it to the claims for the indebitatus claim for money: only certain actions would qualify as a rescission of the contract, which would in turn open the way for a quantum meruit claim. Secondly, while the principle may have been set, the unfortunate result of *Hulle* was the influence it had on how those principles were applied. The effect of the decision was that it denied rescission in the face of a serious breach, albeit based on the right principles.[188] As Ibbetson[189] has pointed out, this set in motion a very restrictive approach to quantum meruit, one which brought it closer to the principle of *Cutter*, and encouraged an atmosphere in which the general rule became 'that while a special contract remains open, i.e. unperformed, the party whose part of it is unperformed, cannot sue in indebitatus assumpsit to recover a compensation for what he has done until the whole is completed'.[190]

In a series of cases in the 1830s, including *Planche*, it was held that a part performing party could under certain circumstances claim for work done;[191] these decisions represented a cutting back of the restrictive atmosphere post *Hulle*. The principle applied in these cases was being rationalised in the following way in Smith's very influential notes:

> And it is further submitted, that it is an invariably true proposition, that, wherever one of the parties to a special contract not under seal has, in an unqualified manner, refused to perform his side of the contract, or has disabled himself from performing it by his own

---

[185] (1802) 4 Esp 75, 170 ER 647.
[186] See n 77 above.
[187] (1802) 4 Esp 75, 83; 170 ER 647.
[188] In his notes to *Cutter*, Smith criticised the decision on this basis: (n 173 above) vol II, 11–12.
[189] Ibbetson (n 123 above) 318.
[190] Smith (n 173 above) vol II, 11.
[191] As well as *Planche* (1831) the cases were *Withers v Reynolds* (1831) 2 B & Ad 882, 109 ER 1370; and *Franklin v Miller* (1836) 4 Ad & E 599, 111 ER 912.

act, the other party has, thereupon, a right to elect to rescind it, and may, on doing so, immediately sue on a quantum meruit for anything which he had done under it previously to rescission.[192]

Although he uses indebitatus and quantum meruit interchangeably, the potential distinctiveness of the claim for wages is noted by him because of the rule (which he tentatively expresses): 'He may wait till the termination of the period for which he was hired, and may then, perhaps, sue for his whole wages, in indebitatus assumpsit, relying on the doctrine of constructive service'.[193]

As Smith assumed, rescission acts as the gateway to claims based on contracts implied by law, namely the general counts.[194] Rescission was understood in the claims for work and labour in the same way as we have discussed in the indebitatus claim for money: only a substantial failure of performance would enable the parties to rely on the MHR count. Despite this commonality, it is worth recording that the difference between the indebitatus claim for money and that for work done, namely one relates to returnable benefits and the other non-returnable, was noted at the time. Smith in pointing out the difference between *Weston* and *Hulle*, says the following:

> but *Weston v Downes* belongs to a somewhat different class of cases; the action was there brought to recover back the price of a horse in consequence of a breach of warranty; so that it was not an attempt to obtain compensation for work done, or goods delivered, under a special contract; but to recover money paid on a consideration which was alleged to have failed, and this the plaintiff, having accepted the horse, was not allowed to do. *Weston v Downes* therefore belongs to the same class with *Street v Blay* . . . and differs from *Hulle v Heightman*, where the action was not MHR to recover back cash paid on a consideration which had failed, but for work and labour done under a special contract which had been only part performed.[195]

The importance of keeping this in mind is discussed later.[196]

(ii) Beneficial Performance Cases

This section will look at cases which appear not to follow the pattern described above, in that they represent what appears to be a more flexible use of a quantum meruit, one which is less sensitive to the contract and focusses in on the 'beneficial service'.[197] It will be shown that these cases are not in fact inconsistent with those analysed above, and that they cover the situations envisaged in the second proposition in the quotation from *LNP*, above.[198]

---

[192] Smith (n 173 above) vol II, 11–12. Note that he states this principle as distinct from that applied in Cutter, which has been quoted above.

[193] *Ibid* 20–1. And see text to n 171 above onwards.

[194] See also J Chitty, *A Practical Treatise on the Law of Contracts Not Under Seal* (2nd edn, London, S Sweet, 1834) 568–75.

[195] *Ibid* 10–11.

[196] See especially Chapter 6, part III.

[197] *Farnsworth v Garrard* (1807) 1 Camp 38, 170 ER 867.

[198] See text to n 176 above.

The starting point is to appreciate what can be described as the quality/quantity distinction.[199] For example, if I am contracted to sell and deliver five boxes of rice and I deliver three, this would be a question of quantity; whereas if I deliver five boxes of rotten rice, this is a question of a quality. The cases discussed in this section were decided against the background where a party could claim the agreed price (or its equivalent for work done) even if there were a shortfall in quality. The quality objection was the subject of the defendant's cross-action. Such a quality shortfall did not qualify as the kind of part performance which we saw in *Cutter* and *Hulle*, which was then thought to raise a question about the inconsistency with the contract.

It is against this background that we can see why the part performance objection does not arise in these cases; they were about badly performed work: for example, in both *Basten v Butter* (1806) ('*Basten*')[200] and *Farnsworth v Garrard* (1807) ('*Farnsworth*'),[201] the defendant's complaint was that the work was very shoddily done. These cases are notable because, starting with *Basten*, the courts, led by Lord Ellenborough, allowed the defendant to raise their objection in the same claim.[202] Balancing each side was easier with the flexibility provided by the quantum meruit (one could adjust what was reasonable in the circumstances, without clashing with, say, a fixed price contract for work). The way Lord Ellenborough rationalised the inquiry in *Farnsworth*, unsurprisingly, was in terms of beneficial service (in the quotation he explains the background too):

> This action is founded on a claim for meritorious service. The plaintiff is to recover what he deserves. It is therefore to be considered how much he deserves, or if he deserves anything. If the defendant has derived no benefit from his services, he deserves nothing, and there must be verdict against him. There was formerly considerable doubt upon this point. The late Mr Justice Buller thought (and I, in deference to so great an authority, have at times ruled the same way) that in cases of this kind, a cross action for the negligence was necessary, but that if the work be done, the plaintiff must recover for it. I have since had a conference with the Judges on the subject; and I now consider this as the correct rule,—that if there has been no beneficial service, there shall be no pay; but if some benefit has been derived, though not to the extent expected, this shall go to the amount of the plaintiff's demand, leaving the defendant to his action for negligence.[203]

The danger with focussing on just benefit, as the reports of these cases suggested, was that there would be a clash with the principle that the law was well aware of at this time: the defendant should not be forced to accept something which they did not bargain for. This principle reflected a controlling mechanism on a claim that would otherwise encourage officious behaviour. And it is this point which probably explains *Ellis v Hamlen*, a case which otherwise appears anomalous to those already considered in this section:

---

[199] See text to n 65 above onwards.

[200] (1806) 7 East 479, 103 ER 185.

[201] See n 197 above.

[202] Barton (n 166 above) 55–6. The first case to establish this in the warranty sphere was *Fielder v Starkin* (1788) 1 H Bl 17, 126 ER 11. See also the note of the relevant cases in Anon, 'Recoupment' (1872–73) 8 *Am L Rev* 389.

[203] See n 197, 38–9.

The defendant agrees to a building of such and such dimensions: is he to have his ground covered with buildings of no use, which he would be glad to see removed, and is he to be forced to pay for them besides? It is said he has a benefit of the houses, and therefore the Plaintiff is entitled to recover on a quantum valebant. To be sure it is hard that he should build houses and not be paid for them; but the difficulty is to know where to draw the line; for if the defendant is obliged to pay in a case where there is one deviation from his contract, he may equally be obliged to pay for anything, how farsoever distant from what the contract stipulated for.[204]

(iii) Planche

Planche provides a challenge for restitution scholars and has rightly been described as 'difficult'.[205] The problem the case poses is that quantum meruit was allowed in a situation where it is difficult to identify a benefit in *the sense of something with a marketable residuum*. Broadly two strategies have been adopted in the modern analysis: (1) to rationalise the case as a contractual damages claim; or (2) to incorporate the case within an unjust enrichment model by adopting a wider notion of benefit. These strategies are discussed in Chapter 6.[206] This section will examine the historical claims made about *Planche*, some of which are the foundation of the modern analysis. This section will then go on to note what *Planche* tells us about the nature of the quantum meruit claim in the contractual context.

The main historical claims for *Planche* fall into two groups.

(1) One suggestion is that the award in *Planche* was for damages for breach of contract, rather than a quantum meruit. The only reason this is not clear is because of the poor reporting.[207] This is an unlikely interpretation, and as Mitchell and Mitchell argue, the comments of Serjeant Spankie, Tindal CJ and Gaselee J are consistent with the view that the award in *Planche* was taken on the quantum meruit count.[208] What reinforces this impression is the near universal reception of the case, as one where a quantum meruit was awarded, in contemporary works.[209] Certainly one imagines that a writer like Smith would have been happy to criticise

---

[204] (1810) 3 Taunt 52, 53; 128 ER 21.

[205] G Virgo, *The Principles of the Law of Restitution* (2nd edn, Oxford, OUP, 2006) 92.

[206] In part III.

[207] C Mitchell and C Mitchell, 'Planche v Colburn (1831)' in C Mitchell and P Mitchell (eds), *Landmark Cases in the Law of Restitution* (Oxford, Hart, 2006) 87–9 outline the case for such a suggestion (which they ultimately reject): The starting point would be the observation by Patteson J in *Goodman v Pocock* (1850) 15 QB 576, 117 ER 577, that the reports in *Planche* do not tell us on what count Mr Planche was successful. This ambiguity perhaps laid the foundation for Lord Campbell's suggestion in *Hochster v De La Tour* (1852) 2 E & B 678, 694; 118 ER 922, that the claim in Planche was for damages. The evidence provided by Mitchell and Mitchell raises a sufficient doubt in J Edelman and E Bant, *Unjust Enrichment in Australia* (Melbourne, OUP, 2006) 114, who state that 'there is even doubt as to whether the claim [in *Planche*] was for a *quantum meruit*'.

[208] Mitchell and Mitchell (n 207 above) 87–8. Eg Gaselee J says this: 'if . . . the declaration had contained no other count than that founded on the special contract, the plaintiff could not have succeeded': (n 165) 53. Interestingly, the editor of the *Jurist* makes the same point in a note to the report of *Goodman v Pocock* (n 207 above): 14 *Jurist* OS 1042.

[209] Chitty (n 194 above) 448; Smith (n 173 above); and C Petersdorff, *A Practical and Elementary Abridgment of the Common Law* (London, V and R Stevens and GS Norton, 1841–44) vol I, 543.

the report had it misrepresented the award or not been clear in any way.[210] Moreover, even if *Planche* was a damages claim, the quantum meruit could have been claimed on the same facts. So that in so far as any argument could be made to ignore *Planche* (and so avoid the problems it causes) by modern restitutionary theorists on the basis that it is really a damages claim, the reality is that their analysis still has to account for the possibility that an award for quantum meruit could be made in the same circumstances.

(2) The second historical interpretation is one put forward by Kull, which was discussed earlier in Chapter 2, namely that the quantum meruit was considered a gap-filler for parties in the absence of a doctrine of anticipatory breach and the ability to claim for reliance losses.[211] As was explained there, this gap-filling thesis is misconceived because (a) it fails to account for quantum meruit claims where the question of anticipatory breach or reliance losses are not relevant; (b) anticipatory breach was a recognised doctrine at the time of *Planche*; and (c) there is no evidence to show that litigants were consciously looking for alternative ways to claim reliance losses.

Part of the reason for raising these arguments is that *Planche* causes problems as it is difficult to fit into an enrichment analysis, because the defendant was not left with a marketable residuum. This forms an interesting contrast to cases above in which beneficial performance is seen as the key. So to what extent was benefit (in the sense of marketable residuum) essential to a claim for quantum meruit? Here, it is important to stress that *Planche* was not exceptional in allowing a quantum meruit in circumstances where the defendant had not been benefited. Consider the following two case examples. The first is the claim by a shipwright, in *Menetone v Athawes* (1764),[212] for work, labour and materials provided in repairing the defendant's ship, which was burnt down before the repairs were complete. Counsel for the defendant's main argument was that 'the defendant has had no *benefit* from the plaintiff's labour or materials: neither was the plaintiff's *undertaking* performed'.[213] Despite the burning down of the ship, the claimant's claim succeeded. The lack of benefit was not critical here.[214]

The second case is *Bull v Sibbs* (1799),[215] in which A agreed to let lands to B, who in turn permitted C to rent them. In such circumstances, A was allowed to claim the rent due from B. Although the case concerned rent, it reflected the general understanding that it could apply to cases where A requested B to work or confer a benefit on C. B could in these circumstances claim on the general counts against A, even though A did not enjoy any direct benefit.[216]

---

[210] He was happy to criticise *Hulle*: see n 188 above.

[211] Chapter 2, part II, section A(ii).

[212] (1764) 3 Burr 1594, 97 ER 998.

[213] Italics in the original report: *ibid* 1594.

[214] See also *Gillett v Mawman* (1808) 1 Taunt 137, 127 ER 784, in which the general law is stated to be that the claimant may be able to claim for work done, even if it has not benefited the defendant; although such a claim would be subject to the usage of the particular trade. Chitty (n 194 above) 452 makes the same point, citing *Gillett* and *Menetone*.

[215] (1799) 8 TR 327, 101 ER 1415.

[216] JS Saunders, *The Law of Pleading and Evidence* (1st edn, London, S Sweet & A Maxwell, 1828) 956, 960. See also *Ambrose v Rowe* (1684) 2 Show KB 421, 89 ER 1018.

The important feature in these cases is that there is the presence of a request. This is reinforced by the view, noted by books especially in the nineteenth century, that a quantum meruit should not be employed in a way which forces a benefit onto a person.[217] Understanding that a request was important but not a benefit (in the sense of a marketable residuum) for the purposes of a quantum meruit, sets clearer parameters for the inquiry into whether the award in *Planche* can be rationalised in the modern law as one founded on unjust enrichment. The key is to determine what definition of benefit one adopts for the law of unjust enrichment. This issue is discussed in Chapter 6, which looks at the modern law.[218]

V. Conclusion

Our historical tracking of the laws relating to performance and conditions before and after *Boone* has enabled us to understand better the dominant model. A substantial failure of consideration left the innocent party free to escape its performance obligations and to rescind the contract (the point that came to be known as termination) because each performance was treated as dependent (conditional) upon one another. A non-substantial failure of consideration did not allow rescission because the performances on each side were treated as independent (not conditional on each other). And it was only in the substantial failure context that MHR or quantum meruit claims were possible. In other words, it was only when performance of the promises were conditional that MHR and quantum meruit claims, which form the basis of the modern law of unjust enrichment, had a role to play.

This chapter also showed that, in so far as rescission discharged each party from its performance obligation, this was not a necessary precondition for a MHR claim. This is because a MHR claim was still possible in the apportioned contract context without each party discharging its overall contractual obligations. However, the conditionality of the transfer of the benefit was important: the money was paid on condition that there would be a return performance of the portion, and the failure generated the right to the restitution of the value of the money.

Finally, this chapter showed that the subsidiarity of the MHR or quantum meruit claims to the claim on the contract is *not* best understood by the requirements that the contract had to be rescinded ab initio or that there had to be a total failure of consideration. This is because absence of the former did not preclude a restitutionary claim, and the latter requirement is best understood as the court's commitment to literal restitution.

---

[217] Saunders (n 216 above) 958–60; and T Starkie, *A Practical Treatise on the Law of Evidence* (1st edn, London, J & WT Clarke, 1824) vol II, 93. See also Chapter 6, part III.

[218] In part III.

In sum then, what we learn from the historical discussion is that in order to bring a claim for quantum meruit or MHR (which today form the basis of a claim founded on unjust enrichment), the presence of a conditional transfer of a benefit was always necessary, but that rescission (what today is described as termination) of the contract was not. It is submitted, therefore, that a much clearer picture emerges about the availability of a claim founded on unjust enrichment in the contractual context if we focus on the conditionality of the transfer of the benefit. This in turn means paying greater attention to the long-established body of laws relating to performance and conditions. How the law would then look is detailed in the next chapter.

6

The True Role of Unjust Enrichment in the Contractual Context

I. Introduction

THROUGH AN HISTORICAL analysis in the last chapter we showed that a much clearer picture emerges about the role of unjust enrichment in the contractual context if we focus on the conditionality of the transfer of the benefit. Informed by the findings in Chapter 5, this chapter maps out a preferable analysis of the role of unjust enrichment in the contractual context (defined in the introduction as concerning contracts which are (a) terminated for breach, (b) subsisting and (c) unenforceable). It will elaborate on the model outlined in Chapter 4, in which it was explained that the right to restitution of the value of a benefit transferred under a contract should be determined by the resolution of two questions: (1) Was the transfer of the benefit conditional? (2) Has there been a qualifying failure of condition?

The core discussion in the chapter is made up of four parts. Part II is split into four sections. Section A defines what is meant by 'condition' in this chapter and clarifies its relationship with other related ideas and concepts. Section B discusses what is meant by a 'qualifying failure of condition'. What qualifies as a failure depends on whether the contract is apportioned or unapportioned, terms which will be defined in this section. In short, it is only in the context of an unapportioned contract that termination[1] is necessary. Once failure of condition is shown, the right to restitution is still subject to accrued rights to receive performance, and these are discussed in section C. This section will also make an important distinction between accrued rights to receive performance, and conditional rights to do the same. Finally, section D will discuss the principle of prevention. Having covered what is a condition and how it may fail, this section addresses the issue of what happens when one of the parties prevents (and then seeks to take advantage of) the condition from occurring.

Part III focuses on the distinctiveness of the quantum meruit, which essentially arises from the non-returnability of the benefit claimed in such an action. This characteristic gives rise to three particular issues, which form the basis of the discussion through three sections. The issues are that the non-returnability of the

---

[1] As to the choice of this term in favour of say rescission, see Chapter 4, part II.

benefit claimed (1) increases the risk of infringing the recipient's freedom of choice; (2) raises questions about the extent to which, if at all, the value of a claim is to be guided by the contract price, and (3) potentially clashes with the entire contract rule in certain circumstances.

Part IV explains the operation of the failure of condition model, described in this chapter, when the claimant is the party in breach and when the claim concerns the restitution of the value of benefits transferred under an unenforceable contract. Part V illustrates how the failure of condition model fits within the absence of basis model for unjust enrichment laid down by Birks and defended in Chapter 3.

With the detail and operation of the failure of condition model set out in parts II-V, the importance of the contract to the restitutionary claim becomes very clear. This reality is, in part, responsible for one of the main objections to the failure of condition model as laid out in this chapter. This is that restitution upon failure of condition is, or should be, a contractual claim, rather than one founded on unjust enrichment. Part VI will assess this objection.

II. Core Principles

A. Meaning of 'Condition'

The definition of 'condition' adopted in the present discussion will broadly follow that which was laid down by Corbin in his classic and influential article near the beginning of the twentieth century:

> In its proper sense the word 'condition' means some operative fact subsequent to acceptance and prior to discharge, a fact upon which the rights and duties of the parties depend. Such a fact may be an act of one of the two contracting parties, an act of a third party, or any other fact of our physical world. It may be a performance that has been promised or a fact as to which there is no promise.[2]

The word 'condition' is employed in many different senses in common law literature.[3] A common use of the term condition occurs in the discussion of the classification of terms (in contrast to a warranty, for example). But it is important to stress that, while this is a different sense of the use of the word condition, it is not wholly unrelated to the definition adopted here, namely the condition as an operative fact or event (I prefer event as it is in more common usage). This is because a term described as a condition states an event of the type referred to in

---

[2] AL Corbin, 'Conditions in the Law of Contract' (1918–19) 28 *Yale LJ* 739, 743. Also see G Treitel, *The Law of Contract* (11th edn, London, Sweet & Maxwell, 2003) 62; S Williston, *The Law of Contracts* (1st edn, Baker, Voorhis & Co, 1920) s 663; and *Restatement (Second) of Contracts* (Philadelphia, American Law Institute, 1981) introductory note and s 224 ('R2C').

[3] Stoljar identifies 12 different senses: S Stoljar, 'The Contractual Concept of Condition' (1953) 69 *LQR* 485, 486–8.

Corbin's quote above, namely one upon which 'the rights and duties of the parties depend'.

Nevertheless, it is still worth emphasising the two senses of condition because they do not overlap. A seller of goods may deliver goods under a contract before payment (and so fulfil the condition precedent (the event)) which gives rise to B's duty to pay, but if the goods are defective in some way, this may be a breach of the condition of a contract (a term stating some fitness for purpose).[4]

The definition in the quotation requires some further clarification, which will be discussed below.

(1) What is meant by the definition when it describes the condition as an operative fact 'upon which the rights and duties of the parties depend'? The language of duties (in some discussions described as obligations, a term which will be preferred in this chapter) and rights needs to be explained here, to appreciate better the effect of a condition.

The creation of a contract generates rights and obligations.[5] At its very simplest in a contract between A and B, each party can place themselves under obligations through the act of promising. A contractual promise generates an obligation in the promisor. In relation to the performance under a contract, A's ability to call upon B to perform can be instructively described as giving A a right to performance and imposing on B an obligation to perform.

A condition will qualify the promise and its performance. As an example to illustrate the distinction so far, consider the contract where, for value received, B promises to pay A £100 after B's ship comes into port. A's right to the £100 is conditional on B's ship coming into port; and correspondingly B's obligation to perform is conditional on the ship coming into port.

(2) It is worth collecting and emphasising here the different types of conditions. As the quotation makes clear, the event may be an act of a third party, an act of one of the contracting parties, or an act of nature. The important point to grasp is that if neither party has promised to bring the event about then this is called a *contingent condition*. This is in contrast to a *promissory condition*, which refers to the event which one of the parties (at least) undertakes to bring about.[6]

(3) Is there a difference between promise and condition? The discussion so far has used these two terms, which raises the question as to their difference, if any. There are differences between the two, the main ones being as follows:

(1) The fulfilment of a promise discharges the obligation. The occurrence of a condition will either create an obligation or terminate the obligation.[7]

---

[4] Treitel (n 2 above) 789.

[5] Corbin (n 2 above) 741, which is in turn adapted from WN Hohfeld, 'Fundamental Legal Conceptions' (1917) 26 *Yale LJ* 710.

[6] Treitel (n 2 above) 62 *et seq.*

[7] The creation and termination of an obligation is often expressed, respectively, by the terms 'condition precedent' and 'condition subsequent'. In employing these distinctions it is important to keep in mind that they are dependent on a fixed reference point, which itself may be manipulated, so that, as Holmes put it: 'In one sense, all conditions are subsequent; in another all are precedent': OW Holmes, *The Common Law* (Boston, Little, Brown, & Co, 1881) 316. In the contractual context,

(2) The non-fulfilment of a promise is called a breach, which gives a right to damages. The non-fulfilment of a condition will, unless it is excused, prevent the obligation to perform in the other person from arising. Such a failure of condition 'may not create any secondary duty at all, and it will not unless someone has promised that it shall occur'.[8] There are two points to emphasise here: first, that non-fulfilment is not necessarily a breach, which is why it does not result in a secondary duty to pay damages. Secondly, unless expressly provided, a secondary duty of any kind cannot arise. All that a failure of condition can do in this instance is to discharge a party from their obligation to perform. If you want a return of the value of the benefit transferred to the discharged party on the basis of a condition which has failed, then you must look elsewhere for the remedy, namely to the law of unjust enrichment. However, it is often the case that the non-fulfilment of a condition is also a breach, because one of the parties has promised to bring the condition about (promissory condition). The following example will illustrate the points made here.[9]

A, a shipowner, promises to carry B's cargo on his ship to Portsmouth. B promises to pay A the stipulated freight on condition that A's ship sails directly there on its next sailing. A's ship carries B's cargo to Portsmouth, but makes a stop on the way. A's failure to go to Portsmouth directly means that the condition has failed and B's obligation to pay does not arise. However, since A did not promise (and therefore is under no obligation) to carry B's cargo directly to Portsmouth, his failure to do so is not a breach.

Now in contrast consider a variation of the facts, where the failure by A is a non-fulfilment of the condition and a breach of promise. This occurs if the party promises to bring the condition about. This would be the case if A promised to carry B's goods directly to Portsmouth. Now B's obligation to pay still does not arise, but the difference is that A's failure sounds in breach.

Although this example (and others that will be given) is about enforcement of contractual obligations rather than restitution, it should not be thought irrelevant, because the principle is applicable in the claim for restitution too: had B paid the money in advance, the failure by A would potentially give B the right to claim its value back in unjust enrichment. This is because B's payment was conditional on fulfilment by A.

(4) What does Corbin mean when he says 'Some operative fact subsequent to acceptance' in the quotation above? Technically, if conditions are events or facts

---

this distinction has been criticised, with the R2C abandoning it altogether: s 224 (reporter's notes). See also B Harnett and JV Thornton, 'The Insurance Condition Subsequent: a Needle in a Semantic Haystack' (1948) 17 *Ford L Rev* 220. Stoljar (n 3 above) 506–9 argues that the condition subsequent is a ghost (as its work can be done by condition precedent) which should be exorcised. However, in the property context, the distinction may still have relevance because a court should in theory construe a condition subsequent more narrowly (in favour of the person in possession) than a condition precedent, because the effect of the former is to divest someone of their proprietary interest: C Harpum, *Megarry and Wade's Law of Real Property* (6th edn, London, Sweet & Maxwell, 2000) 66–7.

[8] Corbin (n 2 above) 745.
[9] Inspired by *Bornmann v Tooke* (1808) 1 Camp 376, 170 ER 991. See also R2C s 225 (comment e).

which affect the rights and obligations of the parties, then an offer and/or an acceptance can be considered as a condition. However, it is not common to speak of offer and acceptance as conditions, which is why the quotation focusses on events after acceptance.[10] Although this quotation focusses on US law, it is likely to be true of English law too.[11]

(5) It is sometimes said that to qualify as a condition, the occurrence of the event must be future and uncertain.[12] While the event is likely to be uncertain because it is to occur in the future after the contract is concluded, this is not always the case. It may be that the event occurred at the time the contract is concluded or even before, as in a case where the insurance policy insures against a pre-existing loss. This raises the question as to how, then, a past event can ever be future and uncertain. It is likely that the event still qualifies as both future and certain in such a case due to the parties' lack of knowledge about its existence (subjective uncertainty).[13] However, Stoljar has persuasively argued that only the future requirement should be retained on the basis that English law recognises as conditions, events which cannot be considered as uncertain subjectively.[14] He gives the example of the case where a seller promises to pay for the unsoundness of the horse, fully aware that the horse is unsound, but hoping the buyer will not realise the defect. As such 'promises [have] always been regarded as effective, being part of the consideration in exchange for the buyer's price . . . the doctrine of "conditional" uncertainty shows itself to be both irrelevant and faulty'.[15]

(6) It is important to appreciate that an obligation can be, and in complex contracts often is, subject to multiple conditions, all of which qualify the obligation in different ways. The various conditions may be cumulative (in which case the performance is not due unless they all occur); alternative (the occurrence of either one will make performance due), or a combination of both. Here are some illustrations:[16]

(a) C sells a painting to D for £1 million with a right to repurchase (a) if the same price is tendered on or before a certain date and (b) that he is in a state to be able to keep it for his enjoyment.

(a) and (b) here are cumulative conditions which must occur before C has a right to order D to perform his promissory obligation to deliver the painting for the set price.

(b) A purchases land from Mrs B, who cannot get Mr B to sign the deed with her because she is engaged in divorce proceedings with him. A agrees to pay Mrs B £10,000 for the land, and will pay a further £5,000 if any one of the following

[10] R2C s 224 (comment c).

[11] Stoljar (n 3 above) 489–92.

[12] RA Lord, *Williston on Contracts* (4th edn, Rochester, Lawyers Co-operative Pub Co, 1990) vol XIII, s 38.1; and R2C s 224 (comment b).

[13] Lord (n 12 above) vol XIII, s 38.2.

[14] Stoljar (n 3 above) 500–4.

[15] Stoljar (n 3 above) 503.

[16] The examples are based on illustrations 5 and 6 in R2C s 224 (comment d).

occur: (a) Mr and Mrs B sign a deed disclaiming any interest in the land; or (b) Mrs B obtains a death certificate for Mr B (assuming Mrs B survives him); or (c) Mrs B signs a deed disclaiming interest in the land, after she is awarded the land in the divorce settlement.

So in this case A's obligation to perform (pay the £5,000) and Mrs B's right to call upon the payment depend on the fulfilment of any one of the conditions above, any one of which is designed to secure the interest A acquires. What this emphasises is that the notion of the *basis* of a transfer of a benefit can be an oversimplification, because in some cases the benefit is transferred subject to a number of *bases* or simply one of an available number.

With the definition of condition clarified, we can see how the first question within the model proposed here will determine whether the contractual transfer of the benefit (eg money, goods or services) is conditional. The condition will be an operative event which in most cases the other contracting party promises to bring about, such as payment or delivery of goods (promissory condition). The condition could be an event whose occurrence has not been promised by the other contracting party, for example an act of a third party (contingent condition). Once it has been determined that the transfer of the benefit is conditional, the second question in the model put forward here will be whether there has been a qualifying failure of condition.

B. A Qualifying Failure of Condition

What is a qualifying failure of condition depends on whether the contract is apportioned or unapportioned. It is only in the latter case that termination of the contract is necessary. Looking at it from a different perspective, the apportioned and unapportioned contracts classification reflects the two types of restitutionary claims possible in the contractual context, which, respectively, are the recovery of a part of a contract and the full reversal of the benefits transferred under a contract.

The meaning of apportioned contracts and how one can recover a part of the contract, without setting aside the whole, will be discussed in section (i). While it is not difficult to see that the term 'apportioned' contracts is broadly the same as severable contracts, the same analogy cannot be made between unapportioned and entire contracts.[17] The reason why will be discussed in section (ii), as well as the meaning and merits of the *total* failure of consideration requirement.

---

[17] Throughout this book I refer to apportioned/unapportioned and severable/entire *contracts* rather than *obligations*. The reason is that this reflects historical usage and the fact that the account (and the text books in the area) is normally focussing on a single central obligation in a contract, eg the obligation to perform work. It would only start to make a difference if one did have a more complex single contract with lots of different central obligations and then some of those could be entire and some severable, as J Beatson, *Anson's Law of Contract* (28th edn, Oxford, OUP, 2002) 510 and Treitel (n 2 above) 782–4 point out.

(i) Apportioned Contracts

This section will challenge the termination precondition within the dominant model on the basis that it proves too much and prevents a party in some circumstances from recovering an apportioned part of a contract. What I mean by this and how the issue arises can be illustrated through the important and much discussed case of *Roxborough v Rothmans ('Roxborough')*.[18]

For many years, a number of Australian States had imposed an indirect tax on sales of tobacco, whose burden was to fall on the consumer. In operation, the tax was paid by wholesalers of tobacco, who included the tax in their charges to the retailers, who in turn passed on the uplift to the consumer. The background to the present proceedings was the High Court's decision in *Ha v New South Wales*[19] that since the States did not have the jurisdiction to impose such a tobacco tax, it was invalid. With the tax no longer payable, the retailers brought an action against the wholesalers to recover the part of the purchase price corresponding to the tax uplift. They failed at first instance, as well as in the Federal Court of Appeal. The retailers succeeded in the High Court of Australia, who held that since the tax uplift was paid on a consideration which failed, it was recoverable. Two points should be noted about the case. First, the tax uplift was 'treated by both parties . . . as separate from the wholesale price'.[20] Secondly, neither party had breached the contract: the wholesalers had not promised to pay over the tax.

Basing themselves on the dominant model, Beatson and Virgo have criticised *Roxborough* for ignoring the termination precondition. They argue that a restitutionary claim is generally only available in the contractual context 'once the contract has been set aside, for example for breach, frustration or because it is unenforceable'.[21] And in *Roxborough*, this condition was not satisfied because 'the sum was paid pursuant to a contract which remained valid'. The reason to insist on this invalidity is to protect a contract from being undermined by the claim founded upon unjust enrichment. It is what Burrows has called the 'anti-circularity principle':

> According to the anti-circularity principle, a plaintiff seeking restitution of a benefit conferred under a contract or apparent contract must first establish that the contract is invalid . . . this is required in order to break the circularity of holding a party contractually liable to confer a benefit which the law of restitution requires the other party to return.[22]

---

[18] (2001) 208 CLR 516.

[19] (2001) 189 CLR 465.

[20] *Roxborough* (n 18 above) [13] per Gleeson, Gaudron and Hayne JJ.

[21] J Beatson and G Virgo, 'Contract, Unjust Enrichment and Unconscionability' (2002) 118 *LQR* 352, 356. Burrows appears to indorse this conclusion and is certainly committed to the termination precondition: AS Burrows, *The Law of Restitution* (2nd edn, London, Butterworths, 2002) 323 (n 1). Although note that Beatson does not think that termination is always necessary: J Beatson, 'Restitution and Contract: Non-Cumul?' (2000) 1 *Theoretical Inquiries in Law* 83. J Edelman and E Bant, *Unjust Enrichment in Australia* (Melbourne, OUP, 2006) esp 266–7 and P Birks, *Unjust Enrichment* (2nd edn, Oxford, OUP, 2005) 122–4 support the result in *Roxborough*.

[22] AS Burrows, 'Solving the Problem of Concurrent Liability' (1995) 48 *CLP* 103, 114.

The discussion which follows is split into two sections. The first section challenges the Beatson and Virgo line and shows that, in certain cases, a claim founded upon unjust enrichment can be made to recover the value of benefits transferred under a contract which has not yet been terminated. The key is whether the contract is apportioned or not. By displacing the dominant model's insistence on termination and recognising the apportioned contract exception, the first section goes on to show that unjust enrichment may be employed in other types of analogous cases which are not normally thought of as within its domain. The discussion in the first section is based on cases in which the contract determines apportionability. The second section outlines other ways in which the contract becomes apportioned. It will focus on the situation in which a contract becomes apportioned by the parties' actions during the performance of the contract.

(a) Challenging the Dominant Model

The error at the heart of Beatson and Virgo's argument, and the dominant model which it follows, is that it ignores the lessons to be learnt from the law relating to the right of a party to recover an apportioned part of a contract. The most important lesson is that recovery in this context has never required the contract to be terminated.[23] Moreover, the law achieves this without undermining the contract between the parties. Two examples will illustrate this, the first from the sales of goods context.

> A owns a sushi stall and contracts with B for the delivery of 1 box of rice a month, for 12 months. Each box costs £100. A pays the full contract price up front. If one box is found defective, and the contract is considered apportioned and the time for correcting the delivery has passed, it is open to A to reject that box and claim back the £100 he paid for it. He can do this without having to terminate the contract.

The key in these types of cases is that (a) the part you want to recover is apportioned, and (b) the circumstances are such that corrective performance cannot be given under the contract.[24] The most helpful test here is one that I take from the

---

[23] On which, see A Guest (ed), *Benjamin's Sale of Goods* (7th edn, London, Sweet & Maxwell, 2006) ('Benjamin') esp paras 8-083 and 8-084; and *Whincup v Hughes* (1871) 24 LT 76, 83. On the independence of an apportioned part from the rest of the contract see *De Oleaga v West Cumberland Iron & Steel* (1879) 4 QBD 472, 475 ('*De Oleaga*'). The immateriality of termination to recovery is clearer in those cases where the parties' actions apportion the contract (see section (b) below). As those cases show, if the part performance is accepted the contract is enforced to that point. However, the cases do not refer to the contract as one which has been rescinded (which in the modern law is substituted by termination) to the extent the part was not delivered. Accordingly, if payment had been made in relation to the whole contract, the innocent party would be free to recover the part of the purchase price which corresponds to the part not performed: *Stevenson v Snow* (1761) 3 Burr 1237, 97 ER 808; *Devaux v Conolly* (1849) 8 CB 640; and *Behrend & Co v Produce Brokers Co* [1920] 3 QB 530. Note that rescission of the contract was not a precondition to recovery in any of these cases. Also see Chapter 5, part IV, section A.

[24] This function is performed by the termination precondition in unapportioned contracts. In apportioned contracts, the termination equivalent may occur because of the passage of time (see *De Oleaga*, (n 23 above)) or, amongst other possible reasons, the impossibility of carrying out the

Second Restatement of Contracts, namely, that the contract can be considered apportioned when 'it is proper to regard parts of pairs of corresponding performances under a contract as agreed equivalents'.[25] An agreed equivalent identifies discrete transfers of benefits: A transfers money on condition that he will get the agreed equivalent (eg some goods); if the goods are not delivered, the condition fails, and the money paid can be recovered in a claim founded in unjust enrichment.

In the simple case above we can see that one bag is the agreed equivalent of the price paid for it. It is important here to stress that the equivalence follows from what the parties have agreed, otherwise the court in allowing a claim in unjust enrichment would undermine the contract between the parties.

> After watching *Bill Kill*, a famous martial arts film, John persuades Paul, a renowned karate master, to take him on as an apprentice. John agrees to be apprenticed to Paul for five years and pays a fee of £1,000 (which covers the duration of the apprenticeship). Two years into the apprenticeship, Paul decides to become a full time actor, and shuts down his centre. John returns home and now seeks to recover three-fifths of the fee, reflecting the lost years of his apprenticeship. It was accepted that the first two years of the apprenticeship were the most difficult and would require the most teaching from Paul. Accordingly, the first two years were worth more than two-fifths, and in the absence of any guidance from the contract on how to apportion the fees for each year, the court held that the contract was unapportioned. John's claim was rejected.[26]

The court's reluctance is understandable because in the absence of any agreed equivalents in the contract (eg if the parties had assigned monetary values to each year of the apprenticeship), if it acceded to John's claim it would be imposing a value on the first two years of Paul's work, which is unlikely to have been agreed by him.

Against this background, *Roxborough* was correctly decided because part of the purchase price (what I called the tax uplift) was an agreed equivalent of the tax liability (which failed), and therefore an apportioned part of the contract. In this type of case, contrary to Beatson and Virgo, there is no need to terminate the contract.

I now come to a case which may benefit from recognising the apportioned contract exception. Consider the following type of case:[27]

> Roger is the owner of a famous nightclub, Pingfellows. As he is dissatisfied with his security, he decides to contract with a new security firm, FELIX, which comes highly recommended by colleagues. The contract is for a month, with FELIX to provide 10 trained

---

condition attached to the transfer of the benefit due to some outside event (in *Roxborough* this was due to the invalidity of the statute, which was out of the control of both parties).

[25] R2C s 240 (comment b). It must be noted that the United States takes a much stricter approach to what qualifies as an 'agreed equivalent', since it aims to reach a result whereby the 'the injured party will not be required to pay for a part of the performance that he has received if he cannot make full use of that part without the remainder of the performance': R2C s 240 (comment e). The English approach does not go as far as this, as is evident from the cases in which a party is obliged to pay an instalment for services which in isolation are useless to him: see part II, section C(iii) below.

[26] Inspired by *Whincup* (n 23 above).

[27] Inspired by *White Arrow v Lamey's Distribution Ltd*, The Times, 21 July 1995; *City of New Orleans v Fireman's Charitable Association*, 9 So 486 (1891).

security guards, made up of three managers, two guards skilled at advanced first aid, and five regular guards. Roger pays the whole contract price of £10,000 in advance and then goes away on holiday. Upon his return after a month, he finds that FELIX had in fact only provided two regular guards on top of the right number of managers and advanced first aiders. Luckily, there were no security issues in the month FELIX was in charge. Nevertheless, Roger is aggrieved that he had to pay for 10 guards in total and only got seven. He realises that there is a possibility that if he brings a claim for breach of contract he may only recover nominal damages as FELIX's breach did not coincide with any loss. His nephew, fresh from a restitution course, tells him that he may be able to found an action in unjust enrichment to recover the excess paid. Is this right?

This is a novel type of case for which there is no authority. However, the nephew's advice may be right based on the cases and principles we have discussed so far. If it can be shown that the excess can be apportioned from the contract, then it may be recoverable as the nephew suggests. This depends on whether the contract sum is apportioned so that each missing guard's *agreed equivalent* (the price that was paid for them) can be assessed and then recovered. In the absence of this information, the court would not apportion the contract sum for the parties, in the form, for example, of dividing the £10,000 by 10 and then adjusting for the two men missing. This is because, as was shown in the example of the karate master, the more senior members, such as the manager guards, are likely to have commanded higher prices, and moreover not all the money would go to salaries. Any attempt to apportion in these circumstances would be to impose a bargain the parties may not have made.

(b) Other Ways of Apportioning

In the cases discussed so far, apportionability is determined by the contract, but it may be imposed by statute[28] or, as will be discussed in this section, arise as a result of the parties' actions in the performance of their contract. The most common example of this is captured in s 30(1) of the Sale of Goods Act 1979:

> Where the seller delivers to the buyer a quantity of goods less than he contracted to sell, the buyer may reject them, but if the buyer accepts the goods so delivered he must pay for them at the contract rate.

If the short delivery is accepted then the contract is 'severed pro tanto'.[29] If the buyer had prepaid for all the goods, then he may recover that part of the purchase price which corresponds to the goods not delivered.[30] This much is well established and is consistent with the approach to apportionability discussed above: (1) the parties' actions subsequent to the conclusion of the contract have created

---

[28] See Edelman and Bant (n 21 above) 257.
[29] *Oxendale v Wetherell* (1829) 9 B & C 386, 109 ER 143. See also *Shipton v Casson* (1826) 5 B & C 378, 108 ER 141; and *Richardson v Dunn* (1841) 2 QB 218, 114 ER 85.
[30] Benjamin (n 23 above) para 8-046, citing the cases in n 29 above.

agreed equivalents,[31] and (2) the background to these cases is that the seller will no longer make the correct delivery.[32]

The principles applied in this area may help shed light on the claim envisaged by two of their Lordships in *Miles v Wakefield*.[33] The situation envisaged was one where an employee works in the form of 'go slow' during industrial action. Working in this way would entitle the employer to reject and refuse to pay the employee. But what if the work done is accepted and the contract has not been terminated? Lords Brightman and Templeman thought that in such circumstances the employee may be entitled to claim for the work done (and accepted). This suggestion has been criticised on the basis that the contract had not been terminated.[34]

However, if we look at this result within the context of the present discussion, it is defensible on the basis that, like the sale of goods cases just discussed, the employer's acceptance effectively apportioned the contract. Accordingly, the employee could claim for the work done. Crucially, as in the sale of goods cases, the quantum meruit award here would be contractual from a modern perspective.[35] Furthermore, if a situation arose in which money for all the work had been paid for in advance, then it would be possible, it is submitted, to claim back that part of the advance which represented the work not done. This would be a claim for the apportioned part, and it would be founded on unjust enrichment.

(ii) Unapportioned Contracts

As a contrast with apportioned contracts, the term 'unapportioned' is preferred rather than 'entire contracts'. This is because entire contracts deal exclusively with the situation in which one contracting party's complete performance is a condition precedent to the other contracting party's performance obligation.[36] However, unapportioned contracts cover cases where each party's performance obligations may be concurrent.

---

[31] Usually there would be two: the first would be the part accepted and the price set for it; the second would be the remainder of the contractual performance that was not performed, whose value would be the contract price minus the value set for the first agreed equivalent.

[32] As was explained earlier, this fact operates as the termination equivalent in the apportioned contract context: see text to n 24 above. The reason is that a claim for the price (or the return of part of the price) should not interfere with, and therefore undermine, the contractual right a party may have to cure the defective performance. This is also why one party cannot unilaterally decide to apportion a contract; acceptance is important: *Walker v Dixon* (1816–19) 2 Stark 281, 171 ER 647; *Waddington v Oliver* (1805) 2 Bos & Pul NR 61, 127 ER 544; and *Kingdom v Cox* (1848) 5 CB 222, 136 ER 982.

[33] [1987] AC 539, 553 (Lord Brightman) and 561 (Lord Templeman).

[34] G Virgo, *The Principles of the Law of Restitution* (2nd edn, Oxford, OUP, 2006) 338. Compare the approach of Beatson (n 21 above) 96, who indorsed the suggestion and argued that this was the type of case in which a claim in unjust enrichment (in the form of a quantum meruit award) would fill the gap in the contractual allocation of risk. The assumption that the quantum meruit here would be restitutionary (and reversing unjust enrichment) as opposed to contract will be challenged below: see text to n 35 below.

[35] Equivalent to an action for agreed sum; for a contrast with historical perspective of such claims, see Chapter 5, text to n 167.

[36] Treitel (n 2 above) 782.

As an example of a contract which is neither 'apportioned' nor 'entire', consider the way the majority of the High Court of Australia treated the contract in *Baltic Shipping v Dillon* ('*Baltic*').[37] The background to the case is that Mrs Dillon was 10 days into her 14-day cruise when the ship she was travelling on, the *Mikhail Lermontov*, struck a shoal and sank. The fare for the whole trip (US$2,205) had been payable in advance. The shipowner had already refunded US$787.50 (representing five days that had been lost). So in this action she sought to recover the balance of US$1,417 (representing nine/fourteenths of the price). Her action for the restitution of the fare failed in the High Court of Australia. For present purposes, the noteworthy point is the way the majority dealt with the agreement between the parties. They held that 'it would not be reasonable to treat the appellant's right to retain the fare as conditional upon complete performance [ie entire contract] when the appellant is under a liability to provide substantial benefits to the respondent during the course of the voyage'.[38] The distinction was between a contract in which Baltic only earnt the right to retain the payment on completion of the voyage (ie entire contract), and a construction in which the money was earnt at various stages before completion (ie apportioned contract), although the moment at which those stages occurred was not set or agreed (ie unapportioned contract).

In unapportioned contracts, the point of termination, as the historical discussion in Chapter 5 showed, operated as the equivalent of a failure of condition, which discharged both parties and opened the way for a claim in unjust enrichment.[39] And broadly speaking, a substantial failure of consideration was enough for termination to occur. This substantial failure requirement was employed to prevent the contract from being undermined by what were money had and received or quantum meruit claims. So what is the function of a total failure of consideration requirement? And should it be retained? As was explained in the overview in Chapter 4, the discussion of total and partial failure has not been clear in the literature. Moreover, recovery in the apportioned contract context was (and should be) more accurately perceived as a case of total failure in relation to a portion, rather than partial failure of consideration.

The best way to view the total failure requirement is as imposing a condition of counter-restitution:[40] in order to claim back the value of a benefit transferred between A and B, A must be prepared to give counter-restitution[41] of any benefit

---

[37] (1993) 176 CLR 344.

[38] Mason CJ (353) (Toohey and Brennan JJ agreeing). See also Gaudron J (386); and Mchugh J (392).

[39] See generally, Chapter 5, part II, esp section D(ii).

[40] 'The word [ie "total"] therefore appears to stand only for counter-restitution as a precondition of restitution': P Birks, 'Failure of Consideration' in F Rose (ed), *Consensus Ad Idem: Essays in Honour of Guenter Treitel* (London, Sweet & Maxwell, 1996) 193.

[41] By counter-restitution I am referring to a *single process*, in which, to use the example above, A's claim to the benefit transferred and B's claim to benefits received by A, is dealt with as a 'single claim for the difference in value between the two performances': Birks (n 21 above) 226. This is opposed to the two claims approach, where each party, A and B, have their separate claims for the performances conferred. The two claims approach increases the risk that procedural bars or other defences may defeat one party's claim for 'slight reasons': *ibid* 226.

he has received (which constituted the condition of A's transfer). The flexibility of what counts as sufficient counter-restitution within the literature poses a real challenge for the law in this area. The key question is whether it is sufficient in cases of non-returnable benefits to give the monetary value of what was received. There are two views on this issue. Under one view ('the strict model of counter-restitution'), a party can only give counter-restitution of returnable benefits. If what he receives is non-returnable then, despite termination, a claim in unjust enrichment is impossible because total failure of consideration will not be achieved (as counter-restitution of non-returnable benefits is impossible).[42] Under the second view ('the flexible model of counter-restitution'), favoured by the majority of writers,[43] as long as a monetary equivalent can be given, it need not matter that some benefits are non-returnable.

The strict version of counter-restitution represents orthodoxy, and fits the majority of the cases. However, in deciding what is the best course for the law to follow, the arguments for and against each model are not susceptible of easy resolution. The main arguments will now be considered.

(1) The main argument against the flexible model of counter-restitution is that the result it produces sits uncomfortably when compared with those reached in the apportioned contract context. Consider a case such as *Whincup*; under a regime applying the flexible model, the father would get back all the money paid, provided he gave value for the two years of training received by his son. The value would represent a substitute for the fact that the services themselves could not be returned. The problem with this is that it effectively achieves an apportionment of the kind the courts were uncomfortable with.[44]

It could be said that in the counter-restitution case, the court is undertaking a different exercise, one which is motivated to prevent unjust enrichment rather than finding an agreed equivalent, so that only superficially does the final result look like apportionment. Moreover, the approach to valuation is different, since in the apportionment cases, there is a greater commitment to the contract price than in the case of determining the appropriate value for counter-restitution (which could refer to the market price, albeit ultimately capped by the contract price). This last point is perhaps more clearly illustrated in claims for quantum meruit made by a part performing party.[45] In so far as the court allows such claims, they too look like apportionment. Yet the court has not denied such claims for this reason, most probably because the source of the claim and approach to valuation distinguishes them from the exercise carried out when apportioning contracts.

(2) The general common law should take its lead from the Law Reform (Frustrated Contracts) Act 1943 ('1943 Act') in which a restitutionary claim is not

---

[42] The leading proponent of this view is Treitel (n 2 above) 1052–3.

[43] Birks (n 21 above) 120–1; Virgo (n 34 above) 325–6; Burrows (n 21 above) 333–6, 541–2; and Edelman and Bant (n 21 above) 258–60 (counter- restitution to the extent that the benefits are incidental).

[44] See the example discussed in the text to n 26 above.

[45] This is discussed in greater detail below: part III, esp section C.

defeated if the benefit received by the claimant is non-returnable. Were *Whincup* to be decided today, the father would not have been denied relief. It might be argued that frustration is a more exceptional situation (as both parties are not at fault, these cases should be treated differently). However, this would be met with the argument that the common law, prior to the 1943 Act, treated frustration and breach cases as falling under the same principles.

Yet in one sense the frustration context does attract greater sympathy, and is therefore arguably deserving of separate treatment. As Treitel puts it, 'restitution is the payor's only remedy, since frustration provides the payee with a defence to a claim in damages'.[46] The argument here would be that the law is justified in providing a remedy in the frustration context, in order to avoid leaving the parties without redress. The same problem does not occur outside frustration cases because of the availability of a damages claim.

It could also be argued that the way the restitutionary remedy operates under the 1943 Act makes the final result less like a case of apportionment than that reached by the flexible model of counter-restitution. For example, under s 1(2) of the 1943 Act, a claimant's success in obtaining restitution does not in any way depend upon the counter-restitution of any benefits he or she may have received. Indeed, the closest one gets to the issue of benefits received by the claimant is the proviso to s 1(2), under which the defendant can claim for expenditure incurred by him in or for the performance of the contract. The aim of this proviso is less to do with effecting counter-restitution of benefits received and more to do with loss apportionment,[47] something which takes into account the claimant's expenditure too.[48] Not having to assess the benefits received means that the final result reached is unlikely ever to look like an apportionment of the contract, a point reinforced when one sees that the application of the proviso may sometimes mean that the claimant is able to retain the benefits received.[49]

(3) Another reason in support of the flexible model is the way in which equity approaches counter-restitution in non-rescission cases.[50] Consider the case of *Atwood v Maude*[51] ('*Atwood*'), in which the court was prepared to apportion a premium transferred between partners, and then claimed back upon dissolution of the partnership. Birks argued that this case compared favourably to *Whincup*. As a later case explained, the approach taken by the court in cases such as *Atwood* was to treat the 'premium as if it were an aggregate of yearly payments made in advance'.[52] It is not clear what would have happened if, as in *Whincup*, evidence had been led to show that such an assumption would be wrong. It seems that even here the court would be willing to impose a value and apportion for the parties, as a later statute indicates:

[46] Treitel (n 2 above) 1051.
[47] Virgo (n 34 above) 369.
[48] *Gamerco SA v ICM/fair Warning (Agency) Ltd* [1995] 1 WLR 126.
[49] *Ibid.*
[50] Birks (n 40 above) 196–7.
[51] (1868) LR 3 Ch App 369.
[52] *Wilson v Johnson* (1873) LR 16 Eq 606.

where one partner has paid a premium to another entering into a partnership for a fixed term, and the partnership dissolved before the expiration of that term otherwise than by the death of the partner, the court may order the repayment of the premium, or of such part thereof it thinks just, having regard to the terms of the partnership contract and to the length of time during which the partnership continued.[53]

It could be agued that the analogy with equity in this context is dangerous, for the ease with which the court is ready to interfere with the bargain and apportion on the basis of notions of what is 'just' was not reflected in the approach taken by the common law at the time or today.

(4) Another reason in support of the flexible model is one which Birks puts in this way:

> If counter restitution in money is not allowed, there will be increasing tension between the literal meaning of 'total' and the actual practice of the courts, producing in effect an ever more inscrutable and unpredictable notion of constructive total failure which will further blur the line between those cases in which there is a good reason why the plaintiff ought not to have to make counter restitution and others in which the court is merely determined that his right to restitution shall not be obstructed by the less than total failure.[54]

In this passage, Birks is referring to cases in which a claim was allowed despite the absence of total failure. Broadly, the cases he cites concern claims in which the court held there was a total failure of consideration even though the parties had used the subject matter that was later rejected. A representative example is *Rowland v Divall* ('*Rowland*'),[55] where the Court of Appeal held that the buyer was entitled to return a car and claim back the purchase price despite two months' use, on the basis that the seller did not pass good title. That the court held that there was a total failure of consideration in such a case despite the use of the car is something which has been criticised by writers.[56]

Arguing that in *Rowland* the use was not the bargained for benefit (and therefore there was a total failure in respect of the benefit bargained for), runs into problems in other cases which have relied on *Rowland*, and where use was arguably part of the benefit bargained for.[57] In so far as these cases represent an instrumental application of the total failure requirement, they may support the argument for a flexible model of counter-restitution.

However, it should be remembered that the court in these cases is not apportioning the non-returnable benefit (the use of the car, for example) but ignoring it, in order to create an artificial total failure. On this basis it could be argued that the court's approach does not meet the criticism made above of the flexible model, namely that its effect is to achieve apportionment of the contract. These cases would only be persuasive if they accounted for the benefits received.

---

[53] Partnership Act 1890, s 40. This section crystallised the principles in the case law: *Belfield v Bourne* [1894] 1 Ch 521, 527.

[54] Birks (n 40 above) 198.

[55] [1923] KB 500.

[56] See Burrows (n 21 above) 329–31, 334; and Virgo (n 34 above) 31–320, 323.

[57] Treitel (n 2 above) 1054–5.

The arguments above are not easy to resolve in favour of one model. It should be noted that the choice of model one follows does not affect the central thesis of this chapter that the law relating to conditions determines the availability of an unjust enrichment claim in the contractual context. I would tentatively suggest that the law in this area would be best served by the adoption of the flexible model of counter-restitution. That this model may interfere with the parties' bargain (by effectively apportioning the contract for them) is most probably a matter of appearance and must in any event give way to the greater purpose of providing a remedy in a situation where there is a failure of condition (which, as we saw in Chapter 5, is what the termination of the contract represents). As Birks put it, the best way forward would be to 'acknowledge the availability of restitution for failure of consideration subject to counter restitution, in money if necessary, of any partial benefits received by the plaintiff'.[58] Such an approach would have reached, with greater clarity, the results broadly achieved in *Ferguson (DO) & Associates v Sohl*[59] and that ultimately obtained, albeit out of court, by Mrs Dillon in *Baltic*.[60]

C. Accrued Rights

In any account on the consequences of a contract terminated for breach, one of the points emphasised is that 'primary obligations falling due after the date of discharge will come to an end; those which have accrued due at the time may be enforceable as such'.[61] The leading text dedicated to this topic puts the matter in this way: 'Rights of the parties which unconditionally accrued prior to election to terminate the performance of the contract for breach or repudiation are not divested by such election'.[62] What is an accrued right and, more importantly, in what way does it impact upon the claim for unjust enrichment in the contractual context, if at all? This section will aim to provide an answer to this and other related questions. In order to do so effectively, it is important to set out some important distinctions and the scope of this section.

This section is concerned with an accrued right *to receive performance* and not an accrued right *to damages*.[63] Similarly, this section does not discuss terms affecting the parties' obligations which survive termination, such as arbitration, agreed

---

[58] Birks (n 40 above) 201.

[59] (1992) 62 BLR 95. In this case the employer had paid substantial sums in advance to builders for a shop fit. However, the builders repudiated their contract, and the employer then successfully claimed back some of his advance payment, representing the difference between the total payment received by the builders (£2,6738) and the value of the work that they had completed (£2,2065). Rather than maintaining the artificial line (see Burrows (n 21 above) 330) that the money recovered represented a total failure of consideration (as the Court of Appeal reasoned), it would be better to say that the sum recovered by the employer represented 'the amount he had paid less the value of the work which they [the builders] had done for him': Birks (n 40 above) 199. The process of accounting for the value received operates as counter-restitution.

[60] Birks (n 40 above) 199–201.

[61] HG Beale (ed), *Chitty on Contracts* (London, Sweet & Maxwell 2004) para 24-048, p 1399.

[62] JW Carter, *Breach of Contract* (2nd edn, London, Sweet & Maxwell, 1991) 439.

[63] A distinction employed by Carter: *ibid* 439.

damages or exclusion clauses. An accrued right to receive performance from another party enables its holder to enforce that performance *unconditionally*, despite termination (although as we will see, termination is not necessary), because (a) no condition is attached to that performance, or (b) the condition has been fulfilled (either, and most commonly, by the holder of the accrued right or due to some external event). Timing is important, since both the accrued right and the obligation to perform must be due before termination.

Accrued rights to receive performance (ie an unconditional right to receive performance) can be contrasted with a conditional right to receive performance. Such a right arises where its holder's ability to call upon and then retain the performance depends on the fulfilment of a condition which is either (i) the holder's performance, or (ii) the occurrence of an external event/contingent event. Sections (i) and (ii) will explain how, respectively, accrued rights and conditional rights to receive performance arise and their impact on a claim for unjust enrichment.

I add two caveats to the discussion which follows. First, the following observation by the leading text in this area is still probably true, even though it is more than a decade since it was made: 'Determining the existence of an accrued right to receive performance is a complex matter, and the law is still developing'.[64] Indeed, section (iii) below looks at a type of situation in which the cases do not provide a satisfactory answer, and which may be resolved by the conditional analysis which it is submitted underpins the nature of the contractual right to receive performance and the availability of the claim founded on unjust enrichment.

Secondly, it is important to stress that the discussion below relates to the general law and is subject to what the contract may say expressly or implicitly on what is to be considered an accrued right to receive performance (eg when performances are due, whether they can be considered genuine agreed equivalents and when the contract itself is considered terminated).

(i) Accrued Rights to Receive Performance

In order to understand what is meant by an accrued right to receive performance, and its relationship with the claim for unjust enrichment, it is best to look at conditional and unconditional transfers of benefits and performances (I use the words interchangeably). One can start with the more common case of conditional transfers.

(a) Conditional Transfers of Benefits

If A, as the contract states, performs before termination he *may* have an accrued right to the return performance by B, which is a condition (of A's) performance. Consider the following factual variations which impact upon whether A has an accrued right to B's performance or not.

---

[64] *Ibid* 440.

(i) If the time for the return performance was to occur *before* termination, then one can say A has an accrued right to B's performance.

(ii) If the time for return performance was to occur *after* termination, then A does not generally have an accrued right to the return performance. This is because termination discharges both parties' obligations, and in this case this would include B's obligation to provide the return performance.

(iii) However, sometimes the *date* for performance may be after termination, merely as a postponement of a right to the return performance which accrued earlier.[65] Lord Brandon neatly summarised the point made here in *Bank of Boston Connecticut v European Grain Shipping*, when discussing the charterer's obligation to pay freight to the owners:

> it is necessary to consider whether the owners' right to the freight had been 'uncondi-tionally acquired' by them before the termination of the charterparty. The circumstance that, by reason of the first phrase of clause 16, the charterer's obligation to pay the freight was postponed until after termination of the charterparty does not . . . mean that the owners' prior acquisition of the right to freight was conditional only . . . It follows that . . . the owners' right to the freight, having been unconditionally acquired before the termination of the charterparty, was not divested or discharged by such termination.[66]

So what bearing do accrued rights have on a claim founded upon unjust enrichment?

(1) If A does have an accrued right, which has been satisfied (by B's perfor-mance), then a claim in unjust enrichment cannot be relied upon to reverse the transfer of benefit from A to B. Consider the following example: an instalment contract in which John is to deliver a box of mangoes to Peter every month for 12 months. Payment is to be made on the first day of the month, with delivery made at the end of the month. After six months of delivery and payment, John's supplies run out and Peter terminates the contract. Peter cannot claim the restitu-tion of the money paid for the six deliveries of mangoes. This is because the money was paid on condition of delivery each month, and the mangoes have been deliv-ered. There is then no failure of condition in relation to the deliveries before termination; or to use the language of accrued rights: Peter's accrued right to the deliveries of the mangoes each month has been satisfied.

(2) If A does have an accrued right but it remains unsatisfied, then the condi-tion attached to the benefit transferred by A fails, and therefore its value can be claimed back in unjust enrichment. Consider the case of Peter and his mangoes again. This time, after five months of successful deliveries and payments, in the sixth month Peter pays but John fails to deliver. The contract is then terminated by John in the seventh month. Here, Peter's payment at the beginning of the month gave him an accrued right to the delivery of the mangoes (which was to occur before termination). But John's failed business means that Peter will not be able to satisfy his accrued right and therefore the condition of his transfer has failed. He can recover the money paid at the beginning of the sixth month.

---

[65] And this is why the expression 'generally' is used in the first sentence in (ii) above.
[66] [1989] AC 1056, 1099.

(3) If A does not have an accrued right (because B's performance is to come after termination and is therefore discharged), the condition (B's performance) attached to the benefit transferred by A fails and therefore here too A can claim back the value of the benefit in unjust enrichment.

The examples in (1) and (2) above are of apportioned contracts because the issue of accrued rights is more likely to arise in this context. In a lump sum building contract, termination will always occur before the builder has completed performance and therefore obtained an accrued right to the return performance. Thus, on termination the condition to the transfer of the benefit (payment) having failed, a claim in unjust enrichment can be made (in the example discussed it would be for quantum meruit).

The point to be emphasised from this section is that it is in the apportioned contract context that accrued rights have an impact on the claim for unjust enrichment. This is because where an accrued right has been satisfied, there is no failure of condition, as the pairs of performances are agreed equivalents.[67]

So far I have been talking about conditional transfers of benefits. The situation in the case of unconditional transfers of benefits is different.

(b) Unconditional Transfers of Benefits

Such cases are very rare, but consider the following theoretical example, in which A, under a contract, pays £100 to B who is to deliver to A a small painting. A is to pay £50 on 1 January 2007 and £50 on 8 January 2007, and his payments, contrary to most if not all contracts of this kind, are *not conditional* on B's performance, but are genuinely unconditional. If A fails to pay on either date, and B terminates the contract on 9 January 2007, B will have an accrued right to A's payments as they fell due before termination.

A may say that if he pays, he can claim it back anyway because B will not deliver the painting as the obligation to do so no longer exists after termination. This argument would fail because A's payment was unconditional and so technically there is no failure of condition and therefore the money cannot be recovered. Finally, payment by A will satisfy B's accrued right.

Now consider a variation, where A makes the first but not the second payment. If B terminates the contract, he still has an accrued right to the unpaid £50. Can A argue for the restitution of the £50? He cannot, because it was an unconditional payment, and without a failure of condition a claim founded on unjust enrichment is not possible. The idea behind the unavailability of the claim is that A took the risk of no performance; although to give such a windfall to B is something which the common law is unlikely to find acceptable (it would strike it down as a penalty or construe the performances as conditional).

---

[67] See text to n 25 above.

(ii) Conditional Rights

A conditional right to call for performance must be distinguished from the accrued right to do the same. Consider the following example of a contract for the sale of land, which the vendor terminates because of a breach by the purchaser. In such a case, as the payment by the purchaser was to occur before termination, can the vendor call for the purchaser to pay? The right the vendor has to call on the performance is conditional: if he received the money it could only be retained if the condition (in this case the transfer of the land) was fulfilled. Due to the termination, this condition will no longer be fulfilled. Accordingly, the purchaser would always be able to claim the money back in a claim founded on unjust enrichment for failure of condition.

Another much discussed example is Proper's claim in *Rover v Cannon Film Sales (No 3)*.[68] Cannon had granted Proper a licence to show films on Italian television. The licence fee was £1,000,000, payable in three instalments. After paying the first two instalments, Proper refused to pay the third. Cannon terminated the contract and sought to claim the third instalment, a claim which Proper successfully resisted. Leaving aside the question of recovering the first two instalments, we can see that Cannon's right to call upon the third instalment was conditional on the fulfilment of the condition, in this case delivery of the films. As they had failed to make the deliveries, Proper could have claimed the restitution of the money, had they paid it (and probably the first two instalments too).[69]

It is important to stress two points at this stage. First, as with accrued rights, conditional rights to receive performance do not only arise in a contract which has been terminated. For example, the accrued right to receive the performance which constituted an agreed equivalent can arise and be enforced without termination. Also, a condition is not always the promised counter-performance by one of the parties; it can be an outside event.

With these points in mind, we can better understand an aspect of *Roxborough*,[70] namely how could the claim for the return of the tax uplift be allowed in the face of a valid term calling on the transfer of the aforementioned tax? Or to put it differently, was not the claim in unjust enrichment inconsistent with (and therefore liable to undermine) the term which allowed the wholesaler to claim the money? This potential inconsistency has generated either a rejection of the result reached in this case[71] or a suggestion that the result is not objectionable because 'there are . . . cases where restitution has been allowed despite the fact that the claimant's payment was made pursuant to a valid obligation'.[72]

It is submitted that this latter view dangerously expands the province of unjust enrichment and has the capacity to disturb other areas of law. This is because it is

---

[68] [1989] 1 WLR 912.
[69] Burrows (n 21 above) 353.
[70] See text from n 18 above onwards.
[71] See n 21 above.
[72] C Mitchell and J Edelman, 'Restitution' (2006) *All ER Rev* 337, 343.

not clear why in some situations a claim founded on unjust enrichment can trump a valid obligation. Moreover, this suggestion is based on the *appearance* that restitution has been awarded, notwithstanding the inconsistency. However, if we see that the right to call upon the tax uplift was conditional, then there is no inconsistency: the wholesalers could only keep it if the money was payable, which it would not be if the statute was void, as was the case in *Roxborough*. Whether the term calling for payment in *Roxborough* was truly conditional is a question that was not investigated in any great detail in the case, but nevertheless the conditional right analysis could arise in a similar fact situation.

(iii) Difficult Cases

Here, I will consider a particular type of situation in which there is no clear answer in the cases. Under a contract between the parties, Mika is to provide Rick, over a 24-month period, parts of a kit car every month. Each part is valued at a certain fixed price, with the total worked out at £24,000. Rick has paid the money upfront. The contract deliveries are to be made on the 15th of each month, commencing 15 January 2007. Mika failed to deliver the relevant part (door) for July 2007, and the time for curing this defect under the contract has passed. Although the subsequent monthly deliveries continue, Rick is keen to get the money back for the door part not delivered in July. This is because he has found the same door at half price, almost new, from a reliable online source. In the situation set out, there is nothing stopping Rick from recovering his money as the contract is likely to be considered apportioned (the part and money are, as evidenced under the contract, agreed equivalents).[73] The claim for the money would be founded on unjust enrichment: the money was transferred to Mika on the condition that Rick would get the door.

Now consider a variation on the facts. After 12 months Mika, due to financial problems, is unable to fulfil the remainder of the contract, leaving Rick with no choice but to accept this failure and terminate the contract. Rather than sue for damages, Rick wants to give back the parts he has got so far over the 12 months and recover the money he paid for them.[74] Understandably, Rick has no interest in having half the parts needed for a kit car. Although there are not many cases on point, it would appear that such a claim may be possible in cases where parts may be considered part of a larger set.[75]

If such a claim is allowed, then there may be a potential inconsistency with the claim where Rick only sought to recover in respect of the one part (the door) that was not delivered. The clash arises in this way: in the second situation, where Rick terminated the contract, his claim for the return of the money is based on the argument that 'I only paid you the money on the condition that I had *all* the parts for the kit car. The monthly payments were not to be conditional on the return

---

[73] See generally part II, section B(i).

[74] The option of finding the replacements on the Internet is no longer available due to the scarcity of parts and the high demand, now that supply has ceased.

[75] Benjamin (n 23 above) para 8-084, nn 90 and 91.

performance of the relevant part for that month'. However, in order to succeed in the non-repudiatory case considered first, the opposite argument would have to be made, namely that each month's instalment was paid for the return of the part. So the inconsistency comes from treating the monthly payment as conditional on the return performance in one situation, and unconditional in the other. One way out of this is to say that Rick can only recover the money back in the repudiatory case. Another solution would be to say that each instalment paid by Rick was subject to the following two conditions: (1) that the part would be delivered, and (2) that the contract would not be terminated on the basis of a failure by Mika to deliver the remaining parts. Failure of either condition would generate a claim, founded on unjust enrichment, for the restitution of the money paid.

The analysis above may help reach a more satisfactory result in cases concerning non-returnable enrichments, where it is more difficult to assess the agreed equivalent. A good case to consider here is *Hyundai Heavy Industries v Papadopoulos* ('*Hyundai*').[76] The case arose out of a shipbuilding contract between C shipbuilders and offshore companies ('the buyers'), whose payment obligations were guaranteed by D. The contract price was to be paid in instalments. The case arose out of a default on the payment of instalments, which caused C to terminate the contracts and bring the claim for instalments due against D. The House of Lords upheld this claim. This section will focus on the rights the shipbuilders may have had against the buyers. A majority held that, after termination, the builders had an accrued right to receive the instalment from the buyers. How this accrued right arose is not clear from their Lordships' speeches. There are a number of different interpretations.

(1) The buyers' obligation to pay was unconditional, that is it was independent of any counter-performance by the builders. Accordingly, when the date for payment arose (and provided it was before termination), the builder had an accrued right to it. The problem with this construction is that it leaves the builders with a windfall: as the buyers' payment is seen as unconditional, the builders need not give any counter-performance. As one text put it:

> for it would follow from the decision [*Hyundai*] that even if the entire price had been payable in advance, the seller could have both exercised his right of cancellation, so sparing him the necessity of delivering the ship at all, and still have sued for the price.[77]

(2) The second interpretation, perhaps one which was in the mind of their Lordships, was that the accrued right arose because of the work that had been carried out already under the contract. It was, after all, a contract to 'build, launch, equip and complete'. In this way, the instalment was an agreed equivalent of the work that had been done. It could be said that this interpretation is hardly better than the first interpretation, above, since it leaves the buyers in no better position because, depending on the circumstances, they may be left with nothing which can be carried over to another contract, to reflect the money they had paid. Another criticism of this second interpretation is that it:

---

[76] [1980] 1 WLR 1129.
[77] PS Atiyah and JN Adams, *Sale of Goods* (11th edn, London, Pearson Longman, 2005) 483.

is hardly satisfying given that it would extend to a situation in which substantially the entire price is payable in advance, and yet the seller may have incurred only minimal advance expenditure prior to cancellation.[78]

(3) A third view, followed by Beatson (he calls it 'construction')[79] is that the instalment payment is 'required not as security for the performance but as payment for work done'.[80] This seems identical to the second interpretation, except Beatson's approach would give the builders a right to claim the instalment even where there are costs that have not been bargained for; as he puts it: 'Thus, he will be able to keep it or claim it whether or not what he did was part of the bargained for performance'.[81]

One of the problems with Beatson's approach[82] is that it is making a bargain for the parties, as its effect is to impose an equivalent to the buyer's instalment, to which he had not agreed: his instalment was paid to purchase part of the contractual performance not costs outside it which may relate to the performance.

Essentially, it is the second approach which is indorsed in the leading case of *Stocznia Gdanska v Latvian Shipping Co.*[83] Although it may leave one party with a relative windfall, if the principles are clear then the parties are aware of this risk and can adjust for it under their contracts.

The problem with a *Hyundai* type case is that while the parties want the instalments to be payable so that the work can be continued, the money also represents payment for something which can only be enjoyed as a whole. There may be a way to give effect to this duality of intention, one which was considered above in the case of the kit cars.

It could be said that the instalments in a case like *Hyundai* were subject to two conditions, namely (a) that the money was transferred subject to the work relating to the particular instalment being done, and (b) that the contract would not be terminated. If either condition failed, the money can be recovered, with the other party having a claim for the restitution of the value of the benefit transferred to the buyer: either a quantum meruit for the services or the money it has paid. One of the advantages of this approach in the situation envisaged above (where a party received the bulk of the money for very little work done) is that if the contract is terminated, then the part performing party will only get money for the work that has been performed, rather than the greater sum which effectively would leave it with a windfall.

By way of conclusion then, A's right to receive B's performance under a contract between the parties may be *conditional* or *unconditional*. If it is unconditional it is called an accrued right. The unconditionality arises either because (a) no condition is attached to B's performance, or (b) the condition to B's performance has

---

[78] *Ibid* 484.
[79] J Beatson, *The Use and Abuse of Unjust Enrichment* (Oxford, Clarendon, 1991) 57.
[80] *Ibid* 57.
[81] *Ibid* 59.
[82] It should be added that Beatson does not claim his solution is perfect: *Ibid* 60–1.
[83] [1998] 1 WLR 574.

been fulfilled (either, and most commonly, by the holder of the accrued right or due to some external event). Where A's performance gives it an accrued right to B's performance, then a claim founded on unjust enrichment for the restitution of the value of A's performance will (a) fail where the accrued right is satisfied (by B's performance) because in such a case there is no identifiable failure of condition, or (b) succeed if B does not perform, for then the condition attached to A's performance will have failed. A contrast to the accrued right is the case where the right to B's performance is *conditional.* Here, if the condition is not fulfilled, any performance by B can be claimed back in an action founded on unjust enrichment.

D. Prevention

Very little attention is usually paid to the doctrine or principle of prevention (I prefer principle) in works on contract and unjust enrichment. Yet this principle is 'very well established'[84] in the common law and should form an important part of any account on the law relating to conditions. A useful definition to begin with is:

> It is a general principle of contract law that if one party to a contract hinders, prevents, or makes impossible performance by the other party, the latter's failure to perform will be excused. This general principle has been referred to as the 'doctrine of prevention'.[85]

Examples of this principle at work include cases where an employer prevents an architect from issuing a certificate or a writer from completing a manuscript, both of which are conditions to the employer's obligation to pay. In both these cases, the employer will not be able to rely on the condition against the claim the other party may bring. So, for example, if the writer seeks to claim for the work done on the manuscript, the employer cannot be heard to say that the delivery of a complete manuscript was a condition precedent to his obligation to pay; and therefore part performance will not suffice. It is important to understand that the reason for this is that prevention excuses the condition, rendering it extinguished in so far as the employer may rely on it.

The independence and scope of the prevention principle is obscured by (a) recent discussion which treats prevention as a basis or a condition of the transfer of the benefit; (b) the unclear relationship of the principle with breach; and (c) the type of claims that are generated once prevention is established. Each of these will be dealt with below.

---

[84] *Roberts v Bury Improvement Commissioners* [1870] LR 5 CP 310, 326. For leading texts on this topic across the centuries, see J Comyns, *A Digest of the Laws of England* (1st edn, London, J Knapton, T Longman and R Horsfield, 1762–67) vol II, 343–5, 349–50; J Chitty, *A Practical Treatise on the Law of Contracts Not Under Seal* (2nd edn, London, S Sweet, 1834) 570–2; CC Langdell, *A Summary of the Law of Contracts* (2nd edn, Boston, Little Brown & Company, 1880) s 171; and Williston (n 2 above) s 677.

[85] Lord (n 12 above) 39.3.

(i) Prevention as a Condition or Basis of the Transfer of the Benefit

Recent discussion has sought to present prevention as a basis or condition of the transfer of the benefit.[86] So for these authors, the *Planche v Colburn* ('*Planche*')[87] type case would be presented in the following way. One of the conditions or bases for the work done by the writer was that the publisher would not prevent the completion of the manuscript. The prevention would thus constitute a failure of basis or condition. There are broadly two problems with this type of analysis:

(1) Historically the principle of prevention has not been treated as a condition. Rather, the principle affects the operation of the condition, depending on the circumstances; it belongs to the category of excuses such as waiver and estoppel.[88]

(2) It seems rather awkward to describe prevention as a basis or condition for a transfer of a benefit because it is highly unlikely to reflect the bargain between the parties. A writer produces a manuscript, a company sells goods, a property company transfers lands, not on the basis that they will not be prevented but because of some likely return.

For these reasons, nothing is gained by perceiving the principle of prevention as another condition.

(ii) Prevention and Breach

Very often, prevention by a party will be a breach of a specific term of cooperation or non-prevention. Another instance of when breach and prevention coincide is when the breach of a term not directed to prevention results in prevention: for example, wrongful dismissal cases or in the sale of goods context, the refusal to take delivery. In both these examples the idea of prevention is submerged in the analysis in the discussion on breach and damages, in one case, and the inquiry into whether the dismissal was wrongful, in the other.

However, the above discussion should not detract from the independence of the prevention principle. Prevention does not always have to coincide with breach. As an example, consider the case where two contracting parties, A and B, make B's obligations to pay for A's work subject to the approval of a third party (eg an architect and the issue of a certificate by him).[89] If the third party does not certify, then A potentially cannot claim payment for the work done. This is especially frustrating where it may be shown that the third party approval has been unfairly withheld. Although there may be ways out of this conundrum, there is a risk that A may not be paid. Another reason for the third party's disapproval may be B's prevention. If this is the case, then the condition of approval can be excused and A can claim payment for the work done. The noteworthy point is that prevention need

---

[86] Edelman and Bant (n 21 above) 252; and B Mcfarlane and R Stevens, 'In Defence of *Sumpter v Hedges*' (2002) 118 *LQR* 569, 578.

[87] (1831) 5 Car & P 57, 172 ER 876; (1831) 8 Bing 14, 131 ER 305.

[88] As well as the treatment of the topic in the references in n 84 above see S Stoljar, 'Prevention and Co-operation in the Law of Contract' (1953) 31 *Can Bar Rev* 231, 233.

[89] A number of the building cases are discussed in Stoljar (n 88 above) 237–43.

not be a breach of the contract between A and B to have the effect of excusing the condition. The fact that such prevention will often be a breach is not material, except for the remedial options that then become available, an issue dealt with in the next section.

(iii) Claims Available After Prevention

If A's performance is a condition of B's performance, then our analysis so far explains that B's prevention of A's performance will excuse the afore-mentioned condition. In practice, this means that A is excused from further performance and as a corollary B cannot claim damages for A's failure to perform. In relation to A, he can claim damages if B's prevention is a breach of contract; or A can make a restitutionary claim in respect of his performance, because the effect of prevention is that the condition attached to the performance has failed.

A more controversial and unclear position in the law relates to whether English law recognises a doctrine of fictional fulfilment. This is where in response to the prevention, the party prevented can ask to be put into the same position as if the condition had been fulfilled. A famous example is in the US case of *Foreman State Trust & Savings Bank v Tauber*,[90] where a man promised his fiancée US$20,000 if she married and survived him. After marriage the husband shot and killed his fiancée. Nevertheless, the wife's estate was able to claim the US$20,000. By awarding the full contractual amount, the court treated the wife as having (fictionally) fulfilled the condition of surviving her husband. Although there are a number of older English authorities recognising the existence of such a doctrine,[91] Treitel has persuasively argued that on principle[92] and more recent authority,[93] such a doctrine is rightly not part of English law.

---

[90] (1932) 180 NE 827.

[91] *Mackay v Dick* (1881) 6 App Case 251; *Holme v Guppy* (1838) 3 M&W 387, 150 ER 1195; *Sir Richard Hotham v East India Company* (1787) 1 TR 638, 99 ER 295. Also see *Jones v Barkley* (1781) 2 Doug 684, 686; 99 ER 434, 687: 'Wherever a man, by doing a previous act, would acquire a right to any debt or duty, by a tender to do a previous act, if the other party refuses to permit him to do it, he acquires the right as completely as it had actually been done; and if the tender is defective, owing to the conduct of the other party, such incomplete tender will be sufficient; because it is a general principle, that he who prevents a thing from being done, shall not avail himself of the non performance which he has occasioned' (per Le Blanc J). And also see Stoljar who assumes that the doctrine of fictional fulfilment is part of English law, a point which he does not criticise: (n 88 above) 232, 237.

[92] G Treitel, *Remedies for Breach of Contract: a Comparative Account* (Oxford, OUP, 1989) 268–9. The argument based on principle was that in the US case mentioned above, the wife was able to claim the full contractual sum even though 'there was no certainty she would have survived her husband': *ibid* 268 . According to Treitel, ignoring such a contingency (namely that the condition may not have been fulfilled even without prevention) makes the award penal.

[93] Treitel (n 2 above) 66: *Thompson v ASDA-MFI plc* [1988] Ch 241, 266; and *Little v Courage* (1995) 70 P & C 469, 474.

III. Distinctiveness of Quantum Meruit

It should perhaps be stressed at the outset that by pointing to the distinctiveness of the quantum meruit, this part does not seek to argue that unjust enrichment can never explain a claim for services because in many situations a service does not provide a marketable residuum (eg pure services). This, as a number of accounts have shown,[94] can be overcome by adopting a wider notion of benefit which is not defined by the identification of a marketable residuum.

Moreover, those that have sought to excise pure services from their model of unjust enrichment do not deny that a claim within their model can still be made in relation to the end products created by the services.[95] Within their model, then, an enrichment action would be brought for the end product and some sort of sui generis claim for the services leading up to it. Such a division is perhaps a more awkward solution than one which describes both the services and end product it produces as benefits because they were requested and valued as such. The foregoing discussion is, of course, subject to what the parties have contracted for: just services or the services and the end product.

Sensitivity in relation to what the parties have bargained for provides a good departure point on the lessons to be learnt from *Planche* and the extent to which the quantum meruit award in that case (and more generally) can be explained through an unjust enrichment analysis.[96] The starting question must be what the parties had contracted for. Looking at the facts of the case, it is unlikely that the parties in *Planche* contracted for anything other than the end product (an MS suitable for inclusion in the Juvenile library).[97] If this is right then the key requirement of a benefit for the purposes of bringing an unjust enrichment claim was not satisfied in *Planche* since an MS was not delivered. If the claim cannot be explained through the law of unjust enrichment, how should it be rationalised within the modern law?

It is important not to rationalise *Planche* as a contractual claim for reliance or expectation damages,[98] because this underplays the breadth of the situations in which a quantum meruit can be claimed, and the potential for etching out (as scholars have with unjust enrichment) a non-contractual claim which does not respond to benefits received. This point is best illustrated if we vary the facts of *Planche* so that the contract between the parties was unenforceable, and the contract in this varied situation was one for the end product. In this type of situation, damages would not be available (because the contract is unenforceable) and

---

[94] Burrows (n 21 above) 16–18 and Virgo (n 34 above) 62–4, 70–2.

[95] Beatson (n 79 above) 21–44; and R Grantham and C Rickett, *Enrichment and Restitution in New Zealand* (Oxford, Hart, 2000) 20–1, 60–1.

[96] See the discussion in Chapter 5, part IV, section B(iii).

[97] C Mitchell and C Mitchell, 'Planche v Colburn (1831)' in C Mitchell and P Mitchell (eds), *Landmark Cases in the Law of Restitution* (Oxford, Hart, 2006) esp 91–2.

[98] Burrows (n 21 above) 343 n 4; and Virgo (n 34 above) 92.

neither would an enrichment claim (because the end product had not been produced). We can be sure that a quantum meruit would be awarded in such a situation, and the question would then be what causative event was this award responding to? It is beyond the scope of this book to resolve this issue, except to add that the usual reference to Treitel's principle of wrongful prevention is unlikely to provide the answer.

Treitel refers to a principle of wrongful prevention as an explanation for a case like *Planche* where there may be no benefit. The problem with this principle is that prevention, as we saw, is not best seen as a cause of action but a mechanism (akin to waiver) which excuses the operation of a condition.[99] It may be that Treitel has a different conception of prevention in mind, one which is distinguished by wrongfulness (as his title suggests). However, on the account he gives it seems unlikely that a special version of prevention is being employed since his use of wrongfulness does not add anything to the way in which prevention applies today.

With this background in mind, we can then move on to seeing the distinctiveness of the quantum meruit. The reason to illuminate the difference is that it enables us to better understand issues which only appear to arise in restitutionary claims for services. The issues all arise because the benefit claimed under a quantum meruit is non-returnable, a feature which is more likely to be inconsistent with (1) the well recognised goal that a benefit should not be forced upon a party, and (2) the entire contract rule. Finally, (3) the non-returnability also gives rise to the issue of the extent to which the contract price plays a role in valuing work done. Each of these issues will be considered in turn. A good starting point for our discussion is to consider the following four situations in which a party may want to claim a quantum meruit in the contractual context:

(1) C agrees to design and build D football club a state of the art stadium. C's work is to be performed under a standard form contract. Part way through the project, D football club is acquired by new owners who have great ambitions for the club and wish the team to play a more expansive game, which ideally requires a larger pitch. Accordingly, C is asked to make the relevant changes, which sees them adjust the stands and extend the pitch on all sides. Such variations are not covered by the contract. C now wants to claim for the work done in making the pitch bigger.[100]

(2) C contracted to build a house for D. C was only to be paid once the house was complete. Part way through the construction works, C abandoned the project. C now wishes to claim for the work he had done before abandoning the project.[101]

(3) D publishers engage C to produce a book on the company history of D. C was to be paid on completion, which for the purposes of the contract was the delivery of a finished manuscript. With the introductory chapters complete, C now asks for access to D's company archives, which are essential for the completion of the manuscript. With a new management installed, D resolve to discontinue the manuscript idea and refuse C access

---

[99] See part II, section D.

[100] For an example of a quantum meruit in respect of extra-contractual performance in the sports context, see *ERDC Group v Brunel University* [2006] EWHC 687.

[101] Based on *Sumpter v Hedges* [1898] 1 QB 673.

to the archives. C takes this as a repudiatory breach and terminates his contract with D. He now wants to claim a quantum meruit for the work done.[102]

(4) C is contracted to develop a software program and integration system for a large multinational corporation, D. Under the contract between the parties, payment was made on set dates corresponding to the completion of discrete parts of C's work (milestone payments, of which there were 30). This was a long term contract, but one which was nevertheless a bad bargain for C. C had failed to claim for the fifth milestone which had been reached under the contract. D's refusal to pay upon milestone six was seen as a general repudiation and the contract was terminated. C now sought a quantum meruit for work done under the contract (corresponding to that specified under milestones 1 to 6).[103]

In the first case, it is well established that a quantum meruit can be claimed in such extra-contractual situations. If the claim is not covered by the contract, the quantum meruit claim here could be seen as preventing unjust enrichment.[104] If this is right, an analogy can be drawn with claims for money in what can be called overperformance cases: misapplying a contractual formula for payment and paying more than was due; or simply mistakenly paying beyond the contractual obligation.[105] We can now move on to the three issues identified above.

A. Infringing the Freedom of Choice

The non-returnability of the services increases the risk that a defendant will be left burdened with an enrichment as if he purchased it. This is why many accounts in this area try to ensure that within their schemes, the defendant's benefit was received in 'circumstances in which the benefit was desired by the defendant'[106] or that the claim in restitution should not 'do violence to the law's respect for the individual's right to choose freely how to employ available resources'.[107] The majority, if not all, of the cases which are covered in the discussion about respecting the parties' freedom of choice arise in the context where the benefit is non-returnable. Consider the following example, loosely based on *Leigh v Dickeson*.[108] John is one-quarter owner of a property of which Mary owns the remaining share. John lives in the property on his own and is to pay Mary rent proportional to her

---

[102] Inspired by *Planche* (n 87 above).

[103] Based on *GEC Marconi v BHP Information Technology* (2003) 128 FCR 1.

[104] It could also be seen as contractual claim: see *Sir Lindsay Parkinson v Commissioners of Works* [1949] 2 KB 632; and Treitel (n 2 above) 1061 and S Furst and V Ramsey, *Keating on Construction Contracts* (8th edn, London, Sweet & Maxwell, 2006) 113. It may be that this is true of the *Parkinson* case because the contract there contained provisions covering extra work, albeit not the full extent of what eventually was carried out.

[105] See Chapter 3, text to n 56.

[106] Edelman and Bant (n 21 above) 98.

[107] Birks (n 21 above) 55. See also Virgo (n 34 above) 68; Burrows (n 21 above) 18; and R Goff of Chieveley and GH Jones, *The Law of Restitution* (7th edn, London, Sweet & Maxwell, 2007) para 1-019 et seq.

[108] (1884) 15 QBD 60.

share. Mary brings a claim for rent owed by John, which John resists generally and in any event seeks to set off by the amount he has spent on refurbishing the whole house. The Court of Appeal rejected this kind of set-off in *Leigh* because as the Master of the Rolls put it:

> The cost of the repairs to the house was a voluntary payment by the defendant, partly for the benefit of himself and partly for the benefit of his co-owner; but the co-owner cannot reject the benefit of the repairs, and if she is held to be liable for a proportionate share of the cost, the defendant will get the advantage of the repairs without allowing his co-owner any liberty to decide whether she will refuse or adopt them.[109]

The problem is that allowing John's claim in these circumstances would leave Mary in a position where she is paying for refurbishments that she did not request.

B. Entire Contracts

Case study 2 is based on *Sumpter v Hedges* ('*Sumpter*'), when the part performing party in breach was unsuccessful in his quantum meruit claim because the contract was held to be entire. This has attracted much criticism because the failure of the quantum meruit would mean that the defendant can benefit without having to pay anything for the part performance received.[110] Macfarlane and Stevens have recently mounted a high profile defence of *Sumpter*, which they argued applied the following general rule: 'a party in breach cannot claim for the value of services rendered or for the value of goods supplied under a contract unless he has an accrued contractual entitlement to be paid'.[111] In relation to the quantum meruit claim, which would be founded on unjust enrichment, they argue there would be no failure of condition (they use the term basis), since the basis was payment only upon completion of the work.[112]

However, the problem with this argument is that the authors accept that a party in breach can claim restitution of money paid pursuant to an entire obligation.[113] A variation of the facts in *Dies v British and International Mining and Finance Corp.* ('*Dies*'),[114] illustrates the point. A agrees to buy 1,000 rifles from B for £10,000, to be paid in advance in five equal instalments. Only when the instalments are fully paid will the obligation to deliver the rifles arise. After paying one instalment of £2,000, A fails to pay the balance, and B accepts this repudiatory breach and terminates the contract. A can then bring a claim for the return of the £2,000, even though payment was a condition precedent to the delivery of the rifles. The authors do not provide an explanation as to how, if the transfer is of money as

---

[109] (1884) 15 QBD 65.
[110] See generally Goff and Jones (n 107 above) 552–5; Burrows (n 21 above) 354–9; and Treitel (n 2 above) 825–6.
[111] Mcfarlane and Stevens (n 86 above) 569.
[112] *Ibid* 577.
[113] *Ibid* 585.
[114] [1939] 1 KB 724.

opposed to services, there can be a failure of the condition. Surely there is a failure of condition in both, since the termination of the contract means that ultimately the rifles will not be delivered and the work not paid for. To the extent then that there is a failure of condition in both cases, there is an inconsistency which needs to be explained.

A more promising explanation, one which Macfarlane and Stevens also rely on, is that there is no inconsistency if we focus on the nature of the benefit: one is returnable and the other is not. As they explain, there would only be an inconsistency if the party in breach in a *Dies* type case was to claim not the part payment but the 200 rifles (representing the corresponding number of rifles his advance would purchase).[115] This illustrates why the quantum meruit is distinctive from the money claims in this context. The nature of the benefit (it is non-returnable) in *Sumpter* means that to allow a quantum meruit in these circumstances would undermine the whole nature of a condition precedent, because it would be open to a party to create a failure by its own action and still claim for part performance (the effect of the quantum meruit), even though it had initially agreed to be awarded only upon complete performance. One could then say that the principle at play in a case such as *Sumpter* is that a part performing party should not be able to take advantage of its own wrong in a way which undermines the condition initially agreed between the parties. A claim for the returnable benefit does not face this problem because its effect is not, as in the quantum meruit claim, to partially enforce the contract (as it would be if rifles were claimed) but to reverse the transfer.

At the heart of this explanation is that the quantum meruit is equivalent to *partial enforcement*. Can it not be said, as those committed to the perfect symmetry between money and non-money benefits could urge, that rather than partially enforcing the contract the quantum meruit award here is really reversing the unjust enrichment? This echoes the arguments rehearsed against adopting a flexible model of counter-restitution,[116] namely that allowing a party to give a monetary value as a substitute for non-returnable benefits would effectively apportion the contract for the parties. And there the debate was resolved in favour of adopting the flexible model. If that is right, it entails the acceptance that the counter-restitution of non-returnable benefits only appears to look like an apportioning of the contract; it is really the reversal of unjust enrichment. Surely then, it could be argued that a quantum meruit in a *Sumpter*-like case only superficially looks like partial enforcement (in the same way counter-restitution appears to apportion the contract), but is really about reversing the unjust enrichment. If this is right, then it follows that the claim in *Sumpter* should have been allowed. What is the best way forward?

As was the case in our discussion of counter-restitution,[117] the non-returnability of the benefit makes the solution difficult. In the end, it is submitted that a quantum

---

[115] Mcfarlane and Stevens (n 86 above) 585.
[116] See text from n 41 above onwards.
[117] See text to nn 40–60 above.

meruit should have been allowed in a case like *Sumpter* for three reasons. First, termination of the contract created the failure of condition. This is why, had the money been paid in a similar situation, a claim for its value would have succeeded. Secondly, this is reinforced when we see that nowhere in the contract was there anything to suggest a forfeiture clause, such that the parties agreed (as they could have done) that the money or work was to be retained if the work was not completed. Thirdly, the innocent party has benefited from the work and it seems unfair to let him enjoy this without payment, unless, of course, this is expressly agreed (through some forfeiture clause) or there is no benefit (which a claim founded on unjust enrichment takes into account).

Under the common law, the existence of an entire contract does not always bar a quantum meruit. Case 3 is an example of that. Here, the defendant publisher has brought about the termination of the contract by refusing C access to the archives, which prevents the completion of the manuscript. In these circumstances the prevention principle applies, as was explained above,[118] which has the effect that the D cannot rely on its condition (namely that payment will only be made upon the submission of a complete manuscript) against the part performing writer C.

C. Valuation

Discussion of the restitutionary quantum meruit is usually taken up by the question of the value one places on the work done: (1) Is it the market value? (2) Is it capped by the contract price? (3) Is the contract price to act as a guide to the value? The difficulty of resolving this problem arises from the tension caused by the presence of the following three factors: (a) the non-returnability of the benefit, which takes us into the debate about whether the quantum meruit is really enforcing the contract (which would suggest option (2)) or reversing the unjust enrichment (which would suggest option (1)); (b) following option (1) or (3) would potentially lead to a party escaping a bad bargain; and (c) even if one follows option (1), what relevance does the contract price have, since termination does not invalidate its significance?

For those that see the quantum meruit as close to partial enforcement of the contract, it seems odd that it could ever be contemplated that part performance could be valued at a higher value than complete performance. The contract price cap here is then perceived as a 'contract ceiling', which prevents the law of restitution from undermining the contract.[119] In support of this view is the rule which says that upon complete performance, a party can only recover the contract

---

[118] See part II, section D.

[119] R Stevens, 'Three Enrichment Issues' in AS Burrows and L Rodger (eds), *Mapping the Law: Essays in Memory of Peter Birks* (Oxford, OUP, 2006) 60; Goff and Jones (n 107 above) 515–18; and some dicta of Cooke J in *Robert Taylor v Motability Finance Ltd* [2004] EWHC 2619, at para [26] ('*Taylor*'). This view also seems to be implicit in the older law: *Thornton v Place* (1832) 1 M & Rob 218, 174 ER 74.

price.[120] A restitutionary quantum meruit for services provided in these circumstances, based on the failure to pay, is not possible. Case study 4 will illustrate this point. C's completion of milestones 1 to 5 gives them an accrued right to the return performance by the defendant, which in this case is the payment of the agreed price. If the money is not paid, then according to the afore-mentioned rule, C is confined to the claim for the price. C cannot, as would be the case if the benefit was money, argue that the failure of condition (refusal to pay) allows the party to bring a restitutionary quantum meruit.

For those that are committed to the principle of symmetry and see the restitutionary quantum meruit as the reversal of unjust enrichment, rather than the partial enforcement of the contract, a defensible line to take is that the contract price should not be a cap. The benefit should be valued at market rates, leading to the possibility, realised or envisaged in a number of cases, that a party is able to claim a quantum meruit for its *part* performance which far exceeds the sum that it would have been entitled to had it *completely* performed the contract.[121] However, this view then leaves the question as to the relevance of the contract price. Here, a number of modern writers follow the line that the contract price should be accounted for as evidence of *value* rather than as what was earlier called a 'contract ceiling'[122] which operated as a mechanism to prevent the contract from being undermined. From this starting point there is a split amongst the writers. One group say that the contract price is a strong, but not determinative, indicator of the value. Accordingly, in some cases it can be ignored.[123] Another group say the contract price should form a valuation cap that cannot be ignored.[124]

The difficulty of identifying the right answer comes from the tension caused by the different directions in which the three factors, identified above, are pulling. It is submitted that the best compromise is to follow the view that the contract price is a valuation cap. It seems counter-intuitive to ignore the clear evidence provided by the contract price about the value both parties put on the performance. It must here be added that the contract price valuation cap will not necessarily operate on a pro rata basis. For example, a claim for services rendered, which constitute three-quarters of the contract performance, should not necessarily be confined to an upper limit of three-quarters of the price. This is because evidence may be led to show that the performance completed was understood by the parties to merit more of the contract price than suggested by a pro rata measurement.[125]

The aim of this part was to emphasise how the non-returnability of the benefit claimed under a quantum meruit explains certain issues which arise only in the

---

[120] Goff and Jones (n 107 above) 516 describe it as 'historically sound and correct in principle'. See also *Taylor* (n 119 above) esp paras [25]–[27]. Cf Burrows (n 21 above) 347.

[121] *Boomer v Muir* (1933) 24 (2d) P 570 and *Renard Constructions (ME) Pty Ltd v Minister for Public Works* (1992) 26 NSWLR 234. See also *Lodder v Slowey* [1904] AC 442.

[122] See n 119 above.

[123] Virgo (n 34 above) 103–4 and Edelman and Bant (n 21 above) 118–19, 263.

[124] Burrows (n 21 above) 346–7; and Birks (n 21 above) 59. For both these authors the cases in n 121 above were wrongly decided.

[125] Birks (n 21 above) 59.

context of a restitutionary claim for services: (1) the courts' concern that a benefit should not be forced upon a party; (2) the entire contract rule; and (3) the extent to which the contract price plays a role in the valuation of the work done. All this raised the question of whether money and services (and more generally money and non-money benefits, which are non-returnable) should not be treated alike. Although the conclusion was not easy to reach, this part concluded that claims for money and services should be treated alike, and that to this end the entire contracts rule should be abandoned. The well known case of *Sumpter* was wrong to deny the quantum meruit of the part performing party in breach. Finally, it was argued that the contract price should be a valuation cap for a quantum meruit award.

IV. Unenforceable Contracts and Claims by the Party In Breach

This part will emphasise what has been implicit in the discussion so far: the fact that the contract is unenforceable or the claim for restitution is made by the party in breach does not impact upon the operation of the failure of condition model detailed in this chapter. The aim is to illustrate the way in which the failure of condition model applies in the afore-mentioned contexts.

As the historical discussion showed, ultimately the same principle determined the availability of the restitutionary claim whether the contract was enforceable or unenforceable.[126] The cases show that where A transfers money or services, for example, to B on condition of some performance by B, then B's failure to perform, and not the unenforceability of the contract, is the reason why A will in principle be able to claim the restitution of the value of the benefit transferred.[127] It follows that if B is 'ready, willing and able' to perform, then there is no qualifying failure of condition that would justify A's claim.[128] The language of termination is not relevant because the contracts are unenforceable. Instead, it is the 'ready willing and able' requirement which operates as the equivalent of the termination requirement in relation to unapportioned contracts[129] and the 'inability to provide corrective performance' requirement, in the context of apportioned contracts.[130] The noteworthy point about recovery in the unenforceable contracts case is that it is

---

[126] See Chapter 5, text to nn 122–4.

[127] *Ibid*: the cases there included *Gosbell v Archer* (1835) 2 Ad & El 500, 111 ER 193; *Pulbrook v Lawes* (1876) 1 QBD 284; and *Scarisbrick v Parkinson* (1869) 20 LT 175. *Monnickendam v Lease* (1923) 39 TLR 445 is a more modern example. The most recent examples come from Australia (*Pavey & Matthews Pty Ltd v Paul* (1986) 162 CLR 221) and Canada (*Deglman v Guaranty Trust Co of Canada and Constantineau* [1954] 3 DLR 786). On these cases, see generally Burrows (n 21 above) 381–6.

[128] *Thomas v Brown* (1876) 1 QBD 714.

[129] See text to n 39 above.

[130] See text to n 24 above.

important to consider carefully the policy or statute which renders the contract unenforceable, since it may outlaw the claim for restitution.[131]

The two situations in which the party in breach is denied a restitutionary claim are when it concerns a deposit or work done under an entire contract. It is important to stress that it is not the wrong of breach which generates the denial of the claim but the particular circumstances, namely the rules relating to deposits and entire contracts. This is why outside these two situations, the case law shows that a party in breach can make a restitutionary claim in the same way as the innocent party.[132]

It has already been argued that a party in breach should not be denied a restitutionary claim in respect of work done pursuant to an entire contract.[133] The following example will illustrate what was argued above. A performs work for B under an entire contract. The condition for A's work is that he will be paid on completion by B. If B will no longer pay, because the contract has been terminated due to A's breach (he abandons the contract part way through), the condition of A's work fails. In these circumstances, A should be allowed to claim restitution of the value of the services provided. It should not matter, as in the case if A was claiming restitution of the value of the money transferred (eg a part payment), that A is the party in breach.

In relation to deposit cases, the money is paid on the condition that it will be forfeited if the payer fails to perform. In such circumstances, the payer's failure to perform *fulfils* the condition, rather than resulting in the qualifying failure of condition required to generate the claim for the value of the deposit. The only way a deposit could then be recovered by the party in breach is by reliance on equitable principles of contract law to obtain relief from forfeiture.[134]

In sum, if it is accepted that a party in breach should be able to make a claim for services rendered under an entire contract, then the position of the party in breach is in theory no different from that enjoyed by the innocent party. The failure of condition model presented in this chapter explains both.

V. Failure of Condition and Absence of Basis

How does the model described in this chapter fit within the absence of basis model of unjust enrichment laid down by Birks in his recent work (what was called the new Birksian approach), and defended in this book?[135] The short answer is that a *qualifying* failure of condition equates with *absence* of basis. However, it is important to

---

[131] *Dimond v Lovell* [2000] 2 WLR 1121. See generally Burrows (n 21 above) 385–6.

[132] See, eg *Dies* (n 114 above) and *Rover International Ltd v Cannon Film Sales Ltd (No 3)* (n 68 above). More generally see Burrows (n 21 above) 351–9, Virgo (n 34 above) 334–42; and Goff and Jones (n 107 above) 507 and paras 20-35–20-57).

[133] See part III, section B.

[134] Burrows (n 21 above) 351.

[135] In Chapter 3.

stress that this view is very different from the way in which Birks explained the right to restitution of initially valid contractual transfers of benefits under his new approach (what he called 'subsequent failure' cases).[136] The explanation for the difference in view becomes clearer upon closer examination of Birks' application of his new approach to the subsequent failure context.

Birks argued that under his new approach, the restitutionary award in *Fibrosa Spolka v Fairbairn Lawson* ('*Fibrosa*')[137] (the leading case in the subsequent failure context) will have to be reanalysed from the way it was analysed under the unjust factors approach. According to him, it would no longer be sufficient to say, as the House of Lords did, that the foundation of recovery in *Fibrosa* was the failure of contractual reciprocation. He argued that the problem with this explanation was that 'it leaves unanswered the objection that the restitutionary right would then have arisen despite the validity of the contractual obligation under which the payment was made'.[138] The most accurate explanation, as *Chandler v Webster* ('*Chandler*')[139] suggested all along, would have to explain how the contractual obligation in *Fibrosa* was invalidated. Birks argued that such an invalidation could be explained by a combination of the failure of reciprocation and termination. In other words, and this is the part where *Chandler* was wrong, a contractual obligation is not only invalidated when it is voidable or void ab initio; it can also be invalidated when the failure of reciprocation results in the termination of the contract.[140] Birks provides the following illustration of his argument:

> If you agree to build me a garage and I pay £10,000 in advance, and you then default, your failure to build the garage invalidates the obligation under which I paid you. I have a power to terminate it and a right to recover the money. That is how the pyramid works: the failure of reciprocation invalidates the obligation and the invalidity of the obligation constitutes the absence of explanatory basis which renders the enrichment unjust.[141]

This account raises a number of difficult questions, to which there is no clear answer. In what way is the invalidation in the subsequent failure context the same as the invalidation when the contract is voidable or void ab intio? It is not usual to group the three situations together in this way. More fundamentally, can it really be right to describe a contract as 'invalidated' when in some situations (discussed earlier) accrued rights to call on performance survive termination?[142] This is not the case in the situations where the contract is voidable or void ab inito. What is the relationship between termination and failure of reciprocation? What does termination add in this context? Moreover, how is the contractual obligation invalidated in cases where an apportioned part of a contract is recovered (something which Birks accommodates under his new approach in limited circumstances),[143]

---

[136] Birks (n 21 above) 140–2.
[137] [1943] AC 32.
[138] Birks (n 21 above) 141.
[139] [1904] 1 KB 493.
[140] Birks (n 21 above) 125–7, 141.
[141] *Ibid.*
[142] In part II, section C(i).
[143] Birks (n 21 above) 122–4.

without the contract ever being terminated? Birks' answer to this question is ultimately unsatisfactory:

> If an item is genuinely non negotiable, the payment of any excess is as much a payment of a non-existent debt as when the contract itself is misapplied so as to cause an overpayment. Provided the excess is cleanly identifiable and independent of the other obligations in the contract ... the basis for that payment totally fails, because the money is paid to discharge a non-existent debt.[144]

This explanation assumes what it needs to prove: why is that we can ignore the contractual right to call upon the payment?[145]

The way to avoid the problems posed by these questions, while at the same time remaining faithful to the new Birksian approach, would be to adopt the model put forward in this chapter: a claim founded on unjust enrichment can be employed for the restitution of the value of a conditional transfer of a benefit if there is a qualifying failure of the afore-mentioned condition. As the discussion so far has shown, this model is better able to explain, unlike Birks' account, the role of termination (that it is not always necessary) and its relationship with failure of reciprocation, as well as the relationship between accrued rights and a claim in unjust enrichment. It does this without sacrificing the overall structure adopted by Birks under his new approach, and defended in Chapter 3: a qualifying failure of condition constitutes an absence of basis.

As a final point, it is worth considering an argument that has been made against the adoption of the absence of basis approach in the contractual context. Adopting the *Fibrosa*[146] case as an illustration, the argument begins by stating that the pre-payment in *Fibrosa* (which was the subject of the claim) was made pursuant to an accrued obligation because had it not been paid, the Polish company could have been sued for it. Accordingly, the recovery of the payment after the frustrating event was allowed despite the existence of a valid basis (the accrued right to payment).

The problem with this argument is that it assumes the pre-payment was accrued because the date for its payment had arisen. However, as was shown earlier in the section on accrued rights, it is not the date of performance which necessarily determines whether the obligation to perform has accrued.[147] Rather, the key question is whether the relevant obligation to perform is unconditional. This will either be

---

[144] *Ibid* 124.

[145] Perhaps it was in acknowledgment of this that in the first edition, Birks recommended an expansion of the law of rectification, because it could effectively erase the contract right and so provide a solution to the problem posed by the question: P Birks, *Unjust Enrichment* (1st edn, Oxford, Clarendon Press, 2003) 109.

[146] See n 137 above.

[147] In part II, section C(i), esp example discussed in text to n 65 above. The distinction between an obligation to perform which has accrued and that which is simply due was understood by their Lordships in *Fibrosa*. The best illustration is from Lord Atkin's example (*Fibrosa* (n 137 above) 50–1) of a contract for the sale of a horse, to be delivered a month from payment. The buyer was to pay the seller an agreed sum per week for the upkeep of the horse during the month before delivery. If the horse died after two weeks, each party would be discharged from further performance. The seller could claim for two weeks' upkeep (as the right to this amount had *accrued*) but had to return the purchase price (the right to this sum had not accrued, although it was *due* before discharge).

because (a) no condition is attached to that performance, or (b) the condition has been fulfilled (either by the person calling on the performance or due to some external event). However, in the *Fibrosa* case the payment was conditional and that condition had not been fulfilled because of the frustrating event. Accordingly, the obligation to pay cannot be described as having been accrued. If, as was the case, the payment had been made, it could be recovered because the condition attached to it had failed, which constitutes the relevant absence of basis.

VI. Restitution Upon Failure of Condition: Contract or Unjust Enrichment?

The failure of condition model outlined in this chapter makes more visible the dependence of unjust enrichment and contract, since it is the construction of the contract which determines the conditionality of the transfer of the benefit. This then raises the following potential argument, which will be considered in this section: if the contract can be construed to explain the conditionality, why can that process of construction not go further and dictate that upon the failure of condition, there is an obligation (contractual) to make restitution? In other words, restitution upon failure of condition should and/or can be a contractual claim rather than one founded on unjust enrichment. Before discussing the reasons for rejecting this argument, it is important to make two preliminary points. First, the argument that the claim for restitution is contractual is one that can be made against any model which seeks to present the same claim as being founded on unjust enrichment. So even if one does not adopt the model proposed in this book and, say, continues with a form of the dominant model, the afore-mentioned argument about the restitutionary claim must be addressed.[148] Secondly, the discussion which follows does not deny that the restitutionary claim could be contractual if the contract provides for such a claim by express or implied term. Accordingly, the present discussion is about the situation when the contract does not contain any express or implied term about the restitution of the value of any benefit transferred.

With the above points in mind, there are three main reasons why it would be wrong to see the restitutionary claim discussed in this book as contractual. First, as the detailed historical discussion has shown, the restitutionary claim in the contractual context has been generally treated as non-contractual. Indeed, this point is well captured in one of the leading cases on the subject, *Fibrosa*:

---

[148] JW Carter and GJ Tolhurst, 'Conditional Payments and Failure of Consideration: Contract or Restitution' (2001) 9 *Asia Pacific Law Rev* 1. This article takes the dominant model as its starting point, when discussing the argument discussed in this section.

The payment was originally conditional. The condition of retaining it is eventual performance. Accordingly, when that condition fails, the right to retain the money must simultaneously fail. It is not like a claim for damages for breach, nor is it a claim under the contract. It is in theory and is expressed to be a claim to recover money, received to the use of the plaintiff.[149]

This is not to deny that there are comments in other cases which may suggest that the claim is contractual,[150] but as Carter and Tolhurst persuasively show, these comments are based on two cases, one of which is problematic[151] and the other misconstrued.[152] Either way, *Fibrosa* represents the binding and most persuasive authority.

Secondly, the argument challenged in this part wrongly perceives the process of construction as a vehicle that can be employed to go beyond the parties' agreement and add terms to the contract which deal with restitution. Using the process of construction in this way contravenes established law that, outside specific circumstances, a court cannot add to the bargain agreed between the parties. And this problem does not arise when a contract is construed to determine the conditionality of the transfer of a benefit, because in such a situation the process of construction seeks to reflect what the parties have agreed.

Of course, following Hedley, one could argue that contract law should not be defined by consent (he calls it the 'express contract fallacy'). Adopting this position would then open the way for courts to be less nervous about adding terms to the contract that were not the subject of the parties' agreement. However, as was explained in Chapter 3, the problem with Hedley's argument is that it leaves a fundamental question unanswered: if contract law is not about consent, what then is the foundation of the law of contract? The failure to answer this question makes Hedley's model methodologically unsound and one that has problems of fit with the current law. More generally, Chapter 3 shows that the same problems affect other prominent attempts to remodel and expand contract law so that it can accommodate the restitutionary claims discussed in this book.

The third reason for maintaining that the restitutionary claim which follows a failure of condition is founded on unjust enrichment and not contract is that this model provides a better explanation of all the situations within the contractual context (as defined in this book). If the restitutionary claim is contractual, then it runs into problems in the case of unenforceable contracts, since the very unenforceability outlaws any contractual claims. So, in such a case, an alternative cause of action would need to be employed to explain the restitutionary claim. Yet the pattern of

---

[149] *Fibrosa* (n 137 above) 65 (per Lord Wright).

[150] *Stocznia* (n 83 above); *Baltic* (n 37 above). Carter and Tolhurst outline the comments and interpretations, (n 148 above) 2–4.

[151] *Dies* (n 114 above), on the basis that Stable J was not clear about the foundation of the claim, although his award has been treated as founded on unjust enrichment. See, eg Carter and Tolhurst (n 148 above) 4; and Burrows (n 21 above) 352.

[152] *Mcdonald v Dennys Lascelles Ltd* (1933) 48 CLR 457. The authors give six reasons why the case actually supports the position laid down by Lord Wright in *Fibrosa*, namely that the restitutionary claim is non-contractual.

the restitutionary claim in the unenforceable contract cases works in the same way as the cases where the contract is terminated and subsisting; the restitutionary claim for the value of the benefit transferred arises if (a) the transfer of the benefit was conditional, and (b) there was a qualifying failure of condition. Accordingly, the better approach is to adopt a theory which reflects this commonality. And the way to do this is to recognise that the restitutionary claim, which follows failure of condition in the contractual context, is founded on unjust enrichment.

VII. Conclusion

The main objective of this chapter was to provide a clear model that can explain when unjust enrichment can be employed to claim restitution in the contractual context. It was shown that two questions will determine whether there is a right to restitution in these circumstances:

(1) Was the transfer of the benefit conditional? The condition attached to the transfer of the money or other benefit can be a promised counter-performance (promissory condition) and/or some other event not promised by either party (contingent condition).

(2) Was there a qualifying failure of condition? If the contract is unapportioned the qualifying failure coincides with termination of the contract, whereas if the contract is apportioned termination is not required.

Building on the historical analysis in Chapter 5, the model presented in this chapter presents a clearer picture than the dominant model in which termination of the contract for breach is a precondition for a claim by an innocent party in unjust enrichment. The proposed model focusses less on termination and more on conditionality of the transfer of the benefit and whether that condition has failed. It applies not just to contracts which are terminated for breach, but also to contracts which are subsisting or unenforceable. The fact that the claim is made by the party in breach does not make any difference in the operation of the failure of condition model. The innocent party and party in breach should be treated alike.

By focussing on the conditionality of the transfer of the benefit we are also better able to understand the impact, if any, that preventative conduct or accrued rights to performance may have on a party's right to the restitution of the value of a benefit transferred under a contract. Prevention is not, as some have recently argued, a condition of the transfer of the benefit, but operates to excuse (and therefore constitutes a failure of) a condition. If A's performance (eg money) gives rise to an accrued right to the return performance by B (eg goods or services), which is satisfied (by B's performance), then a claim founded on unjust enrichment cannot be employed in this situation to claim back the value of the money transferred from A to B. This is because there is no failure of condition in this situation: money was paid on the condition of performance by B, which has been fulfilled.

It was shown how the model in this chapter fits with the absence of basis model adopted by the new Birksian approach: the qualifying failure of condition constitutes the necessary absence of basis. It was shown how this view was an improvement upon the way in which Birks envisaged the operation of his new approach in what he called the subsequent failure context. This is mainly because Birks' account under his new approach is committed to the termination precondition, which as we saw is not necessary for the restitutionary claim in the contractual context.

Part VI of this chapter rejected the argument that restitution upon failure of condition is a contractual claim, rather than one founded upon unjust enrichment. Although the failure of condition model presented in this chapter made the dependence of the restitutionary claim on the contract more visible, it does not follow that the restitutionary claim is or should be contractual. Indeed, it was shown that historically and as a matter of exposition of a number of claims across the contractual context, it made sense to see the restitutionary claim which follows failure of condition as being non-contractual and founded on unjust enrichment.

Conclusion

THIS BOOK CHALLENGED, and sought to replace, what was referred to as the dominant model. According to that dominant model, on termination of a contract for breach, the innocent party can elect to claim for the restitution of the value of benefits transferred under the contract, instead of expectation damages. And this is said to be a claim outside the contract, based on unjust enrichment for failure of consideration. The new model laid down a framework for the availability and operation of restitution, founded on unjust enrichment, in the contractual context, where that context has been defined as covering contracts which are (a) terminated for breach, or (b) subsisting or (c) unenforceable.

The book has comprised six chapters and the key conclusions reached in each chapter are as follows.

Chapter 1 looked at the historical foundations of restitution generally. It sought to build an accurate picture of the development of indebitatus claims (many of which make up the modern law of unjust enrichment) from the late seventeenth century to the nineteenth century, with a particular focus on the eighteenth century. With the help of manuscript evidence the following important conclusions were reached:

(1) Throughout the late seventeenth and eighteenth centuries, indebitatus claims were perceived and understood as being non-contractual. This was facilitated by the fact that during this period there was a sufficiently worked out consensus theory of contract (actual agreement), which was used to contrast the non-contractual nature of indebitatus claims (promise provided-implied-in law). The claims were contractual as a matter of form not substance.

(2) Lord Mansfield's influence on the development of indebitatus claims, specifically the money had and received claim ('MHR'), has been exaggerated because many of the ideas in the classic case of *Moses v Macferlan* ('*Moses*')[1] had been worked out in the common law before. Although he may been influenced by them, the evidence shows that he did not import any specific equitable or Roman law doctrine when he laid down his classic statement in *Moses*. He was applying established common law principles.

(3) Lord Mansfield's main innovation was to couch the MHR action in equity, which turned into an inquiry about whether or not it was unconscionable for the defendant to keep the money. Such a broad inquiry was problematic and caused uncertainty with its potential (which was realised) to interfere with settled commercial bargains or undermine other areas of law and the appropriate limitations they had in place, on the basis of what was considered fair. It is likely that as a result of these problems, by the end of the eighteenth century and certainly by the

---

[1] (1760) 2 Burr 1005; 97 ER 676.

nineteenth century, courts began to be less guided by equitable notions when it came to the MHR claim.

(4) In the nineteenth century, the legacy of employing contractual language for an essentially non-contractual claim came to be a burden. Whereas in the eighteenth century, lawyers and judges were clear about the fictional nature of the promise in indebitatus claims, the same promise began to 'flicker into life' during the nineteenth century. This development witnessed courts asking whether a genuine promise/contract could exist in the circumstances, a requirement which impacted on the results of cases in a way that would not have been the case had the promise been considered fictional as it should have been.

The principal lesson to be learnt from the historical analysis in Chapter 1 is that modern restitution lawyers are correct to search for a non-contractual explanation for many of the indebitatus claims, which they have found in the principle against unjust enrichment. The main reason to support the unjust enrichment model is that it provides the best fit with the cases, as Ames suggested, and the works of the late Professor Birks powerfully showed. Moreover, several of Birks' other arguments are also compelling: recognising unjust enrichment enables us to (a) complete our map of private law, since the law of obligations, as the civil law shows, is not just made up of rights generated by consent or wrongs; and (b) see links with other claims in equity that work in similar ways to indebitatus claims.

Chapter 1 also showed that from an historical perspective, it is problematic to shape the independent restitutionary claim around an equitable notion of unconscentiousness. It was only really during one phase in the development of the law that equitable notions dominated the MHR claim, namely during Lord Mansfield's time. The broader picture of the development of the law does not support the equitable foundation. Moreover, the problems with equity-driven MHR that surfaced during Lord Mansfield's time are just as liable to occur today.

Chapter 2 focussed specifically on the innocent party's claim for restitution after termination for breach. It dealt with the historical and non-historical arguments in support of the view that restitution after termination for breach is not founded on unjust enrichment, but is another contractual remedy (like expectation or reliance damages). Although a number of authors have supported this view, Chapter 3 looked at the work of three leading scholars, whose arguments are representative: Andrew Kull, Steve Hedley and Peter Jaffey. In rejecting the dominant model, all three put forward models which present the restitutionary award as a contractual remedy. All three argue that their models do not cause any upheaval in the law since they broadly fit the results of the cases.

Chapter 2 critically examined each of the three models against the criteria of methodology, history and fit. It was concluded that first, the methodological and/or historical foundations of the models were flawed; and, secondly, that each of the models failed the fit criteria, in so far as they provided a less coherent picture of the law than the dominant model they sought to replace. With the rejection of the argument that restitution in the dominant model should be seen as a contractual remedy, the message of Chapter 1 was reinforced: that is, in the specific context of the innocent party's claim for restitution after termination for breach, the restitutionary claim is best rationalised as founded on unjust enrichment.

Chapter 3 argued that the best model for the law of unjust enrichment to adopt was not, as the law now stands, the unjust factors approach, but the absence of basis model advocated by Birks for the common law ('the new Birksian approach'). The main reason for this was that an ideal system of unjust enrichment incorporated the inquiries from both the unjust factors approach and that from the absence of basis approach. The new Birksian approach is able to achieve that with its pyramid conception of unjust enrichment: restitution is awarded when there exists a reason (the bottom layer where unjust factors reside) why the basis of the transfer of the benefit fails (the top layer). A principal reason for preferring the pyramid conception includes the fact that a purely unjust factors approach generates a tendency to be claimant-focussed, which often results in:

(a) the adoption of wrong reasons being given to explain the restitution award in a particular case;
(b) insufficient attention being paid to existing obligations which unjust enrichment may clash with;
(c) insufficient attention being paid to the basis (eg contract or other type of obligation) of the enrichment, resulting in the risk of the assumption that a basis exists which in fact does not.

With the independence and preferred general model for the law of unjust enrichment clarified in Chapters 1 to 3, Chapter 4 introduced the work of the final two chapters (5 and 6), which work towards mapping out the role of unjust enrichment in the contractual context. Chapters 5 and 6 showed that the key to working out whether a claim for restitution (founded on unjust enrichment) can be made, is to focus on the conditionality of the transfer of the benefit.

Chapter 5 investigated the historical foundations of the modern law of unjust enrichment in the contractual context. The main conclusions reached were as follows.

(1) Three developments explain the evolution and establishment of the dominant model.

(a) The first was the shift from the presumption that each party's promised performances were independent to the presumption, which characterises the modern law, that the afore-mentioned performances are dependent. The shift to the dependency presumption is said to have occurred in the latter part of the eighteenth century in Lord Mansfield's decisions in *Kingston v Preston* (1772)[2] and *Boone v Eyre* (1778) (*'Boone'*).[3] However, it was argued that the shift is very likely to have occurred earlier. The importance of the shift cannot be underestimated because of its importance to the central assumption made by the dominant model that failure of performance by one party (A) can in certain circumstances

---

[2] Cited in argument in *Jones v Barkley* (1781) 2 Doug 684, 99 ER 434.
[3] Cited in argument in *Duke of St Albans v Shore* 1 H Bl 270, 273; 126 ER 160.

justify the refusal to perform by the other party (B). This refusal is only justified because each party's performances are *dependent* on each other in some way: A's performance is a condition precedent or is a concurrent condition to B's performance.

(b) However, the problem with the dependency presumption was that without more it could result in unfair results; a minor failure of performance could justify the other party's refusal to perform. And in the context of the law at the time this could leave B with a windfall of the performance rendered before A's failure. Some further principle was needed and this in turn brings us to the second development, in the form of the principle laid down in *Boone*, although as was indicated it is likely to have existed in the law before, most probably in equity.

Boone laid down the following principle: only a substantial failure of performance by A will justify B's refusal to perform. A non-substantial failure will not justify B's refusal, and in these circumstances B must rely on a damages claim to make up for A's shortfall. Importantly, the *Boone* principle relied on the law relating to conditions and performance for its operation: a substantial failure by A would excuse B from performance because their promises were treated as dependent (conditional upon each other); a non-substantial failure would not justify B's refusal because the promises were treated as independent (unconditional).

(c) Although the principle was not laid down as an illustration of the subsidiarity of the indebitatus claims to the contractual claims (special assumpsit), it was adapted for this purpose in the sale of goods cases during the nineteenth century. It was within these cases that the dominant model emerged: a substantial failure of consideration left the innocent party free to escape their performance obligations and to rescind (the point that came to be known as termination) the contract because each performance was treated as dependent (conditional upon one another). A non-substantial failure of consideration did not allow rescission because the performances on each side were treated as independent (not conditional on each other). As the nineteenth century progressed, what was considered a substantial or non-substantial failure was determined less by the court's view of the quality of the breach and more by the parties' intentions, as evidenced in the contract, usually by reference to conditions (equivalent to substantial failure) and warranties (equivalent to non-substantial failure).

It was only in the substantial failure context that MHR or quantum meruit claims were possible. In other words, it was only when performance of the promises were conditional that MHR and quantum meruit claims, which form the basis of the modern law of unjust enrichment, had a role to play. Furthermore, it was shown that it did not matter whether the claim was made in the context of unenforceable contracts; the same principles applied.

(2) Chapter 5 also showed that setting aside the contract, or discharging each party's performance obligations, was not a necessary precondition for a MHR claim. This is because a MHR claim was still possible in an apportioned contract without each party discharging its overall contractual obligations. However, the conditionality of the transfer of the benefit was important: the money was paid on

condition that there would be a return performance of the portion, whose failure generates the right to the restitution of the value of the money.

(3) Finally, Chapter 5 showed that the subsidiarity of the MHR or quantum meruit claims to the claim on the contract is *not* best understood by the requirements that the contract had to be rescinded ab initio or that there had to be a total failure of consideration. This is because wiping away the contract was not a necessary condition for a restitutionary claim, and, moreover, the term rescission was not used consistently by the courts: there are a number of examples of groups of cases in which the term rescission was used, even though the contract was not wiped away. In relation to the total failure of consideration requirement, this is best understood as the court's commitment to literal restitution.

The main lesson from the historical analysis in Chapter 5 was that in order to bring claims for a quantum meruit or MHR (which today form the basis of a claim founded on unjust enrichment), the presence of a conditional transfer of the benefit was always necessary but rescission (what today is described as termination) of the contract was not.

The challenge taken up in Chapter 6 was to construct a model that reflects the importance of the law relating to conditions and performance, but also the fact that, unlike the dominant model, termination is not a necessary precondition. The conclusions reached here were as follows.

(1) Following the lead from the historical discussion in Chapter 5, the model put forward in Chapter 6 was premised on the following: unjust enrichment can be employed to claim the restitution of the value of a benefit transferred under a contract, only if the transfer is conditional and not when it is unconditional. Two questions will determine whether a party has a right to restitution: (1) was the transfer of the benefit conditional and (2) has there been a qualifying failure of condition?

In relation to the first question, it was shown how a condition of a transfer of a benefit can be a contractually promised counter-performance (promissory condition) or a contingent event (something which neither party has promised). The answer to the second question depends on the circumstances. Here, it is important to note a distinction adopted by this book between apportioned and unapportioned contracts. Essentially, apportioned contracts are those in which the law treats parts of performances as discrete sections of a contract (a typical example is an instalment contract). In relation to the second question, it is only in the context of promissory conditions of an unapportioned contract that the termination of the contract is necessary. In the context of apportioned contracts, termination is not a precondition.

(2) Unlike the majority of modern accounts of unjust enrichment, this book was sensitive to the distinction between money and non-money benefits, to the extent that the former are returnable and the latter are not. In keeping this aspect of returnability in mind, some of the problems with the law in this area became more transparent, including (a) the clash between the argument in favour of allowing flexible counter-restitution and law's policy against apportioning the

contract for the parties, and (b) claiming for part performance of a contract that is said to be entire. All this is not to say that money and non-money benefits should not be treated alike. Indeed, ultimately the model presented here did treat the two types of benefit in the same way, but the route to that conclusion was more difficult than is suggested by those that simply insist on symmetry from the start.

(3) The conditional analysis enabled us to understand better the impact of preventative conduct and accrued rights on the claims for restitution, founded on unjust enrichment, in the contractual context:

(a) The meaning of accrued rights to receive performance and their relationship to conditional rights to receive performance were clarified. A's right to receive B's performance under a contract between the parties may be *conditional* or *unconditional*. If it is unconditional it is called an accrued right. The unconditionality arises either because (a) no condition is attached to B's performance, or (b) the condition to B's performance has been fulfilled (either, and most commonly, by the holder of the accrued right or due to some external event). Where A's performance gives it an accrued right to B's performance, then a claim founded on unjust enrichment for the restitution of the value of A's performance will (a) fail where the accrued right is satisfied (by B's performance) because in such a case there is no identifiable failure of condition; or (b) succeed if B does not perform, for then the condition attached to A's performance will have failed. A contrast to the accrued right is the case where the right to B's performance is *conditional*. Here, if the condition is not fulfilled, any performance by B can be claimed back in an action founded on unjust enrichment.

(b) It was shown that prevention is not, as some have recently argued, a condition of a transfer of a benefit, but operates to excuse (and therefore constitutes a failure of) a condition. This way of looking at prevention is consistent with how the principle has been applied historically. Consider the situation where A's performance is a condition of B's performance. If B prevents A's performance, then the afore-mentioned condition fails. The effect of this is that A is excused from further performance and B cannot claim damages for A's failure. The options available to A are that he can either (i) claim damages if B's prevention is a breach of contract, or (ii) make a restitutionary claim for the value of the benefits transferred until B's prevention.

(4) The fact that a contract is unenforceable, or that the claim is made by the party in breach, did not impact on the operation of the failure of condition model. Indeed, it was concluded that the innocent party and the party in breach should be treated alike in respect of their claims for restitution founded on unjust enrichment.

(5) It was shown how the model presented in this book fitted with the new Birksian approach, which adopted the civilian absence of basis model for the common law which was defended in Chapter 3: a qualifying failure of condition constitutes the necessary absence of basis. Importantly, it was shown how the model presented here was an improvement upon the way in which Birks envisaged the operation of his new approach in the contractual context. The reason essentially is

that Birks remained committed to the view that the contract had to be terminated or wiped away in some way to fulfil the absence of basis model. This approach is unable to explain the fact that termination of the contract is not always necessary for a restitutionary claim founded on unjust enrichment.

(6) Finally, it was shown why the restitutionary claim which follows upon a failure of condition is not a contractual claim. There were good reasons to treat the restitutionary claim as founded on unjust enrichment. These were that historically and as a matter explaining common patterns in claims across the contractual context, the restitutionary claim upon failure of condition is non-contractual. Moreover, Chapter 3 showed the many problems that exist with attempts to treat the afore-mentioned resitutionary claim as contractual.

It is submitted that the failure of condition model presented in this book is clearer and more coherent than the dominant model currently adopted by the common law. It should replace the dominant model, and should be adopted more generally to explain the role of unjust enrichment in the contractual context. It could be adopted without great upheaval because it broadly follows the trends identified in the case law, as was illustrated by the detailed historical analysis which underpins this book.

Bibliography

Anon, *The Gentleman's Assistant, Trademan's Lawyer* (2nd edn, London, T Bever, 1709)

Anon, *A General Abridgment of Cases in Equity* (London, H Lintot and H Shuckburgh, 1734)

Anon, *A General Abridgment of Cases in Equity* (2nd edn, London, J Shuckburgh, 1734)

Anon, *Considerations on Various Grievances in the Practick Part of our Laws, with some observations on the Code Frederick, the Roman Law, and our own Courts of Equity, etc* (Dublin, 1756)

Anon, *Indexes to Mr Viner's General Abridgment of Law and Equity* (Oxford, 1757)

Anon, *An Introduction to the Law Relative to Trials at Nisi Prius* (London, C Bathurst, 1767)

Anon, *The Genuine Letters of Junius* (London, 1771)

Anon, 'On the Sale and Warranty of Horses' (1828–29) 1 *Law Mag Quart Rev Juris* 318

Anon, 'Recoupment' (1872–73) 8 *Am L Rev* 389

Adam, W, *A Practical Treatise and Observations on Trial by Jury in Civil Causes* (Edinburgh, T Clark, 1836)

Albery, M, 'Mr Cyprian Williams' Great Heresy' (1975) 91 *LQR* 337

American Law Institute, *Restatement of the Law of Restitution* (Philadelphia, American Law Institute, 1937)

—— *Restatement (Second) of Contracts* (Philadelphia, American Law Institute, 1981)

—— *Restatement Third, Restitution and Unjust Enrichment* (Philadelphia, American Law Institute, 2000)

Ames, JB, 'The History of Assumpsit' (1888) 2 *Harv L Rev* 1, 53

Andersen, E, 'The Restoration Interest and Damages for Breach of Contract' (1994) 53 *Maryland L Rev* 1

Atiyah, PS, *The Rise and Fall of Freedom of Contract* (Oxford, Clarendon Press, 1979)

—— *Essays on Contract* (Oxford, Clarendon, 1986)

Atiyah PS and Adams, JN, *Sale of Goods* (11th edn, London, Pearson Longman, 2005)

Ayres, I, 'Valuing Modern Contract Scholarship' (2003) 112 *Yale LJ* 881

Bacon, M, *A New Abridgment of the Law* (London, H Lintot, 1736–66)

Baker, JH, 'The Use of Assumpsit for Restitutionary Money Claims 1600–1800' in E Schrage (ed), *Unjust Enrichment: the Comparative Legal History of the Law of Restitution* (1st edn, Berlin, Duncker & Humbolt, 1995)

—— *The Common Law Tradition: Lawyers, Books and the Law* (London, Hambledon Press, 2000)

—— *An Introduction to Legal History* (4th edn, London, Butterworths, 2002)

—— 'Littleton, Sir Thomas (b before 1417, d 1481)' in *Oxford Dictionary of National Biography* (Oxford, OUP, 2004)

[Ballow], *A Treatise of Equity* (London, D Browne and J Shuckburgh, 1737)

Baloch, TA, 'Disguised and Outlawed Interest Claims in Unjust Enrichment' [2006] *RLR* 115

—— 'Law Booksellers and Printers as Agents of Unchange' (2007) 66 *CLJ* 389

Barker, K, 'The Nature and Scope of Restitution' (2001) 9 *RLR* 232

Barton, J, 'Contract and Quantum Meruit: the Antecedents of *Cutter v Powell*' (1987) 8 *J Leg Hist* 48

Beale, HG (ed), *Chitty on Contracts* (London, Sweet & Maxwell, 2004)

Beatson, J, *The Use and Abuse of Unjust Enrichment* (Oxford, Clarendon Press, 1991)

—— 'Restitution and Contract: Non-Cumul?' (2000) 1 *Theoretical Inquiries in Law* 83

—— *Anson's Law of Contract* (28th edn, Oxford, OUP, 2002)

Beatson, J and Virgo, G, 'Contract, Unjust Enrichment and Unconscionability' (2002) 118 *LQR* 352

Beever, A and Rickett, C, 'Interpretive Legal Theory and the Academic Lawyer' (2005) 68 *MLR* 320

Billinghurst, G, *Arcana Clericalia; or, the Mysteries of Clerkship Explained; declaring, defining, and illustrating the essential and formal parts of deeds and their nature* (London, R Sare & E Place, 1705)

Birks, P, 'English and Roman Learning in Moses v Macferlan' (1984) 37 *CLP* 1

—— *An Introduction to the Law of Restitution* (Oxford, Clarendon press, 1985)

—— *An Introduction to the Law of Restitution* (revised edn, Oxford, Clarendon Press, 1989)

—— *Restitution: the Future* (Annandale, NSW, Federation, 1992)

—— 'No Consideration: Restitution After Void Contracts' (1993) 23 *Univ Western Aus LR* 195

—— *The Structure of the English Law of Unjust Enrichment* (Nijmegen, Katholieke Universiteit, 1995)

—— 'Failure of Consideration' in F Rose (ed), *Consensus Ad Idem: Essays in Honour of Guenter Treitel* (London, Sweet & Maxwell, 1996)

____, 'Misnomer' in WR Cornish *et al* (eds), *Restitution, Past, Present and Future: Essays in Honour of Gareth Jones* (Oxford, Hart, 1998)

—— *English Private Law* (Oxford, OUP, 2000)

—— 'At the Expense of the Claimant: Direct and Indirect Enrichment in English Law' (2000) *Oxford U Comparative L Forum* 1, available at ouclf.iuscomp.org

—— 'Failure of Consideration and its Place on the Map' (2002) 2 *OUCLJ* 1

—— *The Foundations of Unjust Enrichment: Six Centennial Lectures* (Wellington, Victoria University Press, 2002)

—— *Unjust Enrichment* (1st edn, Oxford, Clarendon Press, 2003)

—— *Unjust Enrichment* (2nd edn, Oxford, OUP, 2005)

Birks, P and Mcleod, G, 'The Implied Contract Theory of Quasi Contract: Civilian Opinion Current in the Century Before Blackstone' [1986] *OJLS* 46

Birks, P and Mitchell, C, 'Unjust Enrichment' in P Birks (ed), *English Private Law* (Oxford, OUP, 2000)

Blackstone, W, *Commentaries on the Laws of England* (1st edn, Oxford, Clarendon Press, 1765–69)

Blount, T, *Nomo-Lexikon, a Law Dictionary, interpreting such difficult and obscure words and terms as are found in our common or statute, ancient or modern lawes* (London, J Martin and H Herringman, 1670)

Bohun, W, *Declarations and Pleadings, in the Most Usual Actions Brought in the Several Courts of King's Bench and Common Pleas at Westminster* (2nd edn, London, Samuel Birt *et al,* 1743)

Bridge, M, 'Discharge for Breach' (1982–83) 28 *McGill LJ* 867

Brindle, M and Cox, R, *Law of Bank Payments* (London, Sweet & Maxwell, 2004)

Brooks, CW, *Lawyers, Litigation and English Society Since 1450* (London, Hambledon, 1998)

Brooks, CW and Lobban, M, *Communities and Courts in Britain, 1150–1900* (London, Hambledon Press, 1997)

Bryan, M, 'Rescission, Restitution and Contractual Ordering: the Plaintiff Election' in A Robertson (ed), *The Law of Obligations: Connections and Boundaries* (London, UCL, 2004)

—— 'Unjust Enrichment and Unconcsionability in Australia' in JW Neyers, M McInnes and SGA Pitel (eds), *Understanding Unjust Enrichment* (Oxford/Portland, Hart, 2004)

Burn, R, *The Justice of the Peace and Parish Officer* (1st edn, London, A Millar, 1755)

Burrows, AS, *Essays on the Law of Restitution* (Oxford, Clarendon Press, 1991)

—— *The Law of Restitution* (1st edn, London, Butterworths, 1993)

—— 'Solving the Problem of Concurrent Liability' (1995) 48 *CLP* 103

—— 'Swaps and the Friction Between Common Law and Equity' [1995] *RLR* 15

—— *Understanding the Law of Obligations: Essays on Contract, Tort and Restitution* (Oxford, Hart, 1998)

—— *Fusing Common Law and Equity: Remedies, Restitution and Reform*, 2001 Hochelaga Lecture (London, Sweet and Maxwell, Hong Kong, 2002)

—— *The Law of Restitution* (2nd edn, London, Butterworths, 2002)

—— *Remedies for Torts and Breach of Contract* (3rd edn, Oxford, OUP, 2004)

—— 'Restitution in Respect of Mistakenly Paid Tax' (2005) 121 *LQR* 540

—— 'Absence of Basis: the New Birksian Scheme' in AS Burrows and A Rodger (eds), *Mapping the Law: Essays in Honour of Peter Birks* (Oxford, OUP, 2006)

Burrows, AS and McKendrick, E, *Cases and Materials on the Law of Restitution* (Oxford, OUP, 1997)

Burrows, AS, McKendrick, E and Edelman, J, *Cases and Materials on the Law of Restitution* (2nd edn, Oxford, OUP, 2006)

Byles, JB, *A Practical Treatise of the Law of Bills of Exchange, Promissory Notes, Bank-Notes, Bankers' Cash-Notes and Checks* (3rd edn, London, S Sweet, 1839)

Caldwell, J, *A Treatise of the Law of Arbitration* (1st edn, London, J Butterworth, 1817)

Campbell, R, *The London Tradesman, being a compendious view of all the trades, professions, arts, both liberal and mechanic, now practised in the cities of London and Westminster calculated for the information of parents, and instruction of youth in their choice of business* (1st edn, London, T Gardner, 1747)

Carter, JW, *Breach of Contract* (2nd edn, London, Sweet & Maxwell, 1991)

Carter, JW and Tolhurst, GJ, 'Conditional Payments and Failure of Consideration: Contract or Restitution' (2001) 9 *Asia Pacific Law Rev* 1

Cartwright, J, *Misrepresentation, Mistake and Non-Disclosure* (London, Sweet & Maxwell, 2007)

Chen-Wishart, M, 'In Defence of Unjust Factors: a Study of Rescission for Duress, Fraud and Exploitation' in D Johnston and R Zimmermann (eds), *Unjustified Enrichment: Key Issues in Comparative Perspective* (Cambridge, CUP, 2002)

Childres, R and Garamella, J, 'The Law of Restitution and the Reliance Interest in Contract' (1969) 64 *Northwestern U Law Rev* 433

Chitty, J, *A Practical Treatise on Pleading and to the Parties to the Action with a second volume containing Precedents of Pleadings* (1st edn, London, W Clarke 1809)

—— *A Practical Treatise on Bills of Exchange, Checks on Bankers, Promissory Notes, Bankers' Cash Notes, and Bank Notes* (London, 8th edn, S Brooke, 1833)

Chitty, J, *A Practical Treatise on the Law of Contracts Not Under Seal* (2nd edn, London, S Sweet, 1834)
—— *A Practical Treatise on the Law of Contracts Not Under Seal* (3rd edn, London, S Sweet, 1841)
Comyns, J, *A Digest of the Laws of England* (1st edn, London, J Knapton, T Longman and R Horsfield, 1762–67)
Corbin, AL, 'Conditions in the Law of Contract' (1918–19) 28 *Yale LJ* 739
—— *A Comprehensive Treatise on the Rules of Contract Law* (St Paul, West Publishing, 1960)
Cornish, WR, Nolan, R, O'Sullivan, J and Virgo, G, *Restitution: Past, Present and Future: Essays in Honour of Gareth Jones* (Oxford, Hart, 1998)
Craswell, R, 'Against Fuller and Perdue' (2000) 67 *U Chi L Rev* 99
—— 'In That Case, What is the Question? Economics and the Demands of Contract Theory' (2003) 112 *Yale LJ* 903
—— 'Instrumental Theories of Compensation: a Survey' (2003) 40 *San Diego L Rev* 1135
Cunningham, T, *A New and Complete Law Dictionary; or, General Abridgment of the Law* (1st edn, London, W Flexney *et al* 1771)
Dannemann, G, 'Unjust Enrichment by Transfer: Some Comparative Remarks' (2001) 79 *Tex L Rev* 1837
—— 'Absence of Basis: Can English Law Cope?' in AS Burrows and A Rodger (eds), *Mapping the Law: Essays in Honour of Peter Birks* (Oxford, OUP, 2006)
Davies, JC (ed), *Catalogue of Manuscripts in the Library of the Honourable Society of the Inner Temple* (Oxford, OUP, 1972)
Deacon, E, *The Law and Practice of Bankruptcy* (London, J & WT Clarke, 1827)
Devlin, Lord, 'The Treatment of Breach of Contract' (1966) *CLJ* 192
Dockray, M, '*Cutter v Powell*: a Trip outside the Text' (2001) 117 *LQR* 664
Dodd, 'Rescission' (1837) 13 *Leg Obs* 241
Du Plessis, J, 'Fraud, Duress and Unjustified Enrichment' in D Johnston and R Zimmermann (eds), *Unjustified Enrichment: Key Issues in Comparative Perspective* (Cambridge, CUP, 2002)
Edelman, J, 'Limitation Periods and the Theory of Unjust Enrichment' (2005) 68 *MLR* 848
—— 'The Meaning of "Unjust" in the English Law of Unjust Enrichment' (2006) *European Review of Private Law* 309
Edelman, J and Bant, E, *Unjust Enrichment in Australia* (Melbourne, OUP, 2006)
Edelman, J and Cassidy, DI, *Interest Awards in Australia* (Sydney, LexisNexis Butterworths, 2003)
Ellinger, E, Lomnicka, E and Hooley, R, *Ellinger's Modern Banking Law* (Oxford, OUP, 2006)
Elliot, N, Odgers, J and Phillips, J, *Byles on Bills of Exchange and Cheques* (27th edn, London, Sweet & Maxwell, 2002)
England, I, 'Restitution of Benefits Conferred Without Obligation' ch 5 in *International Encyclopaedia of Comparative Law*, vol X, *Restitution: Unjust Enrichment and Negotiorum Gestio* (Tèubingen/Dordrecht/Lancaster, JCB Mohr/Paul Siebeck/Martinus Nijhoff, 1991)
Evans, WD, *Essays: On the Action for Money Had and Received, on the Law of Insurances, and on the Law of Bills of Exchange and Promissory Notes* (Liverpool, Merrit & Wright, 1802)
Fifoot, CHS, *Lord Mansfield* (Oxford, Clarendon Press, 1936)

Fonblanque, J (ed), *A Treatise of Equity* (2nd edn, London, W Clarke & Son, 1799)

Francis, C, 'Practice, Strategy, and Institution: Debt Collection in English Common Law Courts' 80 *Northwestern U Law Rev* (1986) 807

Fuller, L and Perdue, W, 'Reliance Interest in Contract Damages' (1936–37) 46 *Yale LJ* 52, 373

Furst, S and Ramsey, V, *Keating on Construction Contracts* (8th edn, London, Sweet & Maxwell, 2006)

Gava, J and Greene, J, 'Do We Need a Hybrid Law of Contract? Why Hugh Collins is Wrong and Why it Matters?' (2004) 63 *CLJ* 605

Gergen, M, 'Restitution as a Bridge Over Contractual Waters' (2002) 71 *Ford L Rev* 709

—— 'The Restatement Third, Restitution and Unjust Enrichment at Midpoint' (2003) 56 *CLP* 289

—— 'Restitution and Contract: Reflections on the Third Restatement' (2005) 13 *RLR* 224

—— 'Self Interested Intervention in the Law of Unjust Enrichment' in R Zimmermann (ed), *Grundstrukturen eines Europaishen Beriecherungsrechts* (Tubingen, Mohr Siebeck, 2005)

Gilbert, G, *The History and Practice of the High Court of Chancery* (London, J Worrall and W Owen, 1758)

Gilbert, J, *The Law of Evidence* (London, W Owen, 1756)

Goff of Chieveley, RGB and Jones, GH, *The Law of Restitution* (1st edn, London, Sweet and Maxwell, 1966)

—— *The Law of Restitution* (2nd edn, London, Sweet & Maxwell, 1978)

—— *The Law of Restitution* (3rd edn, London, Sweet & Maxwell, 1986)

—— *The Law of Restitution* (4th edn, London, Sweet & Maxwell, 1993)

—— *The Law of Restitution* (5th edn, London, Sweet & Maxwell, 1998)

—— *The Law of Restitution* (6th edn, London, Sweet & Maxwell, 2002)

—— *The Law of Restitution* (7th edn, London, Sweet & Maxwell, 2007)

Gordley, J, 'Common Law in the Twentieth Century: Some Unfinished Business' (2000) 88 *Cal L Rev* 1816

Grantham, R and Rickett, C, *Enrichment and Restitution in New Zealand* (Oxford, Hart, 2000)

Green, TA, *Verdict According to Conscience* (Chicago, University of Chicago Press, 1985)

Guest, A (ed), *Benjamin's Sale of Goods* (7th edn, London, Sweet & Maxwell, 2006)

Hale, MS, *The History and Analysis of the Common Law* (London, J Walthoe, 1713)

Hamburger, P, 'The Development of the Nineteenth-Century Consensus Theory of Contract' (1989) 7 *Law and History Review* 241

—— 'Revolution and Judicial Review: Chief Justice Holt's Opinion in *City of London v Wood*' (1994) 94 *Colum L Rev* 2091

Hammond, A, *Comyns' A Digest of the Law of England* (5th edn, London, J Butterworth *et al*, 1822)

Harnett, B and Thornton, JV, 'The Insurance Condition Subsequent: a Needle in a Semantic Haystack' (1948) 17 *Ford L Rev* 220

Harpum, C, *Megarry and Wade's Law of Real Property* (6th edn, London, Sweet & Maxwell, 2000)

Havinghurst, AR, 'The Judiciary and Politics in the Reign of Charles II' (1950) 66 *LQR* 229

—— 'James II and the Twelve Men in Scarlet' (1953) 69 *LQR* 46

Hazeltine, HD, 'Gossip about Legal History: Unpublished Letters of Maitland and Ames' (1924) 2 *CLJ* 1

Hedley, S, *A Critical Introduction to Restitution* (London, Butterworths, 2001)
—— 'Implied Contract and Restitution' (2004) 63 *CLJ* 435
—— 'Unjust Enrichment: the Same Old Mistake?' in A Robertson (ed), *Law of Obligations: Connections and Boundaries* (London, UCL, 2004)
—— 'Tax Wrongly Paid: Basis of Recovery—Limitation' (2005) 65 *CLJ* 296
—— *Restitution: Its Division and Ordering* (London, Sweet & Maxwell, 2001)
Henderson, EG, 'The Background to the Seventh Amendment' (1966) 80 *Harv L Rev* 289
Hohfeld, WN, 'Fundamental Legal Conceptions' (1917) 26 *Yale LJ* 710
Holdsworth, W, *History of English Law* (London, Methuen, 1922–66)
—— 'The New Rules of Pleading of the Hilary Term, 1834' (1923) 1 *CLJ* 261
Holmes, OW, *The Common Law* (Boston, Little, Brown, & Co, 1881)
Home, H, *Principles of Equity* (1st edn, London/Edinburgh, A Millar/A Kincaid, 1760)
Hoppit, J, *Failed Legislation, 1660–1800, extracted from the Commons and Lords Journals* (London, Hambledon, 1997)
Horwitz, H, 'Changes in the Law and Reform of the Legal Order: England (and Wales) 1689–1760' (2002) 21 *Parliamentary History* 301
Horwitz, M, *Transformation of American Law 1780–1860* (Cambridge, Harvard University Press, 1977)
Ibbetson, D, 'Implied Contracts and Restitution: History in the High Court of Australia' (1988) 8 *OJLS* 312
—— *A Historical Introduction to the Law of Obligations* (Oxford, OUP, 1999)
—— 'Natural Law and Common Law' (2001) 5 *Edin L Rev* 4
—— 'Unjust Enrichment in English Law' in E Schrage (ed), *Unjust Enrichment and the Law of Contract* (The Hague/London, Kluwer Law International, 2001)
Impey, J, *The Modern Pleader, containing several forms of declarations in all actions* (London, J Butterworth, 1794)
Jackson, RM, *The History of Quasi Contract in English Law* (Cambridge, CUP, 1936)
Jacob, G, *The Common Law Common-Plac'd, containing, the substance and effect of all the common law cases, . . . collected as well from abridgments as reports, in a perfect new method* (2nd edn, London, F Clay and H Lintot, 1733)
—— *The Student's Companion; or, the Reason of the Laws of England, shewing the principal reasons and motives whereon our laws and statutes are grounded* (2nd edn, London, W Mears, 1734)
—— *Every Man His Own Lawyer; or, a summary of the Laws of England in a new and instructive method* (1st edn, London, J Hazard, S Birt and C Corbett, 1736)
—— *The General Laws of Estates; or, Freeholders Companion, containing the laws, statutes, and customs relating to freehold and other estates* (London, A Ward, 1740)
—— *A Law Grammar; or, rudiments of the law* (1st edn, London, A Ward, 1744)
—— *The Nature and Scope of Restitution: Vitiated Transfers, Imputed Contracts and Disgorgement* (Oxford, Hart, 2000)
Jones, GH, 'The Role of Equity in the Law of Restitution' in E Schrage (ed), *Unjust Enrichment: the Comparative History of the Law of Restitution* (Berlin, Dunker & Humblot, 1999)
Jones, W, *An Essay on the Law of Bailments* (London, C Dilly, 1781)
Keener, WA, *A Selection of Cases on the Law of Quasi-Contracts* (Cambridge, CW Sever, 1888)
—— *A Treatise on the Law of Quasi-Contracts* (New York, Baker, Voorhis & Co, 1893)

Krebs, T, *Restitution at the Crossroads* (London, Cavendish Press, 2000)

—— 'In Defence of Unjust Factors' in D Johnston and R Zimmermann (eds), *Unjustified Enrichment: Key Issues in Comparative Perspective* (Cambridge, CUP, 2002)

Kremer, B, 'The Action for Money Had and Received' (2001) *Journal of Contract Law* 1

—— 'Restitution and Unconscientiousness: Another View' (2003) 119 *LQR* 188

Kull, A, 'Mistake, Frustration, and the Windfall Principle of Contract Remedies' (1991) 41 *Hastings LJ* 1

—— 'Restitution as a Remedy for Breach of Contract' (1994) 67 *So Calif L Rev* 1465

—— 'Rationalising Restitution' (1995) 83 *Cal L Rev* 1191

—— 'James Barr Ames and the Early Modern History of Unjust Enrichment' (2004) 25 *OJLS* 297

Kyd, S, *A Treatise on the Law of Awards* (1st edn, London, S Crowder, 1791)

—— *Comyns' A Digest of the Laws of England* (4th edn, Dublin, Luke White, 1793)

Lambert, S (ed), *House of Commons Sessional Papers of the Eighteenth Century* (Wilmington, Scholarly Resources, 1975)

Langbein, J, 'Historical Foundations of the Modern Law of Evidence: a View from the Ryder Sources' (1996) 96 *Colum L Rev* 1167

Langdell, CC, *A Summary of the Law of Contracts* (2nd edn, Boston, Little Brown & Company, 1880)

Lawes, E, *A Practical Treatise on Pleading in Assumpsit* (London, W Reed, 1810)

Lemmings, D, 'Blackstone and Law Reform by Education: Preparation for the Bar and Lawyerly Culture in Eighteenth Century England' (1998) 16 *Law and History Rev* 242

—— *Professors of the Law* (Oxford, OUP, 2000)

Lilly, J, *The Practical Conveyancer, in two parts, Part i, containing rules and instructions for drawing all sorts of conveyances of estates and interests* (1st edn, London, T Ward and J Hooke, 1719)

—— *The Practical Register; or, a General Abridgement of the Law, as it is now practised in the several courts of Chancery, King's Bench, Common Pleas and Exchequer* (2nd edn, London, J Walthoe *et al*, 1735)

Lobban, M, *The Common Law and English Jurisprudence 1760–1850* (Oxford, Clarendon Press, 1991)

—— 'Contractual Fraud in Law and Equity, c1750–c1850' (1997) 17 *OJLS* 441

—— 'The English Legal Treatise' (1997) 13 *Iuris Scripta Historica* 69

—— 'The Ambition of Lord Kames' in A Lewis and M Lobban (eds), *Law and History*, Current Legal Issues vol 6 (Oxford, OUP, 2004)

Lord, RA, *Williston on Contracts* (4th edn, Rochester, Lawyers Co-operative Pub Co, 1990)

Macnair, M, 'Vicinage and the Antecedents of the Jury' (1999) 17 *Law and History Rev* 537

—— 'The Court of Exchequer and Equity' (2001) 22 *J Leg Hist* 75

Macqueen, H and Sellar, W, 'Unjust Enrichment in Scots Law' in E Schrage (ed), *Unjust Enrichment: the Comparative Legal History of the Law of Restitution* (2nd edn, Berlin, Dunker & Humblot, 1999)

Maher, F, 'A New Conception of Failure of Basis' (2005) *RLR* 96

Maine, H, *Ancient Law* (London, John Murray, 1861)

Maitland, FW, *The Forms of Action at Common Law* (Cambridge, CUP, 1941 repr)

Mallory, J, *Objections humbly offer'd against passing the bill, intitled, A bill for the more easy and speedy recovery of small debts, into a law* (London, J Roberts, 1730)

Mallory, J, *Modern Entries, in English, being a select collection of pleadings in the Courts of King's Bench, Common Pleas and Exchequer* (London, R Gosling, 1734–35)

Markesinis, BS, W Lorenz and G Dannemann, *The Law of Contracts and Restitution: a Comparative Introduction* (Oxford, Clarendon Press, 1997) vol I

Mcfarlane, B and Stevens, R, 'In Defence of *Sumpter v Hedges*' (2002) 118 *LQR* 569

McGovern, W, 'Dependent Promises in the History of Leases and Other Contracts' (1977–78) 52 *Tul L Rev* 659

Mcgregor, H, *McGregor on Damages* (17th edn, London, Sweet & Maxwell, 2003)

McKendrick, E, 'Total Failure of Consideration and Counter-Restitution: Two Issues or One?' in P Birks (ed), *Laundering and Receipt* (Oxford, Clarendon Press, 1995)

Meier, S, 'Restitution After Executed Void Contracts' in P Birks and F Rose (eds), *Lessons from the Swaps Litigation* (London, Mansfield LLP, 2000)

—— 'Unjust Factors and Legal Grounds' in D Johnston and R Zimmermann (eds), *Unjustified Enrichment: Key Issues in Comparative Perspective* (Cambridge, CUP, 2002)

—— 'No Basis: a Comparative View' in AS Burrows and A Rodger (eds), *Mapping the Law: Essays in Honour of Peter Birks* (Oxford, OUP, 2006)

Meier, S and Zimmermann, R, 'Judicial Development of the Law, *Error Iuris* and the Law of Unjustified Enrichment' (1999) 115 *LQR* 556

Mitchell, C, 'Planche v Colburn (1831)' in C Mitchell and P Mitchell (eds), *Landmark Cases in the Law of Restitution* (Oxford, Hart, 2006)

Mitchell, C and Edelman, J, 'Restitution' (2006) *All ER Rev* 337

Munkman, JH, *The Law of Quasi-Contracts* (London, Sir Isaac Pitman & Sons, 1950)

Nelson, W, *An Abridgment of the Common Law, being a collection of the principal cases argued and adjudged in the several courts of Westminster-Hall* (London, R Gosling *et al*, 1725–26)

Oldham, J, 'The Origins of the Special Jury' (1983) 50 *U Chi L Rev* 137

—— 'Eighteenth Century Judges' Notes: How they Correct, Explain and Enhance Reports' 31 (1987) *Am J Leg Hist* 9

—— *The Mansfield Manuscripts and the Growth of English Law in the Eighteenth Century* (Chapel Hill, University of North Carolina Press, 1992)

—— 'Underreported and Underrated: the Court of Common Pleas in the Eighteenth Century' in H Hartog and W Nelson (eds), *Law as Culture and Culture as Law: Essays in Honour of John Phillip Reid* (Madison, Madison House Publishers, 2000)

—— 'Buller, Sir Francis, first Baronet (1746–1800)' in *Oxford Dictionary of National Biography* (Oxford, OUP, 2004)

—— *English Common Law in the Age of Mansfield*, Studies in Legal History (Chapel Hill, University of North Carolina Press, 2004)

—— 'Murray, William, first earl of Mansfield (1705–1793)' in *Oxford Dictionary of National Biography* (Oxford, OUP, 2004)

—— *Trial by Jury* (New York, New York University Press, 2006)

Perillo, J, 'Restitution in a Contractual Context' (1973) 73 *Colum L Rev* 1208

—— 'Restitution in the Second Restatement of Contracts' (1981) 81 *Colum L Rev* 37

Petersdorff, C, *A Practical and Elementary Abridgment of the Common Law* (London, V and R Stevens and G S Norton, 1841–44)

Plessis, JD, 'Toward a Rational Structure of Liability for Unjustified Enrichment: Thoughts from Two Mixed Jurisdictions' (2005) 122 *South African LJ* 142

Posner, E, 'Economic Analysis of Contract Law After Three Decades: Success or Failure' (2003) 112 *Yale LJ* 829

Pothier, M, *A Treatise on the Law of Obligations* (Philadelphia, R Small, 1826)

Powell, JJ, *Essay upon the Law of Contracts and Agreements* (London, J Johnson and T Whieldon, 1790)

Rogers, JS, *The Early History of the Law of Bills and Notes* (Cambridge, CUP, 1995)

Roscoe, H, *A Digest of the Law of Evidence on the Trial of Actions at Nisi Prius* (London, Butterworth, 1827)

Rose, F, 'The Evolution of the Species' in AS Burrows and L Rodger (eds), *Mapping the Law: Essays in Memory of Peter Birks* (Oxford, OUP, 2006)

Rose, F and Birks, P, *Restitution and Equity* (London, Mansfield, 2000)

Ross, I, *Lord Kames and the Scotland of his Day* (Oxford, Clarendon Press, 1972)

Rubini, DA, 'The Precarious Independence of the Judiciary 1688–1701' (1967) 83 *LQR* 343

Russell, F, *A Treatise on the Power and Duty of an Arbitrator* (1st edn, London, W Benning & Co, 1849)

Saunders, JS, *The Law of Pleading and Evidence* (1st edn, London, S Sweet and A Maxwell, 1828)

Schermaier, MJ, ' "Performance-Based" and "Non Performance Based" Enrichment Claims: the German Pattern' (2006) *European Review of Private Law* 363

Schiefer, JF, *An Explanation of the Practice of Law, containing the elements of special pleading, reduced to the comprehension of every one* (London, J Pheney, 1792)

Scott, H, 'Restitution of Extra-Contractual Transfers: Limits of the Absence of Legal Ground Analysis' (2006) 14 *RLR* 93

Scott, JB, *Cases on Quasi-Contracts* (New York, Baker, Voorhis & Co, 1905)

Seavey, WA and Scott, AW, 'The American Restatement of the Law of Restitution' (1938) 54 *LQR* 29

Shapiro, B, 'Law Reform in Seventeenth Century England' (1975) 19 *Am J Leg Hist* 280

Shea, AM 'Discharge from Performance of Contracts by Failure of Condition' (1979) 42 *MLR* 623

Sheehan, D, 'Natural Obligations in English Law' (2004) *LMCLQ* 172

—— 'Unjust Factors or Restitution of Transfers *Sine Causa*' (2008) *Oxford U Comparative L Forum* 1 available at ouclf.iuscomp.org

Sheppard, W, *Actions Upon the Case for Deeds viz Contracts, Assumpsits, Deceits, Nuisances, Trover and Conversion* (2nd edn, London, SS, 1675)

Simpson, AW, *A History of the Common Law of Contract* (Oxford, OUP, 1975)

—— 'Innovation in Nineteenth Century Contract Law' (1975) 91 *LQR* 247

—— 'The Rise and Fall of the Legal Treatise: Legal Principles and the Forms of Legal Literature' (1981) 48 *U Chi L Rev* 632

Smith, J, *A Selection of Leading Cases* (2nd edn, London, A Maxwell, 1841–42)

Smith, L, 'The Mystery of Juristic Reason' (2000) 12 *Supreme Court Law Revi* (2d) 211

—— 'Demystifying Juristic Reasons' (2007) 45 *Canadian Business J* 281

—— 'Unjust Enrichment; Big or Small' in S Degeling and J Edelman (eds), *Unjust Enrichment in Commercial Law* (Sydney, Thomson LLP, 2008)

Smith, SA, 'Concurrent Liability in Contract and Unjust Enrichment' (1999) 115 *LQR* 245

—— *Contract Theory* (Oxford, OUP, 2004)

Starkie, T, *A Practical Treatise on the Law of Evidence* (1st edn, London, J and WT Clarke, 1824)

Stephen, H, *A Treatise on the Principle of Pleading in Civil Actions* (2nd edn, London, J Butterworth, 1827)

Stevens, R, 'The New Birksian Approach to Unjust Enrichment' (2004) *RLR* 270

—— 'Justified Enrichment' (2005) 5 *OUCLJ* 141

—— 'Three Enrichment Issues' in AS Burrows and L Rodger (eds), *Mapping the Law: Essays in Memory of Peter Birks* (Oxford, OUP, 2006)

—— 'Is There a Law of Unjust Enrichment' in S Degeling and J Edelman (eds), *Unjust Enrichment in Commercial Law* (Sydney, Thomson LLP, 2008)

Stoljar, S, 'Conditions, Warranties and Descriptions of Quality in Sale of Goods (Pt 1)' (1952) 15 *MLR* 425

—— 'Conditions, Warranties and Descriptions of Quality in Sale of Goods (Pt 2)' (1953) 16 *MLR* 174

—— 'The Contractual Concept of Condition' (1953) 69 *LQR* 485

—— 'Prevention and Co-operation in the Law of Contract' (1953) 31 *Can Bar Rev* 231

—— 'Dependent and Independent Promises' (1956–58) 2 *Sydney L Rev* 217

—— 'Some Problems of Anticipatory Breach' (1973–74) 9 *Melbourne Univ L Rev* 355

Story, W, *A Treatise on the Law of Sales of Personal Property* (2nd edn, Boston, Little, Brown & Co, 1853)

Street, TA, *The Foundations of Legal Liability: a Presentation of the Theory and Development of the Common Law* (New York, E Thompson, 1906)

Sugden, E, *Practical Treatise of the Law of Vendors and Purchasers of Estates* (1st edn, London, Brooke & Clarke/Butterworth, 1805)

—— *Practical Treatise of the Law of Vendors and Purchasers of Estates* (11th edn, London, Brooke & Clarke, 1846)

Sutton, D and Gill, J, *Russell on Arbitration* (22nd edn, London, Sweet & Maxwell, 2003)

Swain, W, 'Moses v Macferlan' in C Mitchell and P Mitchell (eds), *Landmark Cases in the Law of Restitution* (Oxford, Hart, 2006)

—— 'Cutter v Powell and the Pleading of Claims in Unjust Enrichment' (2003) *RLR* 46

Swinton, JLS, *Considerations concerning a proposal for dividing the Court of Session into classes or chambers; and for limiting litigation in small causes; and for the revival of jury-trial in certain civil actions* (Edinburgh, 1789)

Sykes, A, 'Impossibility Doctrine in Contract Law' in P Newman (ed), *The New Palgrave Dictionary of Economics and the Law* (London, Palgrave Macmillan, 1998, 2002)

Tettenborn, A, 'Subsisting Contracts and Failure of Consideration: a Little Scepticism' (2002) *RLR* 1

Thayer, J, 'Presumptions and the Law of Evidence' (1889–90) 3 *Harv L Rev* 141

—— '"Law and Fact" in Jury Trials' (1890–91) 4 *Harv L Rev* 147

Treitel, G, 'Some Problems of Breach of Contract' (1967) 30 *MLR* 139

—— *Remedies for Breach of Contract: a Comparative Account* (Oxford, OUP, 1989)

—— *The Law of Contract* (11th edn, London, Sweet & Maxwell, 2003)

Viner, C, *A General Abridgment of Law and Equity, alphabetically digested under proper titles with notes and references to the whole* (Aldershot, C Viner, 1742–57)

Virgo, G, *Principles of the Law of Restitution* (Oxford, OUP, 1999)

—— '*Deutsche Morgan Grenfell*: the Right to Restitution of Tax Paid by Mistake' (2005) 3 *BTR* 281

—— *The Principles of the Law of Restitution* (2nd edn, Oxford, OUP, 2006)

Visser, D, 'Searches for Silver Bullets: Enrichment in Three-Party Situations' in D Johnston and R Zimmermann (eds), *Unjustified Enrichment: Key Issues in Comparative Perspective* (Cambridge, CUP, 2002)

Waddams, S, *Dimensions of Private Law Categories and Concepts in Anglo American Reasoning* (Cambridge, CUP, 2003)

Walker, D, *A Legal History of Scotland* (London, Butterworths, 2001)

Walker, H, 'Rescission of Contracts for Sale of Land' (1932) 6 *ALJ* 49

Weatherill, S and Beaumont, P, *EU Law* (3rd edn, London, Penguin, 1999)

White, M, 'Contract Breach and Contract Discharge Due to Impossibility: a Unified Theory' (1988) 17 *J Leg Stud* 353

Wigmore, H, 'A Summary of Quasi Contracts' (1891) 25 *Am L Rev* 46

Williston, S, 'Rescission for Breach of Warranty' (1903) 16 *Harv L Rev* 465

—— *The Law of Contracts* (1st edn, New York, Baker, Voorhis & Co, 1920)

Winfield, PH, *The Province of the Law of Tort*, Tagore Law Lecture 1930 (Cambridge, CUP, 1931)

—— *The Law of Quasi-Contracts* (London, Sweet & Maxwell, 1952)

Wood, T, *An Institute of the Laws of England; or, the laws of England in their natural order, according to common use* (3rd edn, London, R Sare, 1724)

Woodward, FC, *The Law of Quasi Contracts* (Boston, Little, Brown, & Co, 1913)

Yale, D (ed), *Lord Nottingham's Two Treatises* (Cambridge, CUP, 1965)

Zimmermann, R, *The Law of Obligations: Roman Foundations of the Civilian Tradition* (paperback edn, Oxford, Clarendon Press, 1990)

—— 'Unjustified Enrichment' (1995) 15 *OJLS* 403

Zimmermann, R and Du Plessis, J, 'Basic Features of the German Law of Unjustified Enrichment' (1994) 2 *RLR* 14

Index

Abinger, Lord, 118
  in *Chanter v Hopkins*, 118–9
'Absence of basis', 9, 82
Accrued rights, 156
  see also Conditional rights; Principle of
      prevention
  to payment, 177
  to receive performance, 157, 160, 188
    unconditional, 163–4
  transfer of benefits, 157–8
    unconditional, 159
Advanced Corporation Tax (ACT), 83
AG v Perry, 26
  regarding Money had and received ('MHR'),
      26
*An Introduction to the Law relative to Trials at
      Nisi Prius* ('LNP), 131–2
Apportionability, 150
  are those in which, 187
  determined by contract, 150
Apportioned contracts, *see* Contract
Arris and Arris v Stukeley, 21
Ashburton, Lord, 57–8
Atwood v Maud, 154
Australian High Court, 82, 147
  in *Baltic Shipping v Dillon*, 152

Baltic Shipping v Dillon, 152, 156
  see also Australian High Court
*Bank of Boston Connecticut v European Grain
      Shipping*, 158
  see also Brandon, Lord
Bankruptcy laws, 38
Bannerman v White, 120
Barr v Gibson, 119
  leading authority for, 119
Basten v Butter, 136
Blackstone, Sir William, 7
Blackwell v Nash, 104
Boone principle, *see Boone v Eyre*
Boone v Eyre, 98, 123, 185
  see also Mansfield, Lord, Williams, Serjeant
  details of, 101
  failure of performance, 124
  flexible approach, 120
  greatly influenced modern law, 98
  not so novel, 106, 109
  principle in, 104–6, 112, 116

context of, 107
  in detail, 106–11
  relied on, 108, 186
  reception of, 111
Brightman, Lord, 151
  in *Miles v Wakefield*, 151
Brandon, Lord, 158
  in *Bank of Boston v European Grain Shipping*
Brown v Bullen, 38
Bull v Sibbs, 138
Buller, Francis, 102
Buller, J, 113, 115, 136
Burrow, Sir James, 102, 103

C&P Haulage v Middleton, 67
Chandler v Webster, 176
Chater v Beckett, 115
City of York v Toun, 23
Class of instruments, 25
  extending, 25
Common pleas, 33
  in King's Bench, 32
Condition, 142
  see also Principle of prevention
  apportioned contracts, 147–8
  definition of, 142
    in common law literature, 142–3
  different types of, 143–4
  failure of, 176–8
    Birk's approach, 176
    equates with absence of basis, 176–8
    restitution upon, 178–80
  future/uncertain event, 145
  qualifying failure of, 146
  various, 145–6
Conditional rights, 160–1
Contract, 10
  see also Apportionability; Hedley, B; Quasi
      contract
  ab initio, 125
    test for, 125
  apportioned, 128, 147
    right of party to recover, 148
  classification category, 10–1, 12
  consensual theory, 11
  creation of, 143
  difficult relationship with unjust enrichment,
      124

Index

Contract (*cont.*):
  'express contract fallacy', 60
  implied theory, 41–2
    language of, 45
  must be very precise, 64
  promises by law/parties, 12
  unapportioned, 151–6
    point of termination, 152
  unclear definition, 63
  unenforceable, 174–5
  termination for breach of, 183
    restitution after, 184
    unenforceable, 188
  void, 75
  were considered independent, 98
    promises, 99
Counter-restitution, *see* Restitution
Court of Appeal, 155
Court of Common Pleas, 32
CTN Cash and carry v Gallaher, 79–81
  Court of Appeal's failure, 79
    adopted wrong basis, 80
    to incorporate, 80–1
Cutter v Powell, 133, 136
  see also Kenyon, Lord
  principle of, 134

Decker v Pope, 20, 33
  see also Mansfield, Lord
  reference to equity, 29
Demurrer book, 15
Deutsch Morgan Grenfell v Inland Revenue
    Commissioners, 83
  interest claim in unjust enrichment,
    83–4
  rejected in Court of Appeal, 83
Dies v British and International Mining and
    Finance Corp, 170
  type case, 170
Doctrine of consideration, 74

Ellen v Topp, 119
Ellenborough, Lord, 136
  in *Farnsworth v Gerrard*, 136
Eliot v Von Glehn, 119
Ellis v Hamlen, 136
Equity, 29
  see also Mansfield, Lord
  influence on Lord Mansfield, 29, 35
    principle, 39–40
  in Thomas Sewell's manuscripts, 30–1
  /law divide, 44–5
  relationship with indebitatus claims,
    30
  treatment by Lord Kames, 36–7
European Court of Justice, 83
Expectation principle, 52
Expressum facit cessare taciturn, 115

Farnsworth v Gerrard, 136
  see also Ellenborough, Lord
Federal Court of Appeal, 147
Ferguson (DO) & Associates v Sohl, 156
Fibrosa Spolka Ackcynja v Fairbairn Lawson
    Coombe Barbour Ltd, 124, 177
  conditional payment, 178, 179
  represents binding/most persuasive authority,
    179
  restitutionary award in, 176
First Restatement of Restitution, 51
Floyer v Edwards, 38
Foreman State Trust & Savings Banks v Tauber,
    166
Freedom of choice, 169
  infringing, 169–70

Gaselee, J, 137
German Civil Code, 72
Goodisson v Nunn, 103
Graves v Legg, 119
Grose, Nash, 103, 115
Gummow, J, 46
  principle of unconcientousness, 46

Ha v New South Wales, 147
Hargrave, Francis, 31
Hedley, B, 59, 67, 184
  critic of restitution theorists, 59–61
  'express contract fallacy', 60, 62
  foundation of argument, 60
  law of restitution, 60
  questionable methodology, 61
  use of implied contract, 62–3
    problems of 'fit', 63
Henry v Schroeder, 128
  Cyprian Williams interpretation of, 128
High Court of Australia, *see* Australian High
    Court
Hochster v De La Tour, 55, 56
  two steams of cases, 57–8
Holt, Lord CJ, 7, 8, 34
  fears vindicated, 25
  in *Shuttleworth v Garnet*, 22
  in *Thorp v Thorpe*, 99, 104
  regarding indebitatus claims, 20–9
  regarding Money had and received, 24
  'Horse warranty cases', *see* Subsidiarity
House of Lords, 40, 83
Hulle v Heightman, 133, 135, 136
  case of prevention, 133–4
Hunt v Silk, 123
  contract/unjust enrichment, 124
Hyundai Heavy Industries v Papadopoulos, 162–3
  problem with, 163

'Indebitatus claims', 5, 12–3, 135
  see also Holt, CJ; Mansfield, Lord

count's wording, 18
disunity among, 10
encouraging, 31–3
fictional nature of promises of, 184
for fines by custom, 23
formula, 24
'implied contract theory', 41–2
legal community of, 42
non-contractual, 47, 183
personality/realty world, 22
pleading of, 16
  by passing, 16
  created scope for theorising, 19
procedure/development, 13–9
recovering a wager, 21
suggesting alternatives, 41
understanding, 6
  as non-contractual, 7, 8, 10
'Implied contract theory', *see* 'Indebitatus
  claims'
Isaac Masos v Parker, 27

Jacobs, Giles, 133
  Law Grammar, 133
    regarding quantum meruit, 133
Jaffey, C, 64, 67, 184
  approach to law of restitution, 64
  bold claim 65
    no historical, 66
  methodology, 65–6
    difficulties with model, 66–7

Kames, Lord, 35
  see also Mansfield, Lord
  Treatise on Equity, 35, 105
    groundbreaking work, 35–6
    Pomponius' maxim, 36
Kelly v Solari, 81
Kenyon, Lord, 104, 115, 133
  in *Cutter v Powell*, 133,
King's Bench, 6, 8, 26
  common pleas caseload, 32
  extending pleading category, 24
  rise in business in, 18, 29
Kingston v Preston, 98, 103, 185
  see also Mansfield, Lord
  details of, 100–1
  greatly influence modern law, 98
  is important for, 102
  not so novel, 109
Kull, Professor, 47, 58, 67, 184
  approach to restitution, 52–3
    primacy of contract over, 59
  defends frustration/mistake rules, 54
  defends traditional recission requirements, 51
  gap-filling thesis, 56
  regarding Planche, 138
  regarding remedies, 51

  for contract breach, 54
  historical claims, 55–8
  Third Restatement of Restitution (R3R), 47–8,
    52
    does not exercise unjust enrichment, 50
    least radical of, 48–9
    split into four, 49–50

Lawes, Serjeant Edward, 42
Lawrence, JJ, 115
Le Blanc, J, 134
Legal literature, 19
  law book trade, 19
  poverty of, 101
Leigh v Dickeson, 169
Leigh v Patterson, 57
Leistungkondikition, see Unjust enrichment
Lindon v Hooper, 22
  see also Mansfield, Lord

Maclean v Dunn, 126
  right of resale, 126
Mansfield, Lord, 6, 7, 13, 38, 46, 103, 118
  attractive court of, 33
  debt litigation, 32
  encouraged indebitatus/ Money had and
      received claims, 8, 19–20, 31, 183
    limited, 39
    rationalising, 35
  envisaged equitable principles, 9
  equity principle, 39–40
  in *Boone v Eyre*, 98, 100, 101
    formula, 105
    principle in, 104, 105
  in *Decker v Pope*, 20, 21, 29
  in *Kingston v Preston*, 98, 100, 101, 102
  in *Lindon v Hooper*, 22
  in *Moses v Macferlan*, 12, 25, 26, 37, 45,
    183
    decision in, 33–7
    influence of equity, 29, 30, 31
  in *Stevenson v Snow*, 128
  in *Weston v Downes*, 113–4
  list, 27, 35, 38
  main innovation was to, 183
  regarding Roman law, 27–8
  response to Lord Kames, 36–7
  special juries, 18
Money had and received claims, 7, 9, 26, 27, 35,
    97, 113, 120
  see also Holt, CJ; Mansfield, Lord
  count surprising claimant, 116
  equity-driven, 40
  expanding province of, 39
  for apportioned contract, 128
  foundation of, 42
  high frequency of cases, 38
  in substantial failure context, 139

Money had and received claims (*cont.*):
　subsidiary to, 112, 122, 139, 187
　　special assumpsit, 122, 124
　unconditional promises, 186
　wiping out contract, 127
Miles v Wakefield, 151
　see also Brightman, Lord; Templeman, Lord
Mitigation principle, 52
Moses v Macfarlan, 7, 28, 33
　see also Mansfield, Lord
　discreet circumstances, 40
　Mansfield's decision, 33–7
Motion for new trial, 17
Motion in arrest of judgement, 17

'Non assumpit', 16
New Birksonian approach, *see* Unjust
　　Enrichment
Nichols v Raynbred, 99

Palmer v Temple, 125
　part of problem in, 126
　　absence of resale condition, 126
Paper book, 15
Parks, J, 83, 84
Peel, Edwin, 94
Planche v Colburn, 55–6, 134, 137–9, 165, 167
　see also Kull, Professor
　challenge for restitution scholars, 137
　definition of benefit, 130
　historical claims for, 137–8
Pleading, 14
　stages, 14–5
Pomponius, 36
　maxim as foundation of Money had and
　　received, 42–3
Pordage v Cole, 104
　see also Williams, Serjeant
Power v Wells, 113
Prima facie rules of law, 17
Principle against forced exchange, 49
Principle of pleading, 110
　by Stoljar, 110
Principle of prevention, 164
　as condition/basis of benefit transfer, 165
　/breach, 165–6
　claims available after, 166
　definition of, 164
Principle of wrongful prevention, 168
Principle of unconscientousness, 46

Quantum meruit claims, 124, 135
　see also Subsidiarity
　common perception of, 130
　　modern boundaries of contract, 130
　distinctiveness of, 141, 167–9
　equivalent to partial enforcement, 171, 172
　in contractual context, 128

in substantial failure context, 139
　meaning of term, 129
　more flexible use of, 135
　preventing unjust enrichment, 169
　relationship with special assumpit, 131
　restitutionary, 172, 173
　　reversal of unjust enrichment, 173
　role of policy, 131
　similar actions covering same ground, 130–1
　subsidiarity of, 139, 187
　unconditional promises, 186
　value of work done, 172
Quasi contract, 42, 43

Recovery of small debts, 32
　improving, 32
Reliance, 66
　see also Jaffey, C
　interest, 67
　loss, 67
　theory of contract, 66
　　inability of, 67
Rescission, 122
　acts as gateway to claims, 135
　court did not understand, 125
　horse warranty cases, 125
　　contract ab initio, 125
　　test for, 125
　misuse of word, 125
　recoverability of interest on Money had and
　　　received claim, 127
　replace with 'termination', 122
　right to resale, 126
　total failure of consideration, 122–3
Restatement of Restitution, 41
　reporters of, 44n
Restitution, 60
　see also Jaffey, C
　after termination for breach, 184
　counter, 152–3
　　flexible model of, 154, 155
　　main argument against, 153
　English law, 74–5
　　general approach, 78
　founded of unjust enrichment, 185
　historical foundation of, 183
　invalidity of contract, 75, 78
　is payor's only remedy, 154
　law of, 60
　pyramid/Birksonian approach, 77–8
　upon failure of condition, 178–80
Roman law, 7, 27
Rover v Cannon Film Sales (No3), 160
　conditional right to receive performance, 160
Rowland v Divall, 155
Roxborough v Rothmans of Pall Mall (Austrialia)
　　Ltd, 46, 160, 161
　absence of basis, 82

ignored termination precondition, 147
restitution of tax element, 82
was correctly decided, 149
Rules of practice, 17
Rules of presumption, 17
Ryder, Sir Dudley, 26
notebooks, 26–7

'Sale and Warranty of Horses', 117
Sale of Goods Act, 120
Second Restatement of Contract, 51, 149
Sewell, Sir Thomas, 30
manuscripts, 30
equity theory in, 30–1
Shuttleworth v Garnet, 21
see also Holt, CJ
CJ Holt's resistance, 21–2
similar to, 23
Smith, Lionel, 86
regarding new Birksonian approach,
86
Spankie, Serjeant, 137
St Alban's v Shore, 108
flexible approach, 120
Statute of Frauds, 121
Stevenson v Snow, 128
see also Mansfield, Lord
logic in, 128–9
Stocznia Gdanska v Latvian Shipping Co,
163
Street v Blay, 117, 135
effect of, 118
principle of, 119
Subsidiarity, 112
early forms of, 112–6
horse warranty cases, 112, 118
of Money had and received claim, 122
regarding quantum meruit, 133
Sumpter v Hedges, 170
problem with argument, 170
quantum meruit in, 171–2
wrong to deny, 174

Templeman, Lord, 151
in *Miles v Wakefield*, 151
The Law of Contract, 94
Third Restatement of Restitution, see Kull,
Professor
Thorp v Thorp, 99, 104
see also Holt, Lord CJ
Tindal, CJ, 137
Total failure requirement, 152
best way to view, 152–3
Toussaint v Martinnant, 115
best explanation of, 116
Towers v Barrett, 113
Treatise on Equity, see Kames, Lord
Trial by jury, 18

Ughtred's Case, 99–100, 101
Unapportioned contracts, *see* Contract
Unenforceable contracts, *see* Contract
Unjust enrichment, 5, 89
see also CTN Cash and carry v Gallaher, Kull,
Professor
best model for, 185
claims in common law, 69–70, 180
regarding accrued rights, 92–3
contract must be terminated, 90
termination precondition, 91, 123
current model, 46
definition of benefit in, 129–30
difficult relationship with contract 124
foundation of, 6–7
equitable, 46
framework for claims, 45
German law of, 72
'basis' test, 72–4
notion of, 74–6
objectively/subjectively, 73
problem, 73–4
by transfer/another way, 72
Leistungkondikition, 76
German model, 70, 71
civilian approach, 70–1
historical foundation, 97
favour of dependency, 98
independency, 98–100
presumption, 99
in England, 43
in US, 43–4
Kreb's conclusion, 70
model, 6
modern law of, 9
new Birksonian approach, 72, 74, 81, 87, 176,
177, 188
greater unity, 76
nothing novel about, 76
pyramid, 77, 79, 82, 87
benefit, 78
three criticisms of, 85–7
not confined to contracts set aside, 124
overview, 95
principle of, 60
proposed model, 93
role of, 48
symmetry, 91
'unjustified', 49
Unjustified enrichment, 49

Valuation, 172–4

Waiver of tort, 13
Weston v Downes, 113, 135
see also Mansfield, Lord
inspiration for language, 134
mistake of judges, 114

Whincup v Hughes, 153
White, M, 53
  'damages remedy', 53
  remedial response to breach, 53
Wigmore, Henry, 44n
Williams, Cyprian, *see Henry v Schroeder*

Williams, Serjeant, 108
  five famous rules, 109–10
  criticism of, 110–1
  extremely influential, 110
  in *Pordage v Cole*, 108–9
  observations of *Boone v Eyre*, 119